LAUGHTER FROM THE DARK

MICHAEL PARNELL

Laughter from the Dark

A LIFE OF

Gwyn Thomas

John Murray

For Richard, my son, and Sarah, my daughter,
with love

*Published with the support
of the Welsh Arts Council
and Western Mail & Echo Ltd*

Text © Michael Parnell 1988
Gwyn Thomas quotations © The Estate of Gwyn Thomas 1988
First published 1988
by John Murray (Publishers) Ltd
50 Albemarle Street, London W 1 X 4 BD

Printed and bound in Great Britain
by Butler & Tanner Ltd, Frome and London

British Library CIP Data

Parnell, Michael, *1934–*
    Laughter from the dark: a life of
    Gwyn Thomas.
    1. Fiction in English. Thomas, Gwyn,
    1913–1981 – Biographies
    I. Title
    823'.914

ISBN 0–7195–4426–2

Contents

Illustrations

Sources of Illustrations

John Dd Evans and Century Hutchinson Ltd: 1; Cyril Batstone: 2; Gwyn Jones: 3, 6; Bill Thomas: 4, 5; Lyn Thomas: 7, 12, 13, 14, 15, 18, 20, 21; Jeffrey Robinson: 16; William Hewison and Punch Publications Ltd, London: 17; *Western Mail*: 19; Royal Court Theatre, London: 22; Sherman Theatre, Cardiff: 23

Preface

I first became aware of the existence of a master-humorist called Gwyn Thomas in 1954. On leave from National Service with the Royal Artillery, I called in at my old school in Cornwall and bumped into a favourite teacher, J.B. Boyd Roberts, who had taken us for history. 'I trust you're using your spare time to read widely and voraciously,' he said. 'I should like to think that you were not wasting the two years of grace before you go up to Oxford.' Shame-facedly I confessed that in my soldier's life I had fallen into a kind of mental paralysis, that the physical life had become dominant even in me, that I had read nothing for months on end. He reached into some pocket beneath the swirls of his gown, producing a novel with a vivid yellow paper jacket: *A Frost On My Frolic*, by Gwyn Thomas. 'Here, take this,' he said. 'It will afford you a great deal of amusement and may even reawaken that spark of intelligence I once thought I saw in you.' I have never forgotten his gift. If I knew where he was, nothing would make me happier than to put into his hands, with the utmost gratitude, a copy of this book, the consequence of his generosity.

By the time I came to live and work in Wales, in 1966, Gwyn Thomas had become a national institution. He no longer wrote the novels which had, in my opinion, established his credentials as a writer, but he appeared frequently on television, he wrote plays for theatre, television and radio, and he began, before very long, to write on Saturdays for the *Western Mail* a television column that was unfailingly the high point of the weekend.

To my ear he sounded like the authentic voice of Wales, though liable to spark off controversy or arouse hostility in some quarters.

He was outspoken on the issues of Welsh nationalism (which he deplored, as he deplored any nationalistic – as distinct from patriotic – expression) and the Welsh language (for the development and preservation of which he had little enthusiasm, because of its divisive effect and the way it was dragged into the service of nationalistic extremism) and he had made enemies, some of them among those who failed to understand or care about what he was saying. If some accepted that Gwyn Thomas's love of his country was as great and as sincere as any Welshman's could be, there was also a vocal and powerful minority which saw him as a traitor to the idea of Wales, a puppet performing for the delectation of the English a caricature of Welshness. Some were being won round. However, public recognition came in 1976 when the Welsh Arts Council awarded Gwyn its Honour and £1000 prize. But many persisted in denying that Gwyn Thomas was a true Welshman, and by the time of his death his renown as a writer had diminished.

Though I never met him I always looked out eagerly for Gwyn Thomas's appearances on television and radio, and for his occasional writings in the press. Since he never failed to put on a good show, I, like many others, failed to note his gradual deterioration as ill health destroyed him; we perceived no significant decline in his verbal vigour and inventiveness or in his wicked sense of fun. Thus, it came as a great shock to hear of his death in 1981, and the sense of loss has not gone away.

When I found that Gwyn's widow was prepared to allow me to write a biography of her husband, I embarked upon a fascinating and rewarding exploration. Gwyn had presented himself to the world in a great deal of autobiographical and semi-autobiographical writing, but this proved a fairly unreliable source of firm information. 'The truth was boring to Gwyn,' Lyn Thomas said, and it soon became evident that he had not as a general rule in his writing taken much care to distinguish between truth and fiction. The basis of most of his fiction was clearly the truth as he had perceived it, managed and manoeuvred, expanded and linguistically embroidered, adapted a little here, almost transformed there, as fiction allows and indeed demands; but the basis of his autobiography was almost precisely the same material, treated in a similar way. His mother died in 1919, when he was six years old; but in reporting this on different occasions and in different circumstances he sometimes said he was two when so deprived, sometimes 'about three', and sometimes other ages; it was the loss that mattered, not the petty detail of exactly when it had happened.

It is obvious to anyone acquainted with the work of Gwyn Thomas that it has a strong autobiographical basis. He almost always took very literally the commandment that a writer should 'write what he knows' – and what Gwyn Thomas knew best was what he had lived through, particularly in his first thirty years. He was a prolific and dedicated writer and the total output of his career is impressive: ten novels, three collections of short stories (which include only a small proportion of the 200 he wrote), an autobiography, two collections of essays, six theatre plays, a large number of radio and television plays, films and features, and a wide range of occasional pieces in books, magazines and newspapers. A great deal of what he wrote was never published, including some novels, stories, essays and plays which might yet see print, and a series of journals or commonplace books which were never intended for publication. Making your way through this forest of millions of words, you feel sure you are getting closer to the essential Gwyn Thomas, only to find contradictions and puzzles that are hard to resolve and make him seem as remote and unknowable as ever.

This impression was on the whole compounded when I spoke to those who knew him, either from close contact as brother or cousin or as working colleague and friend, or from more casual acquaintance. I found accounts of some rather different Gwyns, the one common factor being the difficulty of really knowing him at all. Putting it all together, however, I feel as if I have come to know a strange, talented and immensely lovable man whose story is well worth recounting and trying to understand. Although there have been some signs recently of a revival of interest in and appreciation of his work, with the reissue, for instance, of *All Things Betray Thee* and the appearance fifty years after he wrote it of his first novel *Sorrow For Thy Sons*, he is an undeservedly neglected writer. A pity, because he is a great comic writer and it is my hope that this biography may in some measure contribute to a new awareness of what he has to offer.

I am deeply grateful to all those who have helped me in the making of this book. Primarily I am indebted to Lyn Thomas, who has given freely and generously of her time to talk to me about her husband, and who has allowed me a free run of all his papers; her devotion to

Gwyn's interest since his death is even more absolute than when he was alive. Gwyn's sister Nana and her husband Bill Thomas have also been immensely helpful, and the reader will not fail to see how important to me have been the letters written over the years by Gwyn to the sister who became virtually his mother. My thanks are due too to the other members of the family who have helped me to the utmost of their ability: Dil Thomas, in Cinderford; Eddie and Irene Thomas, in London; Gwyn and Beryl Jones, in Abergavenny; and Nest Thomas, Walt's widow, in Neath. Among those of Gwyn's surviving friends who have given invaluable help I owe especial thanks to Howard Fast in Connecticut for sending me all Gwyn's long letters to him, and to Wyn Roberts, MP, for his special help and encouragement.

Many other people have given time to write to me or talk with me, or lend me letters or help in other ways, and it is with heartfelt thanks that I list them here: Graham Allen; Geoffrey Axworthy; Alexander Baron; Edwin Brooks; Gilchrist Calder; Richard Cohen; Alan Coren; Wayne David; Huw Davies; Frank Delaney; Virginia Lewis Dignam; Emyr Edwards; Elwyn Evans; Hywel Francis; Reg George; Livia Gollancz; Viv Grant; Kenneth Griffith; Harold Harris; Geoffrey Hebdon; Sheila Hodges; Emyr Humphreys; Gwyn Ingli James; Alun John; Arthur Jones; Glyn Jones; Professor Gwyn Jones; Owen Vernon Jones; the late Wynford Jones; Vincent Kane; D.M. Lloyd; John Mead; Professor Ian Michael; Gerry Monte; Cliff Morgan; John Morgan; Barry Moore; Juliet O'Hea; John Ormond; Teifion Phillips; Nansi Roberts; the late Mark Roberts; Jeffrey Robinson; Georges Rochat; Hilary Rubinstein; Sir Harry Secombe; Ian Skidmore; Professor Dai Smith; Ray Smith; R.A. Storey; Aled Vaughan; Colin Voisey; Sam Wanamaker; Desmond Watkins; Alun Williams; Alwyn Williams; Mr and Mrs Berwyn Williams; Herbert Williams.

A great deal of my information has come from institutional sources, and I should like to record my gratitude for assistance from the following in particular: Principal Justin Gosling, St Edmund Hall, Oxford; Jean Tranter, HTV Film Library; Cathy Henderson of Harry Ransom Humanities Research Center, University of Texas at Austin; Gareth Morris, BBC Wales Library Services; J. Watts Williams, Assistant Keeper of Manuscripts, the National Library of Wales; Meic Stephens and Tony Bianchi, the Welsh Arts Council. Many other people at the BBC, at HTV, and at Gollancz, Michael Joseph and

Hutchinson helped in various ways, and I am grateful to all these institutions for allowing me to quote from books and documents of which they control the copyright.

I am grateful too to colleagues at the Polytechnic of Wales who helped in many ways, including their tolerance of my preoccupation away from the immediate business of my department. Duncan McAra at John Murray has been a generously supportive and hard-working editor whose assistance and understanding I could not have done without. Above all my thanks to Mary, my wife, upon whose constant encouragement and support I have been totally reliant.

M.P.

I

A CHILD OF THE RHONDDA

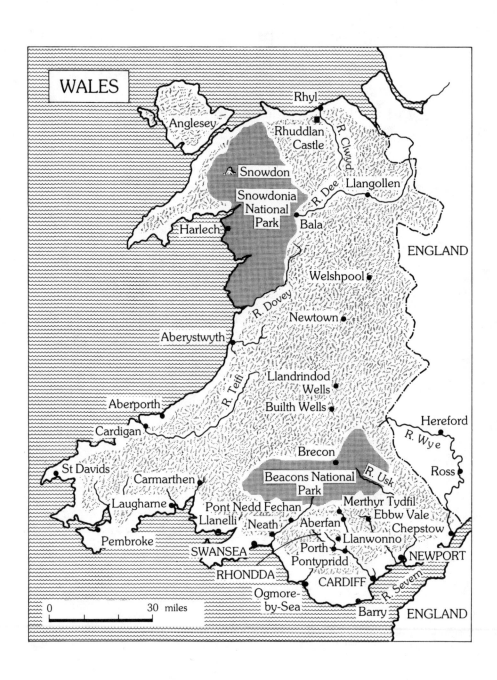

1

A House Full of Children

Engraving a figure Y deeply into the high ground of mid-Glamorgan, the Rhondda rivers Fawr and Fach, Big and Little, meet at Porth and continue south-east for three miles to Pontypridd. Here the Rhondda stream flows into the Taff which has come down the parallel valley from Merthyr Tydfil, and the enlarged river continues south and a little east to Cardiff, twelve miles or so away on the Glamorgan coast. Porth, 'the gateway' in Welsh, marks the southern entrance to the Rhondda, the archetype of South Wales valleys. The main road follows the valley bed, winding down from Treherbert and on to Cardiff, but from Porth an escape road climbs steeply up the enclosing hill on the western side to Trebanog at the summit. Overlooking the township of Porth, and consisting of little more than rows of terraced houses standing on either side of the road as it strains up the hill, is the village of Cymmer. It seems a negligible string of grey, cheerless housing, but Cymmer has its little niche in history, for here, in one of the houses that clings to the face of the mountain on the right hand side going up that arduous gradient, Gwyn Thomas was born.

This is the very heart of what ought to be known as 'Gwyn Thomas country'. Imagine a diamond shape placed over the map of South Wales, stretching from Neath in the west to Chepstow in the east, and from Brecon in the north to Cardiff in the south, and you have defined almost all the area of the earth that seriously mattered to this strange, comical, brilliant Welshman. Though the day came when he travelled widely about the world, and though his search for work actually took him to live for a while in England and in West Wales, he was never happy except when within a dozen miles or so of his birthplace, and almost all the inspiration for his prolific writing

3

came from this small tract of land. So far none of those who compile books about Britain's literary landscape has recorded the Rhondda's debt to Gwyn Thomas, but no doubt that will be remedied in the future as appreciation grows of the skill, idiosyncrasy and love with which he wrote about the Valley.

A closer look at that map of South Wales will help remind the reader of the terrain Gwyn Thomas inhabited. His village of Cymmer lies half way up the inside of the retaining wall, as it were, of the South Wales coalfield. Climb to the village of Trebanog at the top of the slope and you find yourself on a ridge that runs from north-west to south-east. To the south and west the land falls away to the rich green undulations of the Vale of Glamorgan; in the distance the waters of the Bristol Channel wash the coastline that marches more or less parallel to the ridge on which you stand. Twenty miles on across the water you can, on a clear day, see the hills of Somerset and Devon.

Turn round and look back across the valley from which you have climbed, and you can see ridge upon ridge of mountain heights, separating valley after valley not dissimilar to the one at your feet; you cannot see them, but you know they are there, the valleys of the Cynon, the Taff, the Bargoed, the Rhymney, the Sirhowy, the Ebbw, all parallel, all running south by east, all full of endless strings of terraced housing swelling at intervals into townships, each surrounding its colliery or steelworks from which most of the work has finally gone away. And beyond the ridges, a little to the north, sometimes you can see on the horizon the dark masses of the Brecon Beacons.

You are looking down into the Rhondda Fawr; you can just see where, in the town of Porth on the valley floor, the Rhondda Fach or Little Rhondda begins, disappearing from your view behind the intervening height of Troedyrhiw Mountain. The slope directly opposite you, on the far side of Rhondda Fach, rises to the woodclad heights of Cefn Gwyngul where, in the middle of the Gwynno Forest on the plateau, a walker will find the tiny village of Llanwonno – a church, a pub, three or four houses – that represented for Gwyn Thomas the nearest place to heaven on this earth. Distanced from the valley bottom, you appreciate the contrasts always made in Gwyn Thomas's accounts of the place of his beginning:

Porth is dominated by one of the valley's monstrous tips. It covers one half of the plateau of Cymmer mountain. It was once my playground. We found the ravaged part as fascinating as the acres that had been left untouched. We could leap from the world of hot ferns and lark-song into the black and hellish racket of the tippers adding their daily inch to the dunce's cap of refuse.

Down in the valley, he pointed out: 'Streets shoot upwards at angles that suggest a neurotic impulse to be getting away from something, and you don't have to look far to see what. There are streets that tilt. You see dogs, after a quick romp, backing into a corner, foxed and barking for a compass bearing.' From the high places, you could see that nothing had really overwhelmed the serenity of the hills:

> Green tranquil glens and noble domes of hill lie cheek by jowl with some of the most richly concentrated lumps of social living one can ever imagine, the most improbable cocktail of music, laughter, drama and creative toil ever shaken by time, chance and inherited genes.[1]

Gwyn was born on 6 July 1913 – and the following year, as he loved to say, was even worse. He was the twelfth and last child of his mother, Ziphorah, who was already desperately tired in her life's journey, so tired indeed that she gave her latest infant just the one name, Gwyn, although all his elder brothers had been given two; so tired, in the end, that her youngest son went through his life believing that he had been the last, unwanted, straw in the burden that took her to an early grave when he was six years old. Ziphorah was the youngest daughter of a miner called Tom Davies – or Twm Cynffig as he was known, his family having its roots at Kenfig, down in the Vale of Glamorgan. Tom worked at the Cymmer pit, starting at the age of seven, and was luckier than some of his mates, for he had survived two methane explosions while working underground, and was famous for having come out from the pit after one such disaster only after scrambling over the bodies of his father and two brothers. His daughter was only seventeen when in 1892 she married her handsome young sweetheart, Walter Morgan Thomas. On their marriage certificate, Walter laid claim to twenty-four years, though he was barely nineteen. Their first child was born the following year.

Walter's father was a John Thomas of Porth who had emigrated to the United States with his wife Jane in the late 1860s. Finding that

5

Youngstown, in Cleveland, Ohio, was not after all the promised land, they returned to Wales with their American-born children about 1875 and John Thomas set himself up as a cabinet-maker and funeral director in the village of Mountain Ash, on the far side of the mountain separating the Rhondda from the Cynon Valley. Here he thrived, and his children, David, Annie and Walter, spent their childhood in relative and increasing comfort.

Walter was perhaps somewhat spoiled by his upbringing. His taste for reading and music and the finer things of life did not altogether prepare him for the realities which awaited him when at fourteen he had to find work, and the only available employment was in coal-mining. He duly went underground, and in time gravitated towards what seemed to him to be among the more humane and less demanding aspects of colliery work, the care of the pit ponies. But in this he proved little more successful than in other jobs, for he lacked practical ability and found he had neither sufficient sympathy with his charges nor skill to control them – though he was later said to have been kinder to his horses than he was to his children. At the slightest excuse he would miss going down to his work, complaining that the ponies had kicked him or that his health was not good, with the inevitable result that his employers laid him off with increasing frequency.

As a young man above ground, however, he was dashing and stylish, elegantly dressed always, thanks to the suits handed on to him by his more prosperous father. Witty and loquacious, he must have seemed a likely lover, and it was not surprising that Ziphorah Davies should fall under his spell. How long she remained under it, it would be hard to tell, for having made her bed she had no option but to lie in it, that being the way things were in those days. They lived at first in a house in York Terrace that, though small, was not too cramped, for, after a custom not so very uncommon at the time, the firstborn daughter soon went to live with her grandparents in Mountain Ash. There Carrie was brought up in considerably greater comfort than her younger siblings.

By the midsummer of 1898, however, three more children had arrived, Jennie, Emlyn and Minnie, and when Ziphorah found that she was again pregnant it was evident that the York Terrace house would no longer suffice. Somehow or other – and it is still a mystery in the family exactly how it was made possible, though a subvention from John Thomas at Mountain Ash must have had something to do with it — Walter raised sufficient funds to put a deposit on a considerably larger house, and a move was made to 196 High Street, in time for their fifth child, Hannah, to be born there in June 1901.

Although this, too, was a terraced house — like most of the dwellings in the valleys — it had rather larger rooms than others in the terrace, and proved to be somehow capable of accommodating more or less satisfactorily what eventually became an enormous family. In 1904 twin boys were born, Gwilym and Arthur; a year later, another boy, John; and then, at regular two-year intervals, four more sons: Walter (1907); Dilwyn (1909); Eddie (1911); and finally, Gwyn.

By the time Gwyn arrived, the house was bursting at the seams. Not only were there *more* people living in it than it had ever been designed to take, but also they were all rapidly getting larger, and more in need of private space for themselves as they grew into young adults. The time was coming when natural departures would begin to reduce the pressure, for Jennie, who had trained as a nurse, already had a job and had met the young doctor whom she thought to marry, while Minnie, going on sixteen, also had notions about how marriage would be the means to go out into her own life. The new baby's eldest brother, Emlyn, was nearly eighteen, and great events were conspiring to take him away from his parents' hearth all too soon. But for the last few years of her life Ziphorah had too much work to do, and she had to cope, moreover, with less help from some of the elder children than she might have hoped for, and with no help from her husband at all.

Walter turned out to be about as bad a bargain in husbands as a pretty girl could fear to find. Apart from his potency in bed, and the rare charm he could bring to bear when he wished to wriggle out from some responsibility, he had little to offer his family in the way of wisdom, service, or sustenance. Almost all his children regarded him throughout their lives as something of a monster; only Gwyn, in later life, found it possible to bring a measure of understanding to what had made the man what he was, and to recall with some sympathy and affection at least a few memories of good times spent in his company. Not that he was overtly cruel, or ever violent; but he was self-centred, selfish, and quite incapable as a provider or handyman or in any practical role. He could not manage money;

what he got from occasional employment, or from the dole, or from the not ungenerous handouts which sometimes came his way from his father in Mountain Ash, was often spent before he arrived home, and Ziphorah's worries about domestic problems were compounded with financial anxieties. What was spent was rarely spent on the family's needs; Walter bought books when he fancied them, or items of clothing for himself; but mostly he bought drink.

The two parents created between them, however, a bustling and not unhappy domestic life in which the children's intellectual and musical gifts were allowed some scope for development. Several of them went on to notable careers. It is impossible to say which parent provided what talent, but perhaps Ziphorah brought from the Davies family a particular strain of high intelligence. Her sister, Hannah, for instance, who lived just across the road, was also the mother of a brood of children, at least half a dozen, every one of whom went through the primitive education system of the day with flying colours and ended up with university degrees – one of them, John Griffith Jones, became a nationally known specialist in rheumatology, and his brother, Taliesin, was a professor at McGill University. Walter's gift to his children may have been their easy mastery of unusually fluent and fascinating modes of speech. When Gwyn became a writer of wide renown, it was the individuality of his use of the English language that excited the reviewers' praise. The roots of his particular brand of English lay in the family idiolect which the Thomas children learned from their father, whose extensive and eclectic reading had furnished him with many thoughts about the nature of life and the world, and whose peculiar delivery, not quite Welsh and not quite English, made memorable and comical his interpretation and presentation of those ideas.

Walter and Ziphorah were both from Welsh-speaking backgrounds, and Welsh was their natural means of communication with each other. For this reason the first five or six of their children also had Welsh as their first language. Times were changing, though, and all sorts of pressures contributed to an increasing adoption of English as a more satisfactory tongue. South Wales, and especially the Rhondda, had during the nineteenth century seen a huge influx of workers from Cornwall, the West Country, Yorkshire, and Ireland, as well as numerous others from Italy and Spain, and all these brought English either as their own language or as a lingua franca, and none of them understood Welsh at all. At another level, the education system was in various ways promoting English in preference to Welsh, it being far more 'convenient' to deal in one language only, and English, as they saw it, with its worldwide importance and its great heritage of literature to recommend it, was obviously more 'desirable'. Whether to their shame or not, many Welshmen agreed, and even went so far as to assist in trying to forbid the use of Welsh among children altogether. For these and no doubt other reasons, by the beginning of the twentieth century many like Ziphorah and Walter Thomas were changing their habits, and their later-born children were brought up without Welsh both by their parents and by their society. Recalling the situation, Gwyn wrote:

> Our kitchen, about the size of an average hutch, was a busy, bi-lingual bomb of a place. The first six children spoke Welsh, the bottom six English, and all at the same time; politics in English, gossip in Welsh, and downright lies in both.[2]

When Ziphorah died in 1919 she left a gap that was hard to fill. Her energy had been prodigious, both in work and at leisure, if that is not too absurd a word to give to the spaces between her labours when she somehow found time to play with the children, to talk with them and tell them stories, and, above all, to sing with them. In an attempt to supplement her husband's irregular and insufficient contributions to her budget she had, on top of all the endless tasks of shopping, feeding, washing, mending and house-cleaning with which she had somehow to deal, set herself up as a manufacturer and retailer of oilskins for use in the wet underground conditions in the colliery; in a shed in the back garden she was often to be found struggling with mountains of calico and containers of linseed oil and enveloped in the steam and smells from the tub where the material was waterproofed.

What was most severely missed when she died, however, was not the hard worker, the ingenious provider, so much as the faithful spirit of her being, that had kept her going and held her family together, a spirit that manifested itself perhaps even more notably in her singing than in her dauntless coping. She had a glorious singing voice, a thrilling contralto, and, as her daughters had been fortunate enough to follow her in the possession of rich and lovely voices, a central feature of their family life was their constant breaking into song. These were usually the hymns associated with their chapel, and the memory of such occasions was for Gwyn profoundly important. In words which reveal the pain from which he never truly escaped, he said a few years before his death:

> And my mother, a woman of great beauty, I would say – she was in her early forties when she died, a woman of vast creative potential, and this is what of course has created one of the cornerstones of my philosophy: Humanity has been far too prodigal in reproducing itself. Waste is the thing which I detest, the waste of human gifts, the waste of human promise that you have in this vast, ugly proliferation of people in the great slums of the world. . . . I mean, here I was, the twelfth child, a totally unwanted child, and yet, you know, she had this faith in the world and the wind and the sky, and she would look at me, and she would almost forgive me, at times, for being there. Almost forgive me. And this is something I will never forget for as long as I live, these terrible moments when this lovely woman with this marvellous voice – it sort of wrapped the world in velvet, it was a tremendous instrument, in which I'm sure, I'm sure that in the years when I didn't comprehend a stream of human words that she was telling me in some inimitably bitter way of her own plight – that she had been the victim of a monstrous miracle of prolific waste.[3]

Gwyn's life was to be shadowed by a deep-rooted unhappiness and bouts of acute bitterness that can be traced to the subconscious perceptions of his youth. In reaction against a buried trauma, he became a great comic commentator on life, an imaginative recreator of childhood happiness nostalgically recalled. For, whatever may have been the depth of his hurt, his life as a child was, according to his own testimony, for the most part happy. The subject was one of the staples of his writing, and those who want the full flavour of his treatment of it must go to what he wrote, which was delightful and inimitable.

The saviour of the Thomas family after the loss of the mother turned out to be the youngest of Gwyn's sisters, the just eighteen-year-old Hannah, known to everyone then, as now, as Nana. Carrie made no move to return from Mountain Ash; Jennie, the nurse, was too busy working in a local hospital, already well on her way to becoming its youngest ever Matron; and Minnie, although she shouldered for a brief while the burden of being *materfamilias*, had already found a certain way to make her young man, Emlyn Jones, take her earlier than he expected to the altar.

Nana, who sang beautifully and had ideas of her own about making a career in music, who had won the offer of a scholarship to study music in Cardiff, was soon persuaded by her father that women's ambitions were of minor importance in such a situation. A tiny woman, of fierce determination and with the heart of a lioness, she capitulated nevertheless to his blandishments, even wondering whether he was perhaps right about her 'duty' to him and the family. For the next sixteen years she gave everything she had to the difficult job she had inherited, somehow keeping the family together and making possible a childhood and adolescence for Gwyn and his brothers which proved full of golden memories, despite the poverty and political misery of the times, despite her frustrated ambitions (not to mention her frustrated young womanhood, for she put the idea of marriage firmly from her), despite everything.

A hard worker herself, toiling over the iron boiler for the washing, cooking on the open fire and in the side-oven, making clothes for all her men, often from old garments carefully unpicked, Nana laid down conditions herself for the running of the house in a disciplined way, as far at least as was possible when at its core was still a largely idle and undisciplinable father. The younger boys were assigned regular chores which had to be completed to Nana's satisfaction before they were allowed to escape to the football games in the street and the romps over the mountains all around. The place had to be kept tidy or they would all drown in the flood of things that accumulated, she said, and punctuality had to be observed – at meals, in departures for school, at bed-times. Chapel must be attended, the scourge of drink must be kept at bay, people in more trouble than theirs had to be helped. She tried, and did well, gaining in the process a reputation for strictness and rectitude that still kept her brothers in somewhat tremulous respect for her authority as long as they lived – Gwyn, then aged forty-six, and Walter, fifty-two, were not too old to be startled into hiding a bottle of whisky from her when they unexpectedly heard her arrival home from chapel one Sunday in 1959.

The family she took over in 1919 was still large, despite the departure of three sisters. To Gwyn, Emlyn, the eldest brother, a large and handsome twenty-three-year-old, fortunate enough to have survived his war service, was more like a father than his father was; and Nana, ministering to his wants with a strictness that did not wholly conceal her awareness of his need for affection and special care, soon seemed more like a mother than his mother ever had. Then there were the twins, Gwilym and Arthur, an inseparable pair of fifteen-year-olds soon to be separated for ever when Arthur succumbed to rheumatic fever in 1920; that was a blow from which Nana, so recently succeeded to responsibility, found it hard to recover, and it did not help that Gwilym, the surviving twin, suffered deafness more and more acutely for the rest of his life. Next in line was John, fourteen, a serious, responsible lad, precipitated into the world of earning and providing by the circumstances and learning the trade of leather-working and shoe-making from a neighbour who ran a cobbler's shop. Twelve-year-old Walter won Gwyn's greatest adulation; a clever, loquacious boy who already seemed to have read every book in the house – and Walter senior, who would often sit up all night reading and making himself too tired to think of going to work next day, had made it a house full of books – he was destined for the university and great things, and little six-year-old Gwyn thought he was wonderful. Dil was ten, lively and funny and a great favourite with everyone.

Last but one, eight-year-old Eddie became Gwyn's closest companion in undertakings of wickedness and devilry that became legendary in the area. Until Gwyn was about fourteen, there was to add to Nana's troubles a constant procession of farmers, policemen, irate neighbours, pastors and vicars arriving at her door to complain about their exploits. Once the pair of them were hauled before a local magistrate on a charge of repeatedly returning to a local tip to steal bags of coal lumps and annoying the bobby beyond endurance, but escaped justice when the magistrate recognised the angelic pair in front of him, spruced and polished by Nana, as singers in his chapel choir. Emphasising their closeness was the fact that they shared a birthday, both having been born on 6 July; many years later, when someone in a pub remarked to Gwyn that he found this circumstance rather odd, Gwyn replied instantly, with a caustic coarseness which was characteristic of his private wit and which shows something of the bitter disrespect in which his father's memory stood, 'Our father was a precision grinder'.

To the constant comings and goings of all these inhabitants of No. 196 must be added the incessant ins and outs of neighbours, cousins and friends almost without number. The father's cronies came often to smoke and talk politics, or to ask for his advice on the law — for he was considered a true wiseacre as a consequence of all his reading, and was known as a political thinker from his constant and effective heckling at the many political meetings he attended, though too idle or cynical to become sufficiently involved to seek election himself. It was a time for neighbourliness and open doors anyway, and in the specially difficult times that came in the early 1920s the principle of sharing what you had when you had it was ingrained in Nana, so that the throng in the house was even at times augmented by the presence of strangers, little people drawn in by the smell of soup and the cheerful talk. Walt once found himself sitting next to a ragamuffin he'd never seen before who, having cleared the bowl that appeared in front of him, pointed solemnly at Nana and said in a voice preternaturally deep, 'Tell that woman that I want some more.'

Of all the aspects of the life of those early years, that which made the greatest impression on Gwyn was the music by which they were surrounded. It was an easy cliché that the Welsh are a nation of singers, but that does not lessen the truth of the matter. In an age when the religious life was still followed with some enthusiasm, though the great revivals like that of 1904 were already acknowledged to be things of an irrecoverable past, the chapels still flourished, and the basis of their continuing life was in the singing of wonderful, mostly minor-key hymns which they encouraged. Emlyn, like Jennie and Nana, was musically gifted; he played the piano well and, despite the scoffings of his unsympathetic father, who did his best to frustrate his son's ambition, studied music in Cardiff on an 'Interrupted Studies' grant after his war service, and eventually went to the Royal College of Music. Gwyn described the house as 'a cocoon of music', and continued:

> That was just as well, for we were a disputatious lot, curious about all the ideas that man has ever taken up to explain his peculiar fix. The house had two poles: the kitchen where we argued about the new ideologies with passionate intolerance and little understanding; and the front room where the piano was, and we could make the sort of music that would woo us for an hour or two into a pacific neutrality.[4]

Before he left 196, Emlyn, 'who had come back from the first world war in a mood of thoughtfulness that never left him', took singing and piano classes locally, and his brothers all benefited from his teaching. Dil somehow acquired a cello and learned to play it well. Like all his family, Gwyn was deeply involved in the singing, as chorister, duettist with Eddie, and soloist. Possessed of an unexpectedly loud and pure soprano voice for one so diminutive, he became a part of the scene; with dark, curly hair and a round, chubby face, sweetly holding out declaiming arms, he was famous for his temperance songs and recitations, and the love of plangent minor harmonies and vast swelling choral climaxes never left him.

In a busy round of schooling, playing, singing, acting, mountain-walking and cinema-going the family grew through that troubled decade without serious setback despite the economic trials Nana as manager had to endure. Emlyn, Gwilym, John and Dil all contributed to the budget more effectively as time went on, and occasionally some money was wrung from the unwilling father, but Nana had no alternative but to send her youngest boys to the soup-kitchen set up in the chapel a hundred yards down the road in the crisis of strike-torn 1921, and all the boys were dressed as well as they could be in the fashion of make do and mend. One of Gwyn's funniest stories recalls his being fitted for a shirt at about the age of five, and it is typical of his writing in the way it combines the less than ideal reality and the comic stance towards it:

> The finished shirt was brought to us on a Saturday night when I was standing in the bath in front of the kitchen fire.... My father slipped the shirt on to me. My brothers stood around staring and I could taste their astonishment. The front of the garment was about the size of a shirt-front, a dickie. The back fell right down into the water of the bath and was a good inch longer than I was. I was like some new gruesome kind of bird.... My brothers followed me around as if I were a potentate, and my father said he had never seen any bit of raiment that so brought out the dignity in me.[5]

Many of his memories, though transmuted by nostalgic distance and his disposition to laugh rather than to cry (at least, in public), are of times almost unimaginably hard by contemporary standards. Somehow they survived, surmounting difficulties with determination and with a faith in the future that speaks volumes for the resilience of the human spirit. The future they hoped for was a long time coming, and it brought, for Gwyn, ironical consequences. The second phase of his childhood, however, his schooldays, brought him fairly unalloyed delight.

2

County Schoolboy

None of the Thomas boys was dull, though they didn't all take the academic path which might have led them out of the valley to lives of greater freedom and achievement elsewhere. Gwilym, hampered by deafness and perhaps traumatised by the loss of his twin brother, did not take school seriously at all. He became a miner, and after an industrial accident went on in later life to become a gardener; but he, like the rest of the family, had a sharp mind and a sharper turn of phrase, coupled with a keen eye for the ridiculous.

John, who went to work for a local shoemaker to help the family's finances, had shown great promise in the selection examination for the secondary school, but preferred to delay any use of his academic talent until a more appropriate time. He became the mainstay of the family right up until the outbreak of the war and was the eventual purchaser of the house they lived in; then after service in the RAF he trained as a teacher, and might have gone far, had life not had but a brief satisfaction and then an unexpected and undeservedly early end in store for him. Gwyn remembered how John had been the unifying nerve needed to hold the family together: 'He was the odd one out in a band of thrusting egotists.... We ate him alive.... He was an actor of startling gifts and enthusiasm.... He was the only one of us who didn't get seasick in contact with mathematics', and pictured him in his shoe-repair business: 'Around him in his shop he gathered a group of sages and buffoons incomparable in the story of Wales. He sat like Socrates in the midst of these uproarious debaters.'[1]

Dil also left school as soon as he could, and became a shopkeeper's assistant, driven partly by a need to earn money to contribute to the household. During the war he went underground as one of Bevin's conscripted miners and afterwards capitalised on the experience, studying with sufficient success to become a colliery official.

The other four brothers made more of their academic opportunities. After Emlyn had led the way with his musical studies despite their father's opposition, Walter followed brilliantly, and the way was clear for Eddie and Gwyn in their turn. Walt, tall and fit and handsome by the time he was in his mid-teens, was the first to go to the grammar school, or rather to what was then known as the Rhondda Inter-mediate School. Located in fine buildings overlooking Porth from the far side of the valley, it later became known as the Porth County School and was for many years widely regarded as one of the best state-provided schools in Wales. Aggressive in intelligence and graceful and strong in body (he is said to have squared up once to no less an opponent than Tommy Farr during a political debate), as well as diligent and hard-working, Walt was a star pupil, making his way steadily up through the school as First Boy in his class, winning in 1926 a Rhondda Free Studentship to go to the University College in Cardiff. There he gained a First in French, and went on to be a schoolmaster, spending his entire career at Neath Grammar School teaching modern languages; highly effective in the classroom, he was proud that among his pupils there were at least four who went on to become university professors of Spanish.

His example ultimately proved of the utmost importance for the relatively idle and mischievous youngest brother, but first Gwyn went through a long period when academic success looked like the last thing he had in mind. He was the despair of his teachers in the elementary school because, although it was always evident that he was bright as a button, they could rarely find means of directing his nose to the grindstone. His memory was unusually retentive and he never forgot any of the long poems and verses he learned so rapidly for performances in Eisteddfodic competitions or at temperance rallies, even those in Welsh of which he understood barely a word. In school, however, his energies were more concentrated on enjoyment and escape to the joys of life outside. It was not that he did not like school; it had, as he learned early, its rewards. He told an audience, later, in the mid-1960s:

If, as some think, education represents a sort of servitude, I am a willing slave. From mastering the lyric of 'Twinkle, twinkle, little star' in the infants' school at the age of five right through to becoming comatose over mediaeval chronicles at degree level, the act of learning has given me an almost delirious joy. The 'twinkle, twinkle' thing sticks in my mind. A strong voice and an engaging smile which vanished early made me popular with the lady teachers at the infants' school. I was made monitor and was given the daily task of filling inkwells; this duty and the singing wore me out and I have avoided responsibility ever since.[2]

He remembered too how he had occasionally responded to the urgings of the teachers in the next stage of his schooling:

In the elementary school my mind and body were hustled along by some of the grimmest task-masters ever let loose on the young. At the age of nine I won the commendation of an HMI for an essay on Joan of Arc which somehow managed to take a Calvinistic swing against drink and free love.[3]

More often, however, he was drawn by the call of everyday life and its multitude of splendid temptations: the possibilities of the open mountain country within easy reach, and the satisfactions of observing the people, eccentric, peculiar, kindly and dangerous, who thronged the densely packed terraces all around. At that time the slopes behind the High Street had not yet been so extensively built on, and the way to the bare mountain with its rocky outcrops, grassy plateaux, seas of ferns, murky pools and scraggy woods was open. The slopes were the haunt of hundreds of sheep, many of which followed their noses down to the rubbish bins of the back lanes, becoming familiar elements of the street scene and much-sworn-at despoilers of the delicacies of carefully tended gardens. These sheep were far less stupid than legend would have it, and Walter Senior, justifying his existence by some sporadic attempts to make vegetables grow in the back garden, became embroiled in a hilarious saga of ploy and counterploy between himself and a persistent ram which the family called Attila; once, having fortified the defences and built up the rear wall, Walter was congratulating himself on ultimate victory when Attila came flying over the wall clearing a height of at least six feet and sending the triumphant gardener sprawling.

Gwyn and Eddie, sometimes with some of the elder brothers, often without, loved to explore the hillsides. They delighted occasionally in stumbling accidentally or accidentally-on-purpose on the hiding places of young couples who had sought some solitude for their loving, but liked even better to watch those who themselves watched with jealous eyes the activities of the lovers. These *voyeurs*, or pimpers as they were known locally, sometimes went about their business armed with binoculars or telescopes as for bird-watching, and the practice, which the young Gwyn observed with a mixture of derisive pleasure, inner horror and disturbing fascination, stuck deep in his mind, to recur as the subject of or an element in many of his stories later in life.

The pleasures of the mountain were great and provided some compensation for the cramped living conditions in the valley below. Sometimes their father would take a whole group of the boys for long walks over the tops of the hills and into neighbouring valleys, expounding as he went some theory of life or retailing some story which he had picked up about the history of the locality. Just over the summit of the hill immediately behind their house there began a long slope down towards the villages of Tonyrefail and Llantrisant; they would walk round in a northwards arc, keeping to the heights until, looking across the valley at Llantrisant from Mynydd Garth-maelwg − or the 'Smilog' as everyone called it − he would call a halt and tell dramatically the saga of Dr William Price, who 'slipped cremation into the social curriculum and nearly got himself lynched for his pains'. Among Walter's theories was a notion that the earth gave a great cosmic shudder in the small hours of every night; he had experienced it, he said, many a time at about half past two during the night shift underground. When, a little older, Gwyn and a brother or two or a friend went walking over the hills in the night hours, they too felt something:

> Odd things happened on those rambles over the hills and under the moon. There was a wall on the high moorland against which we rested out of the wind at about half past two each night. We would always for a few seconds at a time feel the earth shake beneath us. This might have been the effect of exhaustion or some nervous reaction felt by day people to an excess of darkness. Or it might have been a genuine shake.[4]

In one of his stories, 'Not Even Then', Gwyn made untypical use of the sense of strangeness he sometimes felt up on the mountains. It is also deeply touching in the way it reveals something about his recollections of his mother and of his childhood experience of the educational process. In it the narrator, calling himself Ritchie Beynon, tells of having failed the examination for entry to the secondary school. In the absence of his mother, who died when he was very young, Ritchie has been encouraged and helped in his school work by an elder brother, Cornelius. When the results are announced he flees the anger of his brother and loses himself in an unfamiliar place beyond the mountain ridge, only to find himself in the warm and comforting presence of his long-dead mother – until he confesses his failure, when the ghostly figure fades away in a kind of agony of betrayal and the little boy is 'alone with the pointed, menacing whisper of leaf and water', his 'wet, stricken face pressed into the bark of an ancient oak'.[5] This, the only ghost story and one of the very few completely un-comic stories Gwyn ever wrote, brings together some of the most significant influences upon him: the relatively romantic and beautiful mountain environment high above the industry-fouled valley; the pressures to succeed educationally; and the pain of the loss of his mother, of the conviction that he had never truly had a mother's love.

The best walk of all was one regularly undertaken on a Sunday afternoon, when Walter would lead a proportion of his brood down into Porth and up the hill on the opposite side of the valley on the first stage of a proposed five- or six-mile hike to visit the grandparents in Mountain Ash. They rarely got further than halfway, for up on the plateau in the middle of the Gwynno Forest they would come to the village of Llanwonno, where the landlord of the pub, the Brynffynon Arms (rendered always by Gwyn in his reminiscences as the Tavern of the Fountain or simply the Fountain Inn), would discreetly serve a pint to a man whose talk he loved to listen to, and the afternoon would pass sweetly away. The men sat yarning in the pub, and the boys played happily for hours in the grassy dells and copses, or in the tumbled graveyard. Here they would go to read, as a point of honour, the headstone marking the resting-place of Guto Nyth Brân, the celebrated runner, whose story Gwyn would one day present as a radio play.

Sometimes there were days of adventure which surpassed everything. Gwyn wrote fully himself about such joys as the annual outing on the train or on fleets of buses to the beach at Barry Island, where they would put on hired bathing suits:

We looked like rather derelict druids, you know, with these long blue saggy costumes making our way down to the sea, and we would hit the water, and very often we'd make one gigantic movement of the arms which we thought would take us to the other side of the Channel, and we would leave the costumes well behind, and the sea would become a kind of floating miasma of shed costumes, and the deacons would be patrolling the beach, looking for any sign of un-Christian excitement or levity.[6]

Especially he remembered the glorious summer of 1926 when the miners and their families created a hundred processions and carnivals to pass the time until their strike should end, an experience which furnished him with material for his first radio play.

Nana remembered an occasion when, having provided Gwyn, Eddie, and Dil with sufficient food to last a fortnight and seen them walk off for a week's camping holiday down in the Vale, she was sitting for a rare peaceful evening at home. After furtive rustlings at the door she opened it to discover Gwyn, sheepishly deputed by his elders to announce that they had eaten all their supplies and hence were returned for supper. Both Gwyn and Dil loved to remember a marathon walking expedition they once set out on; in Dil's words:

The tramp to the seaside. Gwyn, Eddie, Vincent Jones and self, complete with blankets and cooking materials. . . . We started very early, Trebanog, Tonyrefail, and then on to Smilog, the wood to the right of Coedely. There on the high ground we saw the sun, a great red ball resting on the clouds. Then on to Cowbridge. Breakfast at Bro Emlyn's. After a hearty meal we pushed on to the sea, Marcross. I can't remember how we got back from there. The only incident I can remember is that of Bro Gwyn being woken by a sheep sniffing his head which was outside the tent. He vowed never to sleep in a tent again.

They were a family of enthusiastic walkers. There was another day Dil remembered well, when the three youngest brothers and John caught a bus to the top of the valley, then walked over the Rhigos Mountain and down to Pont Nedd Fechan at the entrance to the Vale of Neath; here they explored the valley of the Mellte and the great rock called Craig y Dinas, traditionally the site of the grave of King Arthur. Then they caught a bus to Mountain Ash and had tea with their sister Carrie before walking back across the mountain to Cymmer. 'Reached home in time to hear Richard Tauber making his radio début in this country,' Dil recalled. 'Bro Gwyn listened with his feet in a bowl of water for his blisters.'

The people living all around provided a wonderful gallery of individuals for the keen and appreciative eye of the young Gwyn, who early gained a reputation for a satirical turn of mind and phrase. They make the stuff of the world he began to project in his novels and stories about 'The Terraces' and the not very thoroughly disguised townships of 'Meadow Prospect', 'Birchtown', 'Ferncleft' and so on in the years just after the Second World War. Many of them recur in somewhat less fictional form – but not much less – in his 'sort of autobiography', *A Few Selected Exits*. Outside his own teeming family and the houseful of cousins on the opposite side of the road there were innumerable characters, from the teachers and churchmen to the shopkeepers, policemen, colliers, union men, sportsmen, cinema-proprietors and denizens of the various workingmen's clubs like the Non-Pol and the Con (the Constitutional, this latter, not the Conservative Club) constantly crossing each other's path in their daily toings and froings in a rather confined world. And there were the rather terrifying eccentrics who can loom so large in the eye of childhood: tramps and scavengers, or the harmless but unsettling mongol; or those like Louie Lipman, the glazier, who seemed to go everywhere with large and dangerous sheets of glass across his back; or even the genuinely menacing, staring-eyed man called Mortimer, whom Gwyn once encountered in the back lane looking so tall and black-cloaked and evilly intentioned that he fled back to the house, and perhaps just as well, for Mortimer was a little later arraigned on a charge of murder and hanged for it. On another level, Arthur Cook, the miners' leader and Lewis Jones, the communist organiser and novelist, were among those who dropped in to chat, and the talk engaged in by his father and elder brothers with such people began increasingly to engage Gwyn's attention as he grew older. He watched everyone and everything with rapt, unblinkered eye, and loved gossip and yarns; he told stories, too, some perhaps just invented or at least considerably embellished, though an amazing number of his most bizarre accounts had some germ of truth in them, for he was a person all his life to whom ridiculous things tended to happen. It is not difficult to see the origins of Gwyn's impulse to write.

Although he passed the examination to attend the County School,

21

Gwyn's first year or two there were not particularly distinguished. He was known to 'mitch' – or play truant – on occasions when something more interesting distracted his attention on the way to school, and he was often late, thus attracting early the attention of the formidable headmaster, E.T. Griffiths, who believed in beating recalcitrant youth with some enthusiasm where correction seemed necessary. He had early acquired the habit of smoking; inevitably, he later argued during a television interview:

> I was the youngest of eight brothers. They were all very heavy smokers, and by the time that I was eight I thought that this plume of smoke from the nose was a kind of Mendelian appendage, and I felt really deprived.... So I stole their cigarettes until I was eleven, when I could buy my own. And I was on about ten Woodbines a day by the age of ten. I had nicotine stains up to here (*indicating his elbow*). I was the greatest inhaler of my time – I was a good baritone, had good breath control, and whenever I inhaled it was so intense an experience that I was the only man who at twenty-one had cancer of the knee-caps.[7]

Joining the smokers in the boiler-room at the County School similarly qualified him for the cane, and he was caught more than once, each time becoming better known to the headmaster.

E T (as everyone called him) was a man whose influence on Gwyn's life was to be much greater than either could have realised at these early skirmishes. The product of a poor family in a remote west Welsh village, E T had, after the sort of encouragement from a village schoolmaster celebrated in Emlyn Williams' play *The Corn is Green*, and supported by a far-sighted local landowner, gone to Oxford and become a university lecturer, a well-known scholar with the command of several European languages, and a great patriot for Wales. Now he had returned to the country that had given him his chance, determined to play a role in the shaping of better futures for the young, and at the Rhondda County School in the 1920s he found plenty of young men worthy of the best education that could be provided. Among these were two boys in particular whom Gwyn, at about thirteen years of age, suddenly decided to emulate. One of them was his brother Walt, six years older and already a great man at the school when Gwyn joined it. Gwyn had long idolised Walt, sticking close to him whenever he could, willingly running errands for him, enduring his punishment without rancour when Walt, furious at the way his concentration on his books was being disturbed by the noise his younger brothers were making, would suddenly grab them and pitch them into the *cwtch* or cupboard under the stairs. Now Walt was at the University, and the idea began to grow in Gwyn's head that he could do the same.

The other lad was only a couple of years older than Gwyn; his name was John Wynne Roberts, and he came from a comparatively wealthy family living up the valley in Penygraig. Already by the fourth form a by-word for topping examinations and winning prizes, he was a musical, thoughtful, eccentric boy with whom Gwyn somehow or other embarked on a great friendship, perhaps the only real friendship of his life.

With the example of his brother and his friend in mind, Gwyn transformed himself into a dedicated worker of model industry. The walking and talking and cinema-going continued to be great pleasures, but now books and learning joined them as primary interests, and Eddie found himself increasingly left alone to pursue his interests. As these by now included a warm and enthusiastic awareness of his own sexuality, something which came later and more coolly to Gwyn, he did not too much mind that some of his explorations of the possibilities of life, of the hidden hollows in the hillsides and the doorways in back lanes, were unaccompanied by a younger brother. They still went to the cinema together, sometimes two or three times a week, and it was Gwyn who most related to the exotic worlds thrown on the screen when gangster or western pictures were on the programme. For much of his life Gwyn showed from time to time something of the way those films had affected him, for though he parodied and ridiculed them, he imitated his screen heroes too, wearing gangster-type slouch hats pulled over his brow and speaking their language. One of the odd features of his lexis as a writer was the inclusion of some such terms remembered from the westerns of his youth: the local area for instance was for him the 'gulch', or the 'zone'.

In the school he encountered another man whose influence on him was great; this was Georges Rochat, a Swiss teacher of languages whom E T had met in Geneva and with a kind of imperial command had summoned to the Rhondda Valley. Unable to speak English at the time of his appointment, Rochat had quickly mastered yet another tongue and was at about the time of Gwyn's conversion to scholarly ways establishing himself in Porth as a teacher of rare skill. Appointed to teach French, he also spoke German and Turkish fluently, and had as the great thing in his life a passion for Spain and the Spanish language. Gwyn was the first of his pupils to express an interest in Spanish, and a die was cast.

Nobody could ever quite explain why Gwyn became a specialist in Spanish, or why indeed it was languages which he studied at all. His true bent was for literature and history, and as a linguist he seems to have been miscast. According to his own oft-repeated testimony he 'had heard that Buenos Aires was top of the league for sin, sex and sun', and he could not resist the contrast thus suggested with his own gloomy, wet and righteous Rhondda. Although he mastered the grammars of the languages which he studied and became an expert reader in both French and Spanish, he had no love for them as languages, and always felt that it was an odd and artificial thing to be trying to communicate in any other languages but the one he loved best. Speaking the languages was not in those days the primary reason for studying them, however, and Gwyn, when he applied his excellent memory and capacity for sheer hard mental labour to the task, became the most successful student ever to pass through Rochat's hands. His Higher School Certificate results were so good that he was offered State, County and Borough scholarships to see him through university. He would have liked to go to Cardiff, but there was no possibility of doing Spanish there at that time and he was persuaded that he should apply to an Oxford college.

His childhood and youth seemed to have come to a triumphant conclusion, and Nana was full of pride as she began to prepare the clothes and sheets and other paraphernalia he would need to go away with. Her young brother, almost her child, was a phenomenon; difficult at times and impractical he might be, and she was worried about how he would manage to look after himself far away in England, but he had a good brain, was a marvellous talker, and got on well with everybody; surely all would be well.

The signs were hopeful. At school he had not only done well academically but had also participated as enthusiastically in concerts and plays and operettas as he had in the home and chapel environment. He had played rugby, displaying considerable promise as a running, jinking three-quarter, but that had ended when he lost his appetite for the game after a nasty accident in which his spleen had been damaged; his brother-in-law, Jennie's husband Dr Bryan, had perhaps saved his life on that occasion, for a boot had torn a nasty hole in Gwyn's side and rapid and correct attention had been vital. Perhaps his delight in the game would return at Oxford, and help him make friends. As it happened, it never did; Gwyn had never really cared for sport, and was happy enough ever afterwards to seem as ham-handed in that area of physical endeavour as he was in all others, for it left him free for the cerebration which for him was the breath of life. But even if rugby were not to be the *entrée* to a vital life at Oxford, surely his other gifts would stand him in good stead. And his friend Wynne Roberts was already there, a scholar at Magdalen, and there were bound to be other Welsh lads with whom he could make contact. Nana hoped for the best. She could hardly have guessed that he was about to enter on the three most miserable and unhappy years of his life, that it would be the best part of a decade before her Gwyn would find things going well for him again.

II

ADRIFT IN A MAD WORLD

3

Gwyn the Obscure – A Welshman at Oxford

Once he had realised that it would be necessary to go to Oxford if he wanted to read Spanish, and tempted perhaps by the fine promise which the notion of going to Oxford seemed to hold out, Gwyn wrote in confident mood soon after the Higher Certificate results were announced to the Principals of two or three of the Oxford colleges, having picked them out with a pin from the multitude of possibilities. Two replies arrived; one of them, he said, was illegible; the other was in answer to a letter couched in these terms:

> Dear Sir,
>   Having decided to take up my studies at the University of Oxford during the forthcoming year, I am extremely desirous of entering St Edmund Hall as a student, primarily, of Modern Languages. Although I am keenly aware of the belated nature of my application, I am still hopeful of being accepted at your college; I should be very grateful if you would let me know, at your earliest possible convenience, if my hope has any foundation.[1]

After calling Gwyn to Oxford for an interview, the Principal of St Edmund Hall confirmed that the young man's hopes were indeed well founded, and Gwyn accepted this, the first offer made to him. It is now that the difficulties began, the first and most protracted being in the matter of money. Innocently totalling up the value of the awards that had come his way, Gwyn happily informed his family that he would be no burden to them at all; it came as a shock to discover that only the State Scholarship's £80 would be payable, and that his County and Borough awards were merely honorary. Still bitter about it almost forty years later, he began one of his *Punch* pieces with a claim that he had gone up to Oxford 'on the smallest grant in the history of official caution', and went on to describe in his characteristic way some of the frustrating attempts he and his family made at the time to organise supplementary sums from comparatively wealthy relatives or local charities. In a letter to Walt, who was now teaching languages at the Grammar School in Neath, Gwyn wrote:

> I now want about £75 more in order to keep myself from falling into the merciless hands of Oxford's Official Receiver and the subsequent incarceration in one of the city's prisons for recalcitrant debtors.... I have infused our estimable pater with some of my own enthusiasm, and he has been to see approximately 50% of the Glamorgan Council.... I suppose you think I am a fool to have started upon this brainless venture with such slender resources, but my Cynffig blood boils at the thought of capitulation, and I am prepared to go through with it and bag a few scholarships during the first year and obtain by this means some sense of comfort and security during the second year. The worst I have to fear is a nervous breakdown and I have been so near that particular state for the past year that I now treat it as an old friend.

Nothing significant in the way of additional money was forthcoming; he would just have to manage. As he had never had to manage anything before, least of all a budget that had to cater for anything other than a few cigarettes and couple of visits to the cinema, he felt some trepidation, but was able to forget it for a while in the frenetic bouts of activity which now took place to equip him for his momentous excursion. In 'Arrayed Like One of These' he described memorably the business of procuring a tailored overcoat at his father's insistence, and, in *A Few Selected Exits*, the gift from the much-travelled keeper of the nearby sweetshop of a fabulous trunk in which all his belongings could be transported to his new home.

Although worried about the financial quagmire into which he seemed to be advancing and, once the transition had been made, alarmed by the agonies of homesickness that immediately began to assail him, Gwyn started at Oxford in October 1931 on his best behaviour. From his lodgings at 27 Minster Road he trekked daily into Hall, and got started on his courses with books borrowed from Wynne Roberts, who was well established at Magdalen. After a while a letter arrived from Walt offering a small but regular subvention from his salary as a teacher to help his brother pay his dues, and

Gwyn replied relatively cheerfully:

> I accept your offer on condition that you cease payments as soon as you
> find that you need the money for your own purposes because I have a
> positive dread of being a nuisance to someone else.... I enjoyed your
> spirited paragraph concerning my land-lady, but I do not think that I
> shall have to perform any illegal operations with a penknife, rusty or
> otherwise. She is much better than I first thought and the meals she
> cooks are excellent.

Walt had made quite a hard decision in electing to offer Gwyn
some support for he had already undertaken to send a proportion of
his salary home to Nana until times improved; in consequence to
this, he broke off his engagement to Nest Salmon, the sixteen-year-
old daughter of one of his colleagues in Neath, saying that marriage
would have to wait. In the event the match proved good; the two
young people drew close together again and were eventually married
in 1935. It was fortunate for the family that Walt's girl was so very
young, for that must have helped him to see that a delay might be
beneficial as well as necessary.

Perhaps not quite appreciating what the gesture was costing his
brother, Gwyn put financial worries as far from his mind as possible
and pitched into his studies in French and Spanish with a will. As he
met Wynne almost every day, and they were able to spend hours
listening to music on Wynne's gramophone and endlessly talking, he
was at first able to cope reasonably well with Oxford's strangeness
and even to enjoy it; he described the Matriculation ceremony to
Walt:

> We had to tog up in full academic dress (c'est à dire – subfusc suit, white
> bow, cap and gown); we were then shepherded through the streets of
> Oxford like a set of degenerate toffee-apples to the Divinity Hall where
> we were granted a certificate of Matric, together with a Book of Statutes
> (worth 7/6) by the Very Rev, the Vice-Chancellor, accompanied by his
> mace-bearer, who is the most stupid-looking person I've ever seen, but
> then, I don't suppose it takes much culture to be able to carry a mace....
> When we were going out, the New College freshmen were coming in,
> and there, in the middle of them, looking very self-conscious, was R.C.
> Sherriff; he's starting this year, taking Modern History. I'm going to join
> the Oxford University Labour Club and the Society for the furtherance
> of Oswald Mosley's New Party – not because I believe in the efficacy
> of Oswald's proposed measures, but because there are plenty of refresh-

ments.... I'm not going to join the Union this year – £11 is too much of a good thing all at once. I may also become a bulwark of the Hall Debating Society.

Less came of these good intentions than one would expect, because Gwyn very soon found the alien nature of the Oxford he discovered almost more than he could cope with. In his autobiography he treated the period with dazed comic bewilderment:

> Had I been a Venusian I would not have made smaller contact with the place. The high and ancient walls provided an acoustic which was unbearably sharp. The speech of the townpeople reached me in the form of a yelp. That of the students was so languid I had to keep my ear incessantly close to them to gather any of their drift at all.[2]

Equally comic was his explanation of his sense of inferiority that, by being a Celt of average size – i.e. short – he could never get used to having an eye-level which took in the bottom waistcoat button of his infinitely tall Saxon contemporaries, causing him a crick in the neck if he made a real attempt to look them in the face. In 1977 he recalled on television:

> Nothing ever struck me, nothing ever hurt me quite as violently as this contrast when I went up to Oxford, because I'd been brought up, you see, in this warm soup of comradeship, love, singing, understanding; because the South Wales society was the most marvellously inter-penetrating thing, everybody seemed to be sensitive with a thin-skinned awareness of everybody else's problems ... and then you see, from the Rhondda Valley, without preparation, without ever having been to any other kind of place, any other kind of school, I went to Oxford, which was the most glacial, the most forbidding, the most remote place. It was like being taken to Nepal without even the excuse of being a mountaineer and dumped down among those frozen peaks. And you know, the three years I spent there were peaks of total alienation.[3]

At the time he complained to Walt:

> My whole bearing up here is a lie; you strive to speak as others speak and do as others do; your measure of success depends upon your adaptability to a certain atmosphere. I have succeeded pretty well so far merely because I am a fairly proficient actor. The only place that I divest myself of 'la guibba y la farina' is Wynne Roberts's lodgings; we have a big pot of tea and readopt our natural speech and manner. This arduous process is called 'the cultivation of the Oxford Manner'. The pose

becomes part and parcel of one in time and then the cultivation is complete. It's hard for Wynne because he's too honest a soul to be a good actor, or shall we say, a good comedian. You've got to remember that we're not at Jesus, but at colleges where Welshmen are looked upon with the same amazement as would be accorded to a Tibetan yak.

The posing did not last for long; as his energy became depleted and his disillusionment grew, Gwyn withdrew virtually completely from the Oxford experience and became a kind of hermit, hobnobbing only with a few chosen and equally displaced souls. It is not altogether easy to understand what went wrong, despite the explanations he has offered himself. Almost everyone who ever met Gwyn will confirm that he was a most companionable fellow, that wit flowed and laughter sprang wherever he went, and that people were drawn towards him by a force in his personality. One cannot accept that Oxford rejected so totally and so injudiciously a man of Gwyn's potential; he must have brought it at least partly upon himself, and the question is, how?

Part of the answer may lie in the nature of his political thinking at the time. He was already, as a result of all his listening to discussions of the wrongs wrought by capitalism and Toryism, a committed socialist; few came out of the Rhondda with its experience of despoliation and exploitation without being so. He was a romantic, too, an idealist, and his political views at nineteen were couched mostly in extremes, which included routine and vituperative hatred of all that class of people who could be seen as exploiters. Voluble, with a flow of language that already glittered with wild and extravagant metaphor as well as being full of left-wing clichés, an early expert in the employment of heavy and sardonic irony, he may well have seemed a formidable and perhaps not very pleasant opponent to those who wished to offer an alternative way of thinking. There is no record that he used his debating powers in any official forum, but he may have actually felt some of the hatreds which his politics urged him to, and that kind of deadly seriousness and intensity would hardly have endeared him to students of very different backgrounds and convictions.

Part of the answer is to be found in his nature more generally. He was a naïve and inexperienced young man, and being removed from home and from someone dedicated to helping him in practical ways was too much for him. His disposition was to love and to be loved, moreover, but there was no girl to love him at Oxford. There had hardly been anything like a real love affair at home, as far as that goes; there was a beautiful girl from a wealthy home not far from 196 High Street who fascinated him, but she was usually surrounded by a host of eager admirers. The one time Gwyn had a chance to declare his love to her he had ended up by telling her that her head was as empty as the rooms in her father's great house. No more skilled at wooing new friends in the new and strange world of Oxford than he had been at courtship in his native place, Gwyn was doomed to some unhappiness until he could grow through so difficult a stage.

That growth in itself may have been inhibited by a factor Gwyn was not to find out about for sure for another four years; he recognised that he did not enjoy robust good health, but attributed this to too much smoking, a poorly selected diet and too much bending over small print in insufficient light when the truth was that he was already experiencing some of the effects of an inefficient thyroid, something which gradually made him more and more ill until it was finally diagnosed and dealt with.

As things were, Gwyn became an almost invisible student; few people knew who he was and at St Edmund Hall not many cared. As if to emphasise this, his name does not appear in the list of freshmen in the Hall's magazine for 1931–2, though there is one 'G. Thoms' from South Wales; and in the traditional photograph of the freshmen group there is neither a G. Thoms nor a Gwyn Thomas. Perhaps he absented himself deliberately from occasions of fuss and bother of which he did not approve; perhaps he was simply confused or careless or forgetful; in either case the omission of his name and person from the scene seems representative of the mark he was, or rather was not, making.

Not that he neglected his work, for the skill of applying himself to his books was hard won and never to be abandoned, but even here he managed to make things awkward for himself and for his tutors. He insisted, for instance, against the advice of his Spanish tutor, on studying the medieval lyric in Galicia instead of tackling something more satisfying and recent; he read doggedly in areas outside the set curriculum altogether; and he wrote long philosophical essays where brief and pithy critical observations were called for. In the French course which he had to do for Prelims (the First Public or qualifying examination students have to do during their first year),

1 'The Road to the Chapel': one of the drawings by John Dd Evans for Gwyn's *A Welsh Eye* in 1964

2 Porth Square in the early 1930s. In the foreground is the road leading down from Cymmer into Porth. Under the bridge flows the Taff. Commanding the square is the public lavatory in the shadows of which Gwyn once heard himself being discussed as a Red and a spy

3 The younger pair of Gwyn's
four sisters, Nana and Minnie,
in their teens

4 Nana at thirty, the picture carried
by her husband Bill throughout the
Second World War

5 The eight sons of Walter Morgan Thomas in 1915. Emlyn has Gwyn on his knee; the others
are (*back row, l–r*) Eddie and the twins Gwilym and Arthur; (*front row, l–r*) John, Dil and Walt

he complained to Walt, 'I'm back on that Romantic period again. It's great stuff but when you've been hard at it for two years, and your tutor is as dry as the driest dust, it begins to pall.' His hunger for knowledge was insatiable, but it wasn't always the knowledge which was on offer that he cared about, and his assumptions of superior ability to that of his fellow students and sometimes to that of his tutors was not always wholly justified.

In his own way he worked hard, and dealt grumblingly but more or less successfully with the problems of laundry (sending a parcel of dirty clothes and sheets to Nana to wash every fortnight), food (eating hot pies and coffee from a stall more often than not, finding something to object to in the meals supplied at college) and leisure. The last was the easiest, for he was always a great devotee of the cinema and he went as regularly as he could, giving accounts of his favourite films to Nana in his frequent letters home. And there was his friendship with Wynne Roberts, which sustained him throughout his first two years.

In the vacations he and Wynne remained inseparable, endlessly talking as they roamed over the hills or sat in the little Italian-run Rhondda cafés Gwyn loved so much. Their topics were various, of art and literature and music and women, but mostly of politics and how power might be gained in the future to put right the appalling social decline they saw on every side. Whether under Gwyn's guidance or not, Wynne, whose background was really quite comfortable, became a dedicated communist, even joining the party, a step which Gwyn himself never quite took. At the close of every day, late in the evening, still not satiated with talk, they would set out to walk to Wynne's home in Penygraig; when they got there, Wynne would turn and accompany Gwyn back to Cymmer; and then, more often than not, Gwyn would escort Wynne at least halfway back to Penygraig again.

Back in Oxford for a second year, Gwyn battled on with increasing grimness. Besides Wynne he had some friendly acquaintances, particularly a man called Jim Lawless from Sheffield, a fellow student of modern languages at Teddy Hall, with whom he got on well enough. Two other names, John Eric Jackson and Sam Shriberg, crop up from time to time in his letters home, and there were occasional pleasant encounters with students from South Wales: 'Jumbo' Williams; a man called Ashton from Neath; Trevor Morgan from Pontypridd –

Morgan turned out to have a magnificent collection of gramophone recordings of operas and orchestral music, and Gwyn spent several evenings in his company. None of these friendly relationships was more than a matter of temporary convenience, however, for none seems to have survived beyond the university contact. Gwyn was now even more remote from the fraternity of the Hall, having moved out to lodgings at Headington, and his life was painfully lonely. A series of quotations from his letters could easily be arranged to rival the complaints and lamentations of Job; Nana urged him to write more cheerfully and occasionally he would essay a feeble joke, but these more often turned to acerbic surveys of his surroundings and bitter outcries against his fate. A letter to Nana at the end of January 1933, when he had just received a parcel from home, shows him in a slightly better mood:

> With due dispatch and formal salute to the family, I delved deeply into the body of the Welsh cakes and got through about three quarters of them with the help of Lawless to whom I gave three as a kind of jealous ration. He says they're infinitely better than the ones made by his mother with all merited respect to her absent presence. She makes them thin and crisp, a state of cake which comes amiss to comrade Lawless. They call them Welsh cakes in Yorkshire, too. Which, considering the nasty criminal character of the North English is pretty tough on Hen Wlad fy Jake. ['Jake' was the name disrespectfully given by the boys to their father.] Tyshwn Cymreig. Holyname and blessed thing. Let none persist in attitude of unbelieving callousness to the cake Welsh. Soon I shall be asking for more: and with an eye on the wretchedness of my fate here will be grieved if I do not get them.

Readers may detect a somewhat false jollity in these words, which betray something of the young Gwyn's self-absorbed misery as well as his still juvenile cleverness – and perhaps a suggestion that he had been reading Joyce. Improving as it went, his letter continued:

> Last Saturday Hunt gave me some examination-papers lasting from nine o'clock in the morning to six o'clock at night. He allowed an hour's break at one o'clock during which Lawless and I rushed out to drink coffee and chat dismally on the prospect of an afternoon that looked like being as damnable as the morning. However the papers were not so bad and I wrote with a cheerful ease and occasional badness that I knew would please Hunt, our venerably bad tutor in French. So during this toil I had many gaps which I filled with pleasant thoughts of Porth, Pandy and

Penygraig ... beating the point of my nib into the table where I sat. These speculations robbed the day of some of its boredom and the nib of most of its point.

I shattered my vows this morning and went along to a lecture given by Entwistle in the Taylor Institution. I knew the room where these lectures were usually held but inside and around I saw no living soul. Thrusting away the theory that souls can never live, I decided that I was the only one desirous of hearing the lecture. I am not keen on sitting alone in a large lecture-hall, listening to the eloquence of the sometimes interesting professor, bound, by uncontrollable forces, to pay full attention. So down the green stairs I sped, eager to be away. (That sentence reminds me of a song you used to sing, Nan, something by Bantock, maybe.) At the door I met Jackson, my very intelligent partner in restlessness ... and asked him whether he'd like to share a lecture with me. He said that, being member of a good socialist family, he'd share anything with me. So up we went together, wearing expressions of solemn resignation, and Entwistle met us as we were entering the hall. He asked whether we knew if any of the others were coming. Jackson and I exchanged looks of whimsical amusement. I answered that the Spanish school as a whole was too deficient in wit to be attracted by so technical a subject. So he took us both into his private room and there we had a comfortable chat upon all things but the one originally chosen for discussion. We are going to meet him again next Friday. He's a great fellow.

There was some relief from the loneliness of 18 Highfield Avenue, Headington, towards the end of his second year when, granted £90 by the Miners' Welfare Fund, he was able to take up the option offered by his course to go to Spain to improve his knowledge of his preferred language. In April 1933, he travelled with Lawlesss to Madrid and registered as a student in the new people's university there.

Important for him though the experience in Spain was, it was beset as usual by the perversities that life generated about Gwyn – or that he somehow generated about life. He was in Spain during a period of great significance for its own and for Europe's future, and recognised that something special was going on; recalling it for a television programme made just before his death he said:

When you passed over the mountains into Spain you had the awareness of something completely new. Everybody's face radiated somewhat, because ... in 1931, the King, Alfonso XIII, with nobody's blessing had left Spain.... They had the feeling, all the intelligent people of Spain, that these great thick shrouds that had been weighing upon them for three or four hundred years had been shaken off and they were doing the most remarkable things. For the first time the country was sending writers out to be their ambassadors in all the capitals of the world whereas for centuries past only the most immaculate aristocrats had represented Spain.... And of course the great pay-off line was the University of Madrid.... It was new, brand-new, it was the first university ever created in Spain outside the orbit of the church, it was the first attempt by a worldly government to create an educational system for working, living, unbelieving people.[4]

Tortured by his usual ineffable shyness, Gwyn found it hard to become part of what he perceived to be happening, approve of it though he might. He claimed that once or twice he had heard the woman orator known as La Pasionaria in full flight, and had once spoken in a café to Lorca, aware of meeting for a moment a great soul, but for the most part he stayed in his room reading. His texts were Tauchnitz English editions, cheaply available locally, of Shakespeare and the English classics which he longed for in that exotic place as much as in Oxford he longed for the Rhondda. He was entranced by the sight of a girl sitting on the balcony of a house which he passed while on a lonely midnight walk, but did nothing about it other than to walk that way again on subsequent nights. As La Pasionaria's fame did not begin to spread until the Civil War made her an international celebrity, and as Lorca was at the time living in the south, a long way from Madrid, it is probable that these encounters never happened. Certainly Jim Lawless denies knowledge of them. The references show Gwyn's propensity for presenting rather what he conceived to be the artistic rather than the tamer literal or historical truth. He later wrote stories about his frustrated and unrequited love for the girl on the balcony; what might have been was often for Gwyn much more interesting than what was, and both because he was in the business of entertainment and because he preferred life as his fertile imagination was able to reconstruct it to the real, cooler, less satisfying thing, he had no qualms about his cavalier attitude towards mere facts.

Short of money yet again, because the grant failed to come through promptly, and finding his health adversely affected by the change, he was soon in a state of wishing he had never gone there. He wrote to the Bursar at St Edmund Hall, begging that his battels bill be delayed:

> Dear Sir,
>
> As Mr Lawless will no doubt inform you, we are now entering upon our fourth week of study at Madrid and, being a person with body and spirit enough to appreciate suffering in its elementary forms, I would that it were the last. We have experienced little but discomfiture since we arrived.... First, there is the heat of the day, to which I object on parliamentary grounds. Then there is the cold of the night.... In addition, I am not at all pleased with the enthusiasm with which the Spanish nation takes to the delights of bomb-throwing.... They have set up civil slaughter as a rival attraction to the public dispatch of bulls.[5]

A few weeks later, when the official term at the university had been completed, he wrote again:

> I intend proceeding northward, the duration of my course depending upon (a) the ebb and flow of my bodily pain which does not cease to regale my life and (b) my longing for the cold, enduring, studious peace which my native surroundings only can afford. Here, I am on the rack, and only the misplaced enthusiasm of countless thousands could prompt me to say otherwise.[6]

When he came to write an account of this sojourn in Spain for *A Few Selected Exits* he made the whole episode, true to the comic view he had taken up in his maturity, into a hilarious narrative of perversity, bizarre mischance and eccentric encounters, and about half of his tale had to do with the appalling return journey with which it concluded. Caught in unscheduled train manoeuvres in the troubled Basque country, he walked for miles, mostly along the sharp-edged loose chippings beside the rails. His feet in his cheap shoes suffered cuts and blood soaked his socks, sticking them irremovably to his feet as it congealed. There was nowhere to attend to them until he reached Paddington in London where he was able to take a bath and tidy up the worst of the damage, but when he finally arrived home, Nana nearly died of horror as he displayed his shredded feet.

At the end of that year Wynne's university career came to an unsatisfactory end when, after all the promise he had shown, he went down with a poor degree. This was largely in consequence of having curiously but quixotically changed course from the modern languages at which he excelled to English, on the grounds that this would be more useful to someone with a social conscience who intended to work on his own ground among the proletariat. He could not have thought it through for the English course required study of ancient forerunners of the language even less relevant than Italian or French to the requirements of Welsh miners and the children of unemployed steel workers. His departure marked almost the end of any pleasure that might be wrung out of Oxford for Gwyn.

He returned to Oxford late for the beginning of his final year, having spent a vacation of inexplicably poor health. The trouble was that when the particular after-effects of his unhappy stay in Spain wore off he was still suffering from the toxic thyroid which had not yet been diagnosed. It was the beginning of the worst year of all, for now he was lodged in Hall, and his melancholia became profound. It did not help that when he looked out of his window he found himself gazing into an ancient graveyard, so that notions of mortality attacked him from both within and without. He seemed to have hardly any friends, and in a craving for company took to descending into the quadrangles and speaking to the first persons he saw; if they answered pleasantly, he would immediately ask them back up to his room for cocoa. Many thought him more than a little mad, but he had some takers, as he explained to Nana:

> They are as unhappy here as I am.... One of them has fair hair, going dark by neglect of cleanliness; he dresses shabbily ... his father is Lascelles Abercrombie, the poet.... It transpires that as a citizen he's a bigger pain than he is as a poet.... The other fellow is named David Lloyd.... During his vacation he took part in a number of communist agitations. One of them was rather serious and as a legal consequence of his political frenzies, he spent three days in the local jug. The state, which frowns upon these little lapses, retaliated generously by taking away his scholarship indefinitely.

So much did he hate his situation that he took to putting his address at the top of letters as 'St Edmund Hell' or 'St Edmund Hole'; but, as he approached his finals, an even greater worry began, namely, what would he do next year? It was 1934 and unemployment was up to unprecedented levels; in the Rhondda there were no jobs to be had, except occasionally by those who knew the right combination of councillors and could pull a string or two, and Gwyn desperately wanted to return to the Rhondda. Realising how important his result would be, he tackled his work with increasing fervour but little love for much of it. His tutors found him difficult to understand and were worried about him, though it occurred to no one that he might be seriously ill. Professor Entwistle, asked by Principal Emden to furnish a report when Gwyn suddenly asked to be considered for a research studentship after graduation, wrote:

> Confidentially I would say that he is probably the most anxious problem in our department. Coming to Oxford has completely disorganised him mentally in a way that he would have been spared in a junior university. There he would have had prescribed work, terminal examinations, and a wigging when he did less than the conventional minimum; and perhaps such an arrangement, while not enfranchising the mind, would have held him on the rails. Coming here to an atmosphere of self-expression and discussion, he has, I think, lost his way; and his considerable cleverness has been shown in erratic thought, while his inner nervousness seems to have given offence as if it were arrogance. One knows that he is clever and hard-working (perhaps too hard, for his health does not appear good), but one can prophesy little about his future. . . . I very much doubt whether research is his calling, at any rate most doubtfully in Oxford, where he is still far from happy.[7]

Had Gwyn ever seen that report from the professor he considered a 'grand fellow' he might have offered some strong animadversions upon it, but he might too have admitted that it was perceptive, kindly and accurate. A less sympathetic teacher might have written more irascibly of Gwyn's resistance to suggestion, his unwillingness to accept or consider criticism, his refusal to see any other point of view than his own. The trouble undoubtedly had some root in the poor health which Entwistle had plainly discerned, but it lay too in Gwyn's own proud, stubborn character and in the deep prejudices against much of what Oxford stood for which he had brought with him from his Rhondda background. All about him were people of wealth, privilege and physical superiority, and he could not or would not at the time see beyond those trappings to the essential decency and mental and cultural excellence which were also there.

Deepest of all was the sense of his own dignity which made it important for him then, as throughout his life, to rely wholly on his own efforts. He would never ask for help even when he needed it, and he regarded with suspicion and usually ignored any suggestion that he might change his ways. Though he always worked unremittingly hard at what seemed to him important, he never found a proper self-discipline which might have allowed him to refine his considerable giftedness and release his genius fully, nor was he destined to find an editor who would help him achieve that end. Aware of his own shortcomings, he agonised over them privately but never found a way to deal with them, preferring always to escape into his writing and his talking where he found it possible to entertain and turn enough pennies to keep going.

The idea of doing postgraduate research at Oxford might have been a serious one, but more likely it was part of the programme of grasping at straws upon which he entered as his finals came closer and the need to find some kind of employment loomed larger. He considered the possibility of the Civil Service and told Nana:

> I should like my life to be of profit to myself and to someone else. In order to achieve this end, it is of vital moment I select for myself a job near home. But the days are over when people could select jobs for themselves. Nowadays, with a hundred persons slitting each other's throats to obtain one single job, the honours go usually to that human being blessed with the greatest capacity for evil. But, little as you may suspect it, I have a number of ideas about advancing myself to a position of formidable prosperity that will allow us to knock that wall down in the middle room and construct that iron staircase with a loud-speaker on every rail that I have dreamed about.... As far as the most obvious avenues are concerned, teaching and the Civil Service are enough.

His student days came towards their end in a fine delirium of hard work and contemptuous dismissal of the ideas, abilities and characteristic qualities of his contemporary undergraduates. The Marxists and socialists he found most sympathetic, but even they often irritated him with their juvenescent twitterings. Those he found most objectionable were the overt Christians, for he could not stand their anxiety to convert him back to the ways of chapel and church which he had long found intellectually untenable and socially nefarious. Nobody could have made him happy until the whole period at Oxford was over, for he had taken an unshakable set against it. His moments of comparative delight were all in the cinema, and he wrote to a friend of the family who had emigrated to the United States:

These days I derive my only satisfaction from the pictures. I go regularly; sometimes three, sometimes four times a week. I never tire. I am as indefatigable as the Cymmer ash-man. If I can, I'm going to get into the film business: as a critic or as a scenario-writer or something else as leisurely and as prettily paid.

I regard gangsters as the finest film-subjects. They may be untrue. I suppose they are. A glorification and Christian baptism and purging of vermin. But that does not alter the fact of their greatness as types of civilisation that started off by being lousy and ending up by being lousier. Take Paul Muni's *Scarface*. From my point of view of the drama a greater film will never be made. Equally great were Edward G. Robinson's *Little Caesar* and Wallace Beery's *Secret Six*. They were classics.[8]

The idea of somehow finding a niche in the world of film-making was probably no more than the wildest and most momentary of dreams; in practice he made no attempt whatever to move in that direction until invited to do so in the 1960s. What is perhaps more interesting is that it does not yet seem to have occurred to him that he might write for a living, though he observed prophetically to Walt in a letter of 1932: 'Our pilgrimage ends in childhood and the remaining days are spent in commenting topographically upon the pilgrimage.'

He certainly wrote letters very copiously during this heavily introspective and dejected stage of his life, as he never would again, but there was as yet no attempt at fiction in any form. A certain self-awareness made him halt himself in his tracks in the middle of almost his last letter home from Oxford; starting by sounding off about 'the various abominable objects that in the eyes of the world's tourists constitute "the Beauty of Oxford",' to which 'sickening sore' he hopes to 'wave a contemptuous fond farewell' on leaving for the last time, he suddenly says:

> And now I shall leave those desperate thoughts that, however stimulating they may appear to me, can only be depressing for you. It may yet be my function to bring laughter to those who have known misery too long: even though I give myself a pain in the neck.

He approached the seven continuous days of final examinations in 'worried, worked up, flurried, burned up, angry, prostrate, weary' state of mind, arguing:

43

I sit some dozen papers, set me by a man who has probably forgotten the answers to whatever questions he may care to ask me. If that was all, Thomas would have but little cause for protest. But after asking them, they take good care to consult friends and books with an eye to discovering the answers. And then, when I have offered up my small sacrifice in the Small Examination Schools (the sacrifice smaller than the Schools) with innocence in my heart, they pounce upon me with the information that I've got a wrong line on every subject that fell my way. I will have to express surprise at that revelation, and suggest that I am not yet of an age to compete with their powers of mature judgment and discretion. That remark, without having any relevance to my status as a Lover of the Book will possibly make the difference between one degree-class and another. So I may as well go and pay my compliments to them now and get a First without sitting the papers. That will save me thirty-three hours, thirty-three head-aches, thirty-three heartburns and roughly one square foot from the seat of my subfusc trousers.

When the results of the examinations were announced Gwyn had, to his intense disappointment, missed a First by a thickish whisker. Walt had shown himself to be the more successful scholar. A good Second would be a perfectly good qualification for a job, if there were any job to be had, but it wasn't the same. Still, at least he had finished his purgatorial stint at Oxford.

4

First Death

GWYN THOMAS, BA (OXON). He wrote his name with its new appendage a dozen or so times inside the cover of one of the notebooks that he began to keep at about this time. He had gone through a kind of hell to get his degree. It looked encouraging when written down. Now, what would it do for him? Despite his awareness of the worsening economic plight of the country since the slump at the beginning of the 1930s, intensified by the knowledge that Wynne and numbers like him had been unable to find regular employment, he could not help hoping that things would be different for him. It was not long before disillusionment set in.

He was pleased to be back in Cymmer, to feel that 196 High Street was genuinely his home again and that the Rhondda was henceforth his stamping ground. He had sampled foreign parts and did not care for them. Oxford was unmentionable. England generally was not quite right for him; he later gave a macabre account of what happened when he went to stay with a friend on a farm near Worcester during his first long vacation. He had accepted the invitation, he said, to get away from home for an interlude in his fruitless courtship of Mary, the girl whose father had the biggest house in town:

> She had a great collection of vivid tartan skirts on the short side, which stood out like a sunrise in a place where the garments of women tended to be long and dun.
>
> ... Her skirts were attracting a fine audience. She was a well-trained flirt. She had dozens of lads dancing around her, and I was the most laggard, least confident member of this band. She would lure the others and then call them to a halt with a tinkling laugh. For me she did not even tinkle. Whenever I managed to pronounce an audible word in her

45

presence and got my eyes close enough to hers to suggest ardour, she would bring me crashing down with a series of crushing rebuffs.... So I looked forward to a fortnight of not having to moon about this enchantress.[1]

But the rural retreats of Worcestershire concealed something quite as nasty as anything in the woodshed of *Cold Comfort Farm*, and Gwyn was glad to leave earlier than planned rather than continue to stay in a house that turned out to be sheltering, in the elder brother of his friend, a homicidal lunatic.[2] So much for England.

Romantic Spain had hardly been better, though there had been compensations for the heat of the sun and the inefficiency of the young and incomplete university. In the weeks he had spent slowly working his way home through northern Spain he had come, in the mining villages of the Asturias, upon scenes and people so reminiscent of his warm-hearted and essentially decent Rhondda Valley that the name of the town of Oviedo remained dear to him as long as he lived. But Spain was a long way off, and was in any case becoming increasingly dangerous. Gwyn did not yet realise that a civil war there was virtually inevitable, but he had spoken with enough people, who thought that violence was the only answer, to be fearful of the consequences.

Even if he had wanted to return to Spain, circumstances were hardly propitious. Something had to be done about finding a job before anything else could be considered. He needed, too, some time to adjust to living in a home where changes had taken place and a bigger change was in the offing. Emlyn had already left before Gwyn went to Oxford; finding it impossible to make a living from his music alone, he had taken a course in Public Health administration in Cardiff and had become a sanitary inspector in Cowbridge. Now married to Bessie, he was living in Mount Pleasant; in another year or two he went north to Deeside to become Public Health Inspector for Hawarden, and he and his talent for choral conducting were lost to the valley for good. Eddie had trained as a teacher in Exeter while Gwyn was at Oxford; he had a post at a school in Ealing and was to all intents and purposes a Londoner. John had left after marrying Gwen in 1933, but he was living nearby. Gwilym, at this stage a miner, and Dil, who worked in a shoe-shop, were still at home, and of course Walter Senior was a permanent resident.

If they thought that they had enslaved Nana for ever, however, they were in for a rude awakening. She had given up a great deal to look after the family after her mother's death; there was no reason why she should give up everything. When Gwyn came down from Oxford she was thirty-three. There was still time for her to marry and have a family of her own, if she had the energy to contemplate such a step. And she did.

Nearby there lived another family of Thomases, unrelated to the inhabitants of 196 High Street but friendly enough all through the years of growing up. In it were several brothers, one of whom, Bill, had had eyes for nobody else but Nana for several years, since, indeed, they were children together. A well-set-up young man, a great lover of sport and a good footballer, he was a tailor by trade and had been working in Barry when he first began dropping in at weekends to visit Nana and the family. In 1928 his calling took him to Wells, where he continued to wait patiently until he was able finally to persuade her that, her duty to her brothers well and truly done, she could come and join him.

Although this was but an unspoken something in the air when Gwyn came home after his last term at Oxford, it was one of a number of factors that helped make the next twelve months for him 'a daft, hallucinated year'. Already by October he was beginning to worry seriously about his prospects of employment. He wrote to the Principal of St Edmund Hall for help, telling him:

> I was advised by my doctor to forget surgical operations and the general onus of medical imposition that have been my lot for the past five years and use up my resources in finding some solid base on which to place the fragmentary elements of my life.
>
> In obedience to this advice, I hobbled up and down Wales, casting my eyes to left and right, searching for anything that might qualify as a solid base.... I returned home after two months of an interesting but fruitless itinerary, there to relapse into a coma of bodily discomfort and mental frustration.[3]

He had applied, he said, for a teaching position in Egypt, there being little available domestically; the task had involved him in putting more words onto a form than there were in the complete works of Balzac, but they still wanted more, which perhaps Mr Emden would be good enough to supply on his behalf. The Principal duly sent a testimonial which spoke of Gwyn's 'thoroughly satisfactory record in all subjects' and his 'keenness and industry', and E.T. Griffiths, now the Headmaster of Barry County School, also provided an enthusiastic testimonial. It was to no avail.

The trouble with being jobless in 1934, if you had never had a job before, was that you did not qualify for unemployment benefit as you had not paid the insurance. Supplementary benefit did not exist. If you were truly destitute you might be able to get some relief from the local Poor Law authority, the Public Assistance Board, but that was a step many people, including Gwyn, found themselves too proud to take. He had therefore to rely on the generosity of his family to keep him while he sought a solution, and the situation did nothing for his confidence in himself or for his respect for a society that could let such things be.

For a year or so he went about in moods veering between wild anger and searing bewilderment. He was not totally without money, as he had somehow contrived to leave Oxford with a positive bank balance; but he still owed £25 to E.T. Griffiths, who had staked him on his original departure for Oxford, and debts which he owed for books at Blackwells were not paid for several years. He walked and talked a great deal with Wynne Roberts, conceiving with him a number of possible undertakings in the writing line, but, though some paper was scribbled on, little came of it. He went to the Labour Exchange a good deal, and found himself once talking to an energetic but unemployed miner called Will Paynter, now working his way through union management to political influence, who was kicking against the pricks in a positive way that Gwyn much admired. But though he poured over the *Daily Worker* every day, diligently writing into one of his notebooks a rich succession of news items and editorial expressions of opinion which seemed particularly accusing of the government and all the ways of British bourgeois society, he had not the energy to become politically active. Much of the time he felt so low that he was convinced there was something wrong with him, but his doctor could find nothing. Recalling the period, Gwyn wrote:

I would die of natural causes. This thought caused me no misgivings. The world was full of marching maniacs and wounded economies. I was spent. The years of study with no relief of change or pleasure had burned my nerve-ends to ashes. I felt I had reached a point beyond the power of any miracle to revivify.

I approached my end with a kind of sinister jollity. I knew that, dying at twenty-two, I would regret not having travelled a little more, not having heard more music, not having made genuine love with willing women, but these things took second place to my desire to ease myself slyly and without fuss through the next door.[4]

In the late summer of 1935 two family weddings took place. Having arranged with her brother John that he and his wife would move into No. 196 to look after the house and the remaining menfolk, Nana allowed Bill Thomas to claim her, and off she went with him to Wells. A few weeks later, down in Neath, Walt finally took Nest to the altar, and set up home with her in a house next door to her parents' house in Bryncoch. Gwyn took one startled look at the new regime in Cymmer and decided to have as little to do with its settling-in period as possible. Though he had the highest regard for John, he was not so fond of Gwen, nor of the two sisters, Dilys and Kit, who forever seemed to be dropping in to natter with her. Gwen was something of a clairvoyante, or so she claimed, and to the house came women from up and down the street anxious to have their fortunes told from the tea-leaf patterns in their tea-cups. Kit ran a Chocolate Christmas Club, collecting money in dribs and drabs for parcels of goodies when the money was sufficient and the season due, and this too attracted more people to the house than the melancholic Gwyn could tolerate. As the years went on his objections to the female gabble that filled the place grew insuperable, though for one young woman visitor to his sister-in-law's circle he was to be eternally grateful. That was still a year or two ahead, however, when, as soon as Walt and Nest had settled in to their new home, he took a bus up the valley to Treherbert, walked the ten miles or so to Neath and announced he had come to stay.

He was there for more than a month before having to return to Porth to see Dr Clarke again. Well received by his tolerant brother and new sister-in-law, he was not unhappy in Bryncoch. Nest's grandmother kept a little shop, whither Gwyn would frequently repair for a chat, returning always with cigarettes and sweets from her store. The old woman could not help mothering him. No longer cherubic, tending now rather to be pale and thin, he brought out all her maternal desires to see him fed and fattened, and rewarded her with his mordantly funny company, for even when unwell he could, if he wanted, make laughter out of anything. He talked enthusiastically with his brother about Walt's idea of writing a short book about the Labour movement in South Wales in the nineteenth century, centring on the activities of Dr Price, the Chartist and active revolutionary, of Llantrisant, and Dic Penderyn, and told Nana:

> But Walt has laid aside the idea for a while. So he and I are now collaborating in dead earnest on a book dealing with every aspect of life in the Rhondda Valley from unemployment to this lump in my neck. He's doing it for fame. I'm doing it for fags. He's writing the facts. I'm writing the fiction. As yet neither is able to decide which is which.

Although Gwyn could sometimes be cheerful, Walt and Nest were worried about him, about the aimlessness of his frustrated life but also about the swelling in his neck, the goitre which was becoming more and more apparent, and which they felt was responsible for his poor condition.

The doctor was still baffled. It was, he thought, just an exophthalmic goitre. He prescribed 'Logule Mixture' – a weak solution of iodine to be taken with milk – and told Gwyn to stop worrying. Mental exhaustion was the cause of it, and rest the only cure.

Fortunately the G P's diagnosis was shortly superseded by one better informed. According to Gwyn's autobiography it was his brother-in-law, Dr Charles Bryan, who was the agent of his delivery:

> I made my way to the bridge in the middle of the town. Its steel was no harder than my dilemma. I was penniless, unfitted for entry into any market and overdue at the grave.... I was in a mood to do something defiantly Roman like throwing myself into the river. But that tactic at the time was being overworked and in personal conduct I always aimed at a bit of distinction. Besides the river was running shallow.... The only other alternative was a walk to the North Pole. I had always been attracted by the idea of a gradual, lethal numbness and a long absence of daylight.
>
> I was picking over these notions when my brother-in-law Charles, the doctor, pulled up alongside me.... He was shocked by the sight of me, the gauntness of my cheeks, the skeletal bareness of my frame, the general impression of a life hastening into the sunset. He had me lodged in hospital.[5]

As with the proposed book about Rhondda life embarked on in collaboration with Walt, and indeed in life generally, Gwyn in his autobiography often confused fact and fiction, or at any rate let the

6 The four youngest boys in 1931 (l–r) Dil, Gwyn, Walter and Eddie

7 Walking on the plateau near Llanwonno in the summer of 1933: Gwyn and, on the wall, his great friend, John Wynne Roberts

8 Unemployed workers on a protest march in the Rhondda in the mid 1930s

9 Excitement in the Puerta del Sol in Madrid on the outbreak of the Spanish Civil War in 1936

one flow seamlessly into the other. Whether he really felt so near-suicidal, whether it was Bryan who introduced him to a specialist, do not appear from an immensely long letter which he wrote to Nana in December 1935, but it is evident from the events which followed that he was not far from the death he said he was craving. He had seen a specialist, he said, who realised that his real trouble was in his thyroid:

> For the past year it has been excreting some kind of dangerous poison which accounts for my sleeplessness, my debilitated nerves and the unusual pallor and sunkenness of my face and body.... The gland has also forced my windpipe into a dangerous position. The specialist remarked that I've been lucky to be able to swallow.

Within a matter of days he was called into the hospital at Llwynypia to be the patient of Mr Melbourne Thomas (again no relation), a widely respected surgeon of the day. For well over a month, up to and past Christmas and on into the early days of 1936, while Gwyn was driven to the limits of his patience, an operation was delayed until it was deemed he was strong enough to bear the shock. '*Five weeks!*' he complained to Nana:

> Five weeks, stowed away in this white-sheeted, pasty-faced, moribund bogey-hole where life is so fundamentally dull, tedious and repulsively monotonous that it cheers me up to see someone dying for a change.

He gave as an example a homeless and hopeless old man called Walker in the same ward, who wanted the hospital to get on with it, do the operation, and kill him off if they pleased:

> Yesterday he went on the long journey, leaving even his toothbrush behind. I was quite happy to hear it. To die, when you are in Walker's position, is like winning a very good scholarship. Only you don't have to worry about getting a job at the end of it.

When the day for his operation arrived at last, he told John that he didn't care if he did die. Kill or cure was what he wanted, because life as he had been living it simply wasn't worth while. As he slipped under the anaesthetic it felt like death and he went towards it without reluctance.

5

A Not So Merry Merry-go-round

Restored to life by the skilful knifework of Mr Melbourne Thomas, Gwyn burgeoned with the spring of 1936. Looking back, he said:

> When I came back into the world, the years of frenzy were finished. My jungle juices had been thinned out. The pressures that had driven my mind in and out of storm-clouds had been eased. I had been brought back to something like normal, and it was a peculiar feeling: utter sobriety after a long, cheap jag.[1]

At the time he told Nana:

> I went out for the first time today. I enjoyed every sight and smell of March.... I found something more ramshackle about Porth than I had seen previous to my admission to hospital. Perhaps it was an increased sensitiveness on my part.

But he warned her that his operation had not transformed him into 'a happy young and carefree boy'. He was still aware of the 'filthy, rotten, damnable system' under which hundreds of thousands of people had to live with, 'death, disease and drab unhappiness', and he was going to do something about it:

> What my father took in in drink, I give out in truth. He wished to drown himself to the extinction of his responsibilities. I wish to drown a world to the extinction of its miseries.

Just before his admission to hospital, Gwyn had at last been offered a teaching job. It was in a private school at Ystalyfera in the Swansea valley, and although it was against all his principles to have anything to do with such an institution he had accepted, in desperate conviction that it was his only chance. It would not, as he admitted to Nana, be the most desirable of positions:

> As a job, it is lousy. Intellectually it will make me feel as miserable as if I were forced to sit on top of Coedcae tip through a year of December mornings.

But it was a job, and he hoped, he said, that 'this neck and its deviations will not interfere with my beginning to teach in Ystalyfera. It's not of myself I'm thinking. It is of Ystalyfera.' After a short period of convalescence he duly reported at the school for what must have been one of the shortest teaching engagements in history, as he explained many years later:

> The Principal told me the pupils would have a whole morning of French. . . . I went to work. Pedagogically no one has shot his bolt more swiftly. At 9.30 I was on the Definite Article. At 10.00 I was on the Agreement of Adjectives. At 10.45 I was on the Agreement of the Past Participle with a Preceding Direct Object. At 11.30 I was on the Imperfect Subjunctive. At 12.15 I was on the floor. At 12.45 I was on the bus home and I never went back.[2]

In the absence of a teaching post, Gwyn cast around for alternatives that would allow him to stay in the valley. While waiting for something to turn up, he returned to some of the ideas he had been discussing with Wynne Roberts during the months previous to his admission to hospital. With a new discipline made possible by his better health and calmer mind, and convinced that his true destiny was to be a writer, he began to work seriously on a novel that would draw the attention of the haves to the dreadful predicament of the have-nots in the Britain of 1936. As he worked he became more excited about what he was doing, and Wynne shared his enthusiasm. The pages were typed, not without eccentricities of spelling and presentation, on Wynne's portable typewriter; Gwyn kept Nana in touch:

> I'm trying to finish a novel. A few more weeks should see the thing done. Wynne is typing it as I go along. He can't understand my writing. I don't understand his typing. We'll both have to be present when the thing is read by a publisher.

It was a larger undertaking than he had expected. Six months later, just before Christmas 1936, he was telling Nana:

My novel proceeds slowly to a close. This is its third month. [Gwyn's dealings with absolute facts were always somewhat cavalier when they didn't much matter, as the next sentence also suggests – for he had been working on his book for well over a year at this stage.] Not bad going. A year is not considered too long for a novel. It should take a year to read, and a less profitable way of spending twelve months I cannot imagine.

Eventually it was deemed to be finished and sent off, grandly entitled *Sorrow For Thy Sons*, to Gollancz in the early months of 1937, a house chosen because both Gwyn and Wynne recognised and treasured the contribution to the socialist debate being made by the Left Book Club and other of Gollancz's enterprises.

It was inevitably a novel strongly influenced by autobiography. Covering the five-year period between 1930 and 1935, it followed the experiences of three Rhondda brothers: Herbert, the eldest, a shopkeeper; Alf, a miner who in the opening pages faces the first day of idleness after being made redundant; and Hugh, a schoolboy of eighteen, a thoughtful, still hopeful youngster whose growing bitterness and disillusionment are the central theme of the whole book. More conscious of his political message and his story than of technique, Gwyn wrote it down as it came to him, and a reader used to the Gwyn Thomas 'voice' of his published novels will find *Sorrow For Thy Sons* relatively straightforward; there are elements in it of the mordant tone and verbal wit which are so notable a feature of his later writing, but not very much of the comic hyperbole and tumbling imagery which his name on the title page came to promise. What was unmissable in it was the anger against the government of the day, against bourgeois values, fascist politics, cynical business and industrial combines, and everything that could possibly be blamed for the misery of those who in places like his Rhondda Valley were condemned to unemployment, means test, charity handout and all the rest of the undignified and unhappy circumstances of the mid-1930s. It is hard to guess what Gwyn would have made of his book's eventually finding publication, in an edited version (which surgically removed some of the more macabre and melodramatic elements in the novel for reasons of compression), fifty years after he wrote it. At the time of its submission Gwyn's hopes were high at first; he had not received a cent so far, he informed Nana, but Gollancz had been making encouraging noises:

Exactly what the position and possibilities of that novel are, I couldn't say. To me it is a mystery. I submitted it on its own merits just as a novel. Apparently it's got caught up in some competition for the best novel on unemployment. I had a letter from them stating that it had been selected as one of the best half-dozen manuscripts of those submitted. I heard that several weeks ago. Since then, silence.

The silence continued, until the typescript was returned with little more than a brief 'Sorry' at the end of the year. There was some consolation when Gollancz wrote inviting Gwyn to come and see him at Henrietta Street, saying that he liked the raw power in his book and that he was sure there was a future for him as a novelist. Gwyn made the journey to London and got as far as the stairs that led up to the Gollancz offices, but was then so overcome by a panic of shyness that he turned tail and went straight back to Paddington. With a shrug he put his typescript away in a drawer. There were other things to be done, and no time to weep over past failures. In retrospect he commented:

> [The book] had a few good suicides, some inept sex, and plenty of hunger.... Gollancz said he liked the fervour of the book, but its facts were so raw, its wrath so pitiless, its commercial prospects were nil unless he could issue a free pair of asbestos underdrawers to every reader.[3]

From the moment he first set his pen to paper to write *Sorrow For Thy Sons* he had delighted in the enterprise and business of writing stories. His long-cherished idea that his calling was to be a writer was reinforced by the experience and unshaken by its lack of success. From that day on and for the next forty years there was rarely a moment when he was not observing the scene with a writer's eye, scribbling down ideas for projects, notes of snatches of overheard conversations, or producing stories. For the next decade few people would show any great interest in his writing but he never stopped; in a way the writing was not for an audience anyway, but for himself, to give him the satisfaction of getting onto paper the ideas and thoughts that teemed in his mind. Once he had written something, he had more or less finished with it; after his early disappointments with publishers, he wrote almost as if publication were a matter of no moment. The exercise books and sheaves of papers he filled with his bold, rapid handwriting were often left lying about to be tidied away by whoever was currently looking after him.

During the year of his renewal in intervals between seeking employment and writing his novel, he turned his hand to other kinds of writing, too. Not feeling as much at home in Cymmer as he had done previously, he went to stay at intervals with Walt and Nest in Neath or with Nana and Bill in Wells. In both places, between drinking immense quantities of tea (Nest was certain that in one perhaps exceptional day he and she got through sixty cups) and talking with staunchless inspiration, he would sometimes sit and write into exercise books. After his death Nana found in her house in Wells a pile of notebooks from the period in which there were a score of stories which had never been read by anyone except their writer, pages and pages of dialogue for proposed plays, and hundreds of quotations from newspapers epitomising the state of the nation.

The stories, if made available, would also surprise most of his readers, for they were rarely funny, even in the grim idiom of his early published stories; on the contrary, they were intense, powerful and melodramatic, rather in the manner of Caradoc Evans. In tone and content they reflect the fury and the hurt of a sensitive man who perceives that the world about him is unacceptably cruel and unfair. In one called 'Agony in the Skull', for instance, a young woman worn out with looking after a dole-stricken family and exhausted by a new, unwanted pregnancy suffers a major blow when in a stupid accident the family's pig is killed. Esther's well-meaning but insensitive and incompetent husband leaves the gate to the pig's cot unfastened and the animal crashes fatally down into a ravine at the side of the house. Aware that something was wrong,

> Esther limped towards the ravine. She stumbled. Her hands landed in a little black puddle.... Esther's mouth came near. Her head-nerves jangled. Hunger, weakness, a great insensate wanting to vomit, to have her toes forced upwards through her body to between her teeth. She wanted to dip her lips into the festering pool and fill herself with it. She sobbed in a musical singsong.
>
> She did not get to her feet. She continued to crawl. She stared in front of her, avoiding the broken jars and bottles that strewed the ground, wanting to tear her flesh open.
>
> She peered into the ravine. Menna lay at the bottom.... Her head was twisted. Blood streamed from her distended belly. A rat that had crawled out of the culvert sniffed at her leg. Esther wanted to slip over

the ravine's edge and strangle the life out of that dirty, brown rat that
dared defile the dead, white Menna.[4]

Some of his work was published. Like his hero, Hugh, in *Sorrow
For Thy Sons*, Gwyn more than once approached the local newspapers
for commissions and was given a chance by the *Rhondda Leader* not
only to report some local funerals but also to review an amateur
concert or two; for a while he became 'our Porth correspondent',
contributing accounts of a billiards championship and of the enthusiastic involvement of children in the events of a local polling day. It
was thin stuff and poorly paid, but it was better than nothing.

Something a little better did now begin to become available.
Although there was no school post for him, the very fact of widespread unemployment threw up a string of opportunities to give
classes and lectures to groups of men and boys in clubs and institutes.
Financed partly by government, which had an interest in keeping the
unemployed sufficiently occupied to prevent active disaffection, and
partly by educational charities, there was an increasing amount of
such provision, and Gwyn found a fair number of appointments over
the next year or two. In the winter of 1936–7 he gave regular lectures
on the topic of 'International Relations' at Trebanog, Porth and
Ynyshir for the Workers' Educational Association, and the following
year had classes on the political history of South Wales at Ton Pentre,
Cwmparc, Ferndale, Cymmer and Llwynypia. From the beginning he
had some success as a lecturer. Blessed with a good, resonant voice,
an acute sense of humour, a quenchless flow of language and a passion
for justice, equality and fair play, he attracted audiences and his
reputation spread through the valleys.

It was not particularly satisfactory, lacking certainty and perma-
nence. A class might simply disappear, leaving its tutor financially
embarrassed because he could not expect to be paid for classes not
taken. The travelling about and the part-time nature of the job left
him feeling rootless and purposeless. As long as there was no
alternative he put a good deal of energy into it and took on every
challenge that could be thrown up. He lectured at various YMCA
clubs and took part in their debates. For the Ynyshir branch with a
friend called Tecwyn Evans he undertook to write a play about Spain
and contemplated the possibility of helping to establish a Left Theatre
in the area. Disagreeing after a while with the local organisers of

the WEA he looked further afield and found some classes in the Monmouthshire valleys. The outbreak of the Spanish Civil War became a great talking point, and Gwyn's experience of Spain was reckoned to make him an expert on the subject; he lectured to the Porth Unemployed Club in such an exciting and vital fashion that the *Rhondda Leader* wrote up his talk in detail:

> Spain today is a subject of arresting and challenging importance, and Mr Thomas proved himself to be a vivid and eloquent political thinker, more concerned with presenting a full, clear and eloquent picture of the truth about Spain than with conserving the prejudices and comfortable nationalist misconceptions of his audience.

The interest in the Spanish tragedy which flared as brightly in South Wales as anywhere sent a number of Welsh miners to their deaths as soldiers of the International Brigade, some of them as virtual ambassadors of the Communist Party, rather as Lewis Jones sacrificed his Rhondda hero in his novel *We Live*. At the height of the excitement Gwyn may well have felt desirous of doing something to help, but he later denied that he had actually volunteered for the International Brigade himself, as he romantically claimed in his autobiography to have done. Even with good health it is doubtful whether the impractical, rebellious young Gwyn Thomas would have made a very desirable soldier; with his history of illness, and the long and livid scar across his neck left by the thyroid operation, and his nervous, excitable disposition, he would never have been accepted anyway. Down in Neath Walt and Nest set a good example to the rest of the family by taking in and providing a temporary home for several evacuee children brought to Wales from Spanish towns particularly affected by the violence and destruction of the war. When large groups of refugee young people arrived in Newport in 1937, to be housed rather miserably in a big old empty warehouse, Gwyn was called in as translator to aid in their reception, and amazed his fellow-workers by the energy with which he lectured the children on the principles of Marxism.

He was certainly at the time working hard on being a communist, and had adopted their rhetoric and rationale with as much emotion as ratiocination. Together he and Wynne talked of a day when the red revolution would include South Wales, and the extreme tenor of their views alarmed Nana when she heard them. Anxiously she besought Walt, whose influence upon Gwyn had always been greatest, to see if he could not persuade him to a more moderate outlook and expression. Walt cheerfully undertook the commission, telling his wife all about it in a note:

> The great work shall be commenced when I see the young reprobate tomorrow. I shall set about it quietly and subtly, with no heat, no acrimony, no noise. I shall appeal not to his head with political argument and philosophical claptrap, but to his heart and bowels because they are easily and profitably attacked.

Anything that Walt had to say on the subject would have been respectfully considered and positively rejected, for Gwyn was full of loathing for the system and everything which prospered under it. He hated the Monarchy, the Tories, the landowners, the banks, the turncoat socialists of the National Government, all with an equal disgust, and said so frequently to anyone who would listen, with a rare turn of persuasive eloquence. He was young, he was attacked by and suffering under the prevailing set-up, and he wanted change. He did not, however, join the Communist Party, even after Wynne did; and he resisted with laughter the idea put to him somewhat later that a man with his gifts and feelings ought to be standing for Parliament in the Labour cause. Change must be brought about by those with a gift for government, he said. All he offered was language in support. He was a writer, not an activist. When reproached by Nana for having had a malign influence on Wynne, he replied:

> I took no part in bringing him to Communism. For a man to become a Bolshevik he need be just the two following things: (a) sensitive, (b) exposed to the vileness of the private profit system. Wynne was both. I disclaim all responsibility.

Close though he was to Wynne, there were some aspects of his friend's behaviour which were beginning to disturb him. Light-heartedly he told Nana:

> There's something funny about Wynne. I do not say that as a solemn charge against his character. I have been his bosom friend for many years and the remark is a kindly commentary on the fact that he does funnier things than a professional comic without getting a ha'porth of pay for it.

He told her of Wynne's spy mania, of his conviction that he had a special ability to sniff out traitors, of how he would sometimes disguise his voice on the telephone not apparently as a joke but with some serious intent to escape detection. Gwyn was a little puzzled by Wynne's eccentricities which seemed at times to be getting out of hand; they were probably in fact the early warning signs of the depressive illness which twenty years later was to make Wynne seek treatment in hospital. He was a little embarrassed, too, by Wynne's almost literal inseparability from him when in the Rhondda, and this was because, for the first time in his life, he had found a young woman with whom he thought he would like to be occasionally alone and who seemed to return the compliment.

Eiluned Thomas – again no relation; if there were people not called Thomas in Gwyn's ambience they seem to have been few and far between – was the daughter of a miner at the Lewis Merthyr colliery in Trehafod, a mile or so further down the valley. She had come to work as a typist in Porth, had fallen in with Dilys, the sister of Gwen who now ruled the roost at 196 High Street, and had thus been introduced into the household. She was a petite, auburn-haired girl, fashionable and attractive in a slim way, and called herself Lyn. She was astonished and delighted by the lively family whom she encountered there. Although she had a boyfriend – his name was Ivor Thomas, and his teacher-politician brother George was said to be a coming man – she found herself returning more often to the house than her friendship with Gwen and John would normally warrant, and the object of her attention was John's strange, witty, clever, darkly personable if moody youngest brother.

His shyness merely represented for her an element of challenge. There was something attractive about this young man that she had never encountered before. Almost skeletally thin – at twenty-three years of age he lacked physical robustness, weighing no more than nine stone – but with a mop of dark, curly hair and browny-green eyes, he seemed, despite the loquacity into which he sometimes broke, to be a child, lost and alone. They began to go out occasionally together, at first to the cinema to sit in the sevenpenny seats, accompanied often by Wynne. Sometimes they would take walks over the mountain slopes, their favourite destination being the village of Llanwonno to which Gwyn's father had taken him in the Sundays of his childhood. Again Wynne accompanied them more often than not, and Lyn seemed to have joined them as an extra friend rather than as one being romantically courted. As time went on, Gwyn discovered he was depending more and more on her frequent appearance and constant presence. Wanting her more to himself, he tried to find ways of suggesting to Wynne that there were times when he needed to be alone. When that didn't work – for Wynne, when in high flight about politics or music, hardly heard what was said to him – Gwyn began to see him in a new light. He complained to Nana:

> Wynne and I are not so conspicuously friendly these days. He hasn't even got an elementary sense of manners.... Why he should think he's got a gift for politics, I don't know, but in his own imagination he's already made Lenin look infantile.

Secretive as ever, he did not hint to Nana, or to Wynne, or to anyone else, that the main reason for his temporary disaffection with his old friend was his too constant presence when he wanted to concentrate on the new and delightful feelings evoked in him by Lyn.

Pleasant though these developments were, however, Gwyn's pattern of life was very frustrating and he longed to get away. Even as his affection for Lyn grew, his savage dissatisfaction with the lack of a proper job made him consider even the most exotic alternatives. In one of his letters to Nana he outlined his thinking:

> I am intrigued by the personality of A.J. Cook. If I can gather enough material from those who knew him in the Rhondda, and from the archives of the Miners' Federation, I will write his biography. There is too much darkness round his name. I also find there is too much darkness around mine. I hope to dispel both lots with this bit of work ...
>
> About myself, as usual, there is a good deal of doubt.... Four weeks ago, I was practically *en route* for Mexico. Three weeks ago I was practically *en route* for China to write a book about the Red Army. A fortnight ago, South Africa came within an ace of claiming me. I'm still here and quite bronzed after each of the three journeys. All I have to do now is unpack my case and write my memoirs.

In the end it was a letter from Eddie and the example of Wynne that convinced him that he should give London a try. Eddie spoke well of life in the great city, and Gwyn could stay with him in his flat in Hanwell. Wynne had done a teaching course at Exeter after leaving Oxford and was particularly well qualified for a teaching post, but when time went by and nothing turned up he too lost heart.

A man of strong principle, he declined his one offer of a post when he discovered that his wealthy and socially aware mother had pulled strings to get it for him. When his mother dismissed him from her home with nothing but his grandfather's gold watch and a £5 note in fury at his rejection of her gift, he decided to go to London for a while. There he tramped from door to door on behalf of the Electrolux company trying to dispose of their vacuum cleaners, and there, in the autumn of 1937, Gwyn was offered a job as a trainee manager at Selfridge's and decided to submit himself to the exigencies of the world of commerce. His brother described it as one of the weirdest appointments in the history of department store business. It was certainly one of the shortest. Instructed to take up a position in the children's area and attempt to interest the passers-by in an ingenious toy called Stick-a-Brick, he realised that shopkeeping in any form was not for him. After three weeks he gave in his notice and returned to Eddie's flat in Hanwell in the darkest of moods.

For a while he remained in London to see if anything else turned up. Eddie had found his niche in a number of settings, many of them with gatherings of other ex-patriate Welshmen, and there were many meetings, much talk, much singing. Gwyn recalled in a television programme in 1975 how, being poverty-ridden, he had had to do his own washing. Leaving the body of the shirt for less frequent attention, he would wash out the separate collars in soapy water and put them on the window-sill to dry:

> And then, on Sunday evening, we would go, like many Welsh exiles in London, we would go to Hyde Park Corner, and there the exiles would meet, you know, it was almost like the meeting of the Jews after the Diaspora, this great occasion of coming together again, the broken body coming together, and we would sing the great hymns and tears would be shed, and there we'd be, you know, whipping ourselves into this kind of climactic sadness.
>
> And it started to rain one Sunday night, and we had no money for the bus, and we had to get to Ealing which was about eight miles away; and there we were, going through the rain now, walking those eight miles in London, hard streets, hard streets, indifferent, hostile things, you know; and terribly cruel eyes kept looking at you all the time. But this was all right, we didn't mind, we were thinking about the abdication of dignity and grace and the taking over of the earth by fools and scoundrels and murderers, and then I became aware of a strange thing: all the

imprisoned soap in our collars was starting to come up, you see, and by the time I looked at my brother the bubbles were just about level with the top of his head. And it created quite a sight, really, because the people walking behind us must have thought from our conversation that we were maniacs of some sort or another, and then I heard a woman's voice say, 'By God, they're frothing at the neck!'[5]

The expedition to London proving abortive, Gwyn returned to the Rhondda, preferring frustration at home to that offered in England. At least here he had the constant and strengthening support of Lyn to help him through his disappointments. So great was the attachment between them that he never mentioned her being employed as a typist-clerk by the hated Unemployment Assistance Board, which administered the means test. Her job was her business; he was glad for anyone who had one. For himself there were more temporary classes, including courses of lectures at Maes-yr-Haf, a so-called Educational Settlement at Trealaw, which catered for some of the great mass of unemployed people in the valley. This led eventually to his applying for and being offered a series of posts in settlements and 'instructional centres' overseen by the National Council for Social Services − the period of employment which he called in his autobiography 'some of the most confusing bits of social work ever recorded'.

When Eddie announced that he was going to marry his girl, Nancy, Gwyn travelled down to Torpoint, her home town, by train to be his best man. Upset either by the journey or by something he had eaten, Gwyn found the last stage, the crossing by ferry of the Tamar, too much. He was violently ill. Unusually, the vomiting did not clear up the trouble, and next day, without staying for the wedding, he was put on a train back to South Wales by his anxious brother. The episode seemed somehow typical of the bizarre and unhappy way life chose to treat Gwyn, but about this one he told no funny stories.

The idea of marriage was now in his head, though. Economically it made little sense, for he was virtually penniless and could not offer her the protected and cosseted life that a wealthy suitor might represent. Both of them were less − or more − romantic in certain ways than was expected of young people, however. He told Lyn that he had wanted to be married to her from the first day he had seen her. On 5 January 1938, without a word to their families, friends and relations, they walked into the Registry Office at Pontypridd and were married in a brief ceremony witnessed only by two strangers brought in from another room for the purpose.

There was no way they could properly set up home together. They could not even announce officially that they were married, for that would have resulted in Lyn's losing her job, and neither of them wanted that to happen. They lived together in Lyn's mother's house in Trehafod, but otherwise carried on much as before. The news was broken to John and Gwen at 196, as it had to be to explain Gwyn's absences overnight from his room, but they told no one else for some time.

Between his occasional lectures and classes, Gwyn continued to write whenever he had a moment. He had been talking with Wynne about a project to write the political and cultural history of the Rhondda, but this fell into abeyance as he returned to fiction, with which he felt much more at home. Remembering Gollancz's encouragement he began a draft of a new novel. There was no problem with ideas for subject matter, for they poured from his mind as if he had some inexhaustible well at his centre. Still in the grip to some extent of his fascination with the manner and method of Caradoc Evans, and deeply interested in the long-term effects of this kind of restrictions on behaviour imposed by puritanical nonconformist sects like Calvinistic Methodism, he conceived the story of Abel Hicks. Abel comes from a strict and uncompromising North Wales background to the valleys of South Wales, and the story is of his slow and agonised escape from the repressions of upbringing to a compromise with the new freedoms, particularly sexual, of the south. With a hard and honest irony Gwyn's story leads inexorably to Abel's destruction by the very forces that had seemed to offer him life. Though he worked at the book sporadically for some time, it never quite took satisfactory shape for him, and eventually he abandoned it; he may partly have been unprepared to face the consequences if a book so open about and concerned with sexual perversion and excess had been published under his name. Some years later he returned to his manuscript and, in a manner which became habitual with him, extracted a part which he saw might have validity as a short story; it was published with the title, 'My Fist Upon The Stone'.

Another novel began to take shape as the months went by, and in September 1938 he wrote to Gollancz again, describing it as a story arising from his experience as a teacher in the instructional camps for the unemployed and asking whether he might send it to be considered. An answer arrived from Norman Collins, saying that he was looking forward enormously to seeing Gwyn's new novel, but reminding him why *Sorrow For Thy Sons* had not been acceptable:

> All three readers commented on the fact that some of your physical descriptions were so realistic as to produce actual nausea in the reader. Your reply to this probably is that you *wanted* to nauseate the reader, but it is worth while to remember that, as your audience will be ninety per cent more or less tender-stomached, you will frighten them all away if you write in this fashion.

Nothing more was ever heard of this novel either. Gwyn's response to rejection was always in accordance with what he conceived to be his dignity. He would neither protest nor, usually, seek a second opinion. Into a cupboard the manuscript would go, to be forgotten or lost, and he would start again on something else.

At this stage of 1938 the main something else was to find another of the lecturing positions he had been undertaking under the auspices of the NCSS. His marriage had reinforced his determination to be employed in some way or another, and quite soon after their first days together Gwyn had accepted a posting which took him out of Wales altogether. Leaving Lyn to carry on with her job in Porth, he went to Thetford in Norfolk to work in an instructional camp on Cranwich Heath for nearly three months. It was, he told Nana, the most maddening place that ever he had struck:

> Here you see the pitch-black tragedy of unwanted men against the snow-white background of Norfolk desolation. You might think you see it in its entirety in the Rhondda. I thought so too. But you don't, not by a mile ...
>
> There is scarcely a man in these camps who is not saddled with the Nazarene error of some hire-purchase swindle.... Apparently, the wives get the idea that the fact of their husbands being in a Training Centre gives them immunity from the debt. Babes in the wood. If any of these trainees is found to be in debt and trying to escape the responsibility, the Centre management co-operate with the police to put him in the jug. When he has done his term, the management make sure to get him back here to finish his twelve weeks. Between jail and training centres there is little difference.

In a paragraph of acute self-analysis he attempted some explanation of 'the extreme contradictions' of his own personality, which made him seem to the world and himself a different person every day. Perhaps it was his uncomfortable awareness that his talents were being wasted which made him so desperate:

> There is nothing here, nothing, from the work of the place to the state of my soul, that does not make me snarl.... Looking back, I seem to have been so terribly unhappy, so needlessly unhappy for so many years. In my lighter moments it makes me think that there must be a period of glorious and brilliant fulfilment waiting for me.

It was to be some time yet before that last wishful thought turned out to have any foundation, but, as the world rolled onward towards the cataclysmic war which Gwyn began to realise was unavoidable, things did slowly, for him, begin to get better. After his period in Norfolk, he was offered and accepted further similar posts in England; in them he felt no more usefully employed than in the first, but there were suggestions that a more permanent post might be his for the asking once he had gained enough experience in the field. As an Education Officer in a Staffordshire camp, accordingly, he duly took his classes, one item of his instruction being in the art of knot-making, about which he knew nothing until he'd had a chance to consult some esoteric handbooks, as he explained in another interview:

> The poor chaps in the camp, they were very desperate men, very sad men, and I gave these lessons in knotting, now; you know, how to attach a yacht to a mooring point – these chaps were on about four shillings a week, you know – but it's a very funny thing, because so many of these lads would come up to me and ask, 'What is the Execution Knot?' Well, I didn't have much of an idea, but I gave them some sort of demonstration.... One of them at least acted on the information and killed himself.[6]

Early in 1939 he became an officer of the Derbyshire Association of Social Service Centres. While working in Mansfield he visited a camp where the majority of the men were from the North-East. Here there was an even more harrowing experience in store for him:

> And these were men of great strength, great dignity, who had had their backs broken by an act of social idiocy – you know, the number of people in Britain at that time who thought the world was lovely because the investments were coming in from Africa and the Argentine, and yet they were allowing one half of the nation to die under their noses and

they did not give the sliver of a damn about this. And these men were bitter, but impotent, of course, impotent.... And there they would sit in these awful bunks – there were nine great huts – and there'd be silence, terrible silence for half an hour in the evening. Maybe the odd crooning of a Northumbrian song, something of that sort, you know, and then a voice would cry: 'Nie mair!' – No more. 'Nie mair!' And it would be taken up until it became a great prairie fire of wrath and anguish and despair. 'Nie mair!'[7]

In February he was suddenly called upon to replace the Secretary, Rowland Hill, who was struck down by flu just before an important conference. To his own surprise he found himself able to handle the organisation that now fell upon his shoulders with competence and even confidence, and he told Nana:

Then I had to give two speeches on 'Cultural Developments'. My speeches were good.... At the end of my second speech two ladies advanced excitedly to shake my hand, saying that they were enraptured. What is it that I have got that other people haven't got? God alone can tell.

He was gaining in cheerfulness as his work became more respon- sible, and he outlined his plans to 'implant in the minds of the younger and least spoiled members of the Social Service movement a curiosity about the world in which they live', though adding sardonically at the end of a long and enthusiastic broadside: 'That's the idea. I won't start putting it into practice until I get my pay raised.'

Presumably his work was noted, for later in the year he was invited to go to Manchester and take responsibility as Education Officer for the area all around. Lyn gave up her job and she and her mother went to make a new home with Gwyn in the north. Surely a new phase was about to begin, one in which, perhaps, that intimation of greater things which he had confided to his sister might prove true.

III

THE SCRIBBLING USHER

6

A Weird Traffic

The Manchester appointment gave Gwyn and Lyn their long-awaited but curiously timed opportunity to begin to settle down just as the world was lurching into its most searing period of unrest. No sooner were they there than Europe slipped over the edge into the war whose accelerating approach Gwyn had noted with contempt and disgust. A whole-hearted internationalist, an idealistic socialist both by experience and intellectual conviction, his belief was that the war had been brought about by the cynical and self-interested forces of capitalism, which, harnessing the energies of fascist authoritarian thinking and dyed-in-the-wool Toryism, had seen a chance to recover its old-time domination of the many by the rich and ugly few. Yet even as he fulminated against the 'traitors of the people' who had plunged the world again into war, he recognised somewhere deep inside that the matter was not quite so simple. It was not until after the revelations of the bestiality of Hitler's final 'solution' to the Jewish 'problem' that he publicly acknowledged that force might have been the only answer, and even then he felt that there must have been more civilised ways of dealing with it. At the time, whether inwardly understanding the need for war or merely reacting with unexpected patriotism, he went quickly to offer his services to the army.

Perhaps he was not surprised to be graded C3 and rejected. Although he had felt much better generally since the thyroid operation, his health was never of the most vibrant. He was very thin, gaunt and hollow-cheeked; he smoked far too much and his lungs were not good; and his doctor had told him that he would be troubled all his life with the Graves' disease which had led to the thyroid trouble and the exophthalmic goitre. Even so, he thought at first that a man of his intelligence and linguistic ability was bound to be needed in some non-violent capacity by the army's servicing departments. He had no wish whatever personally to smite the enemy. Unlike his brothers Emlyn, who had fought in the first war, and Walt, who was something of a boxer when young, Gwyn was almost completely a-physical. Aggressive enough verbally, when his ire was raised or when he was forced into a position of self-defence and took attack as its best means, he hated everything to do with violence and slaughter, but something told him that he had at least to offer. He was not too much troubled when his offer was turned down.

As the machinery of war ground slowly into action while the 'phoney war' of 1939 led some to think that it would soon be all over, Gwyn took up his functions as an area Education Officer, travelling all about the Manchester–Rochdale region for meetings and classes. His heart was not wholly in his work, but it was a responsible job and a steady one and he took it seriously. In an article written twenty years later in praise of local government he recalled:

> I myself once did, in those dim twilit days of the late Thirties, a semi-governmental job which required me to attend endless sub-committees of a whole group of municipal councils. It was a period of black and maddening tedium. It was a nightmare of brain-rusting triviality and bland unreason. And luck would always have me sitting next to the least civilised member of the council: some crafty, sub-literate schemer with eyes like clinker and apparently dead except when he gave me a fierce nudge and said it was bra-a-ass that made the mare go round or, his only other punch-line, that life was the best university.[1]

While the experience was to stand him in good stead years later when he came to write a novel such as *A Point of Order* or a play such as *The Alderman*, it did little at the time to shake his longing to find a job as a teacher which, he thought, would suit him much better. The fact that the job had taken him to live in Lancashire was not in its favour, either, for although Lyn had settled in to life in the north with considerable pleasure, Gwyn considered himself to be in a forced exile, fiercely missing his home territory.

Lyn was adaptable and brisk, and would have been perfectly happy anywhere as long as she was near Gwyn. Since the only job he could get was in Manchester, then Manchester was home as far as she was concerned. In comfortable lodgings in Rochdale Square, with her mother for company and with plenty of friendly neighbours, Lyn saw no reason why they should not make the best of it and enjoy life. It troubled her that Gwyn was not really happy in his inappropriate employment, but the people were delightful and she thought that when he had made some friends after his own heart things would be better.

He did soon make one particular friend, Leslie Smith, another Education Officer and fellow-toiler in the service of the NCSS. He had graduated in modern languages at Cambridge and had a sense of humour which matched Gwyn's; he was a handsome, vital man and his literate, music-loving, fun-filled nature made life much more tolerable for his friends. So good-looking that 'he took your breath away' (said Lyn), and so capable in practical as well as intellectual ways, he seemed destined for great things. On the outbreak of the war he too volunteered for service early on, and was accepted, like Gwyn's brother John at about the same time, into the RAF. Although the Thomases were still enlivened by his visits when he was on leave, they badly missed his constant company.

Meanwhile Gwyn's own energy for communication was unabated. For a while he wrote less fiction into his notebooks, for the times brought his political thinking to a head and he was happy to find that there were plenty of outlets for the expression of his furious ideas. He had long formed the habit of going out to a favoured pub practically every night, not so much to drink as to find company, and not so much to find company as to find listeners. Once the edge had been taken off his shyness by a pint of beer he would start to talk to a neighbour, and so compelling and pleasant was his voice, so comical and attractive his stories, so devastating and effective his rhetorical flights, that soon all the occupants of his corner of the room would be engaged in capping his stories and countering his debating points. A short, slight, haggard-looking twenty-six-year-old, his presence was strangely commanding, depending mainly on his clear, Welsh baritone voice and his verbal inventiveness, but also on the compassionate sincerity of the message that was plainly to be heard behind the comic incidents and metaphors that first attracted.

He was already gaining a reputation as a public speaker, too. More restrained in his verbal manner when addressing, for instance, the Bury Rotary Club, as he did in February 1940, he was yet entertaining as well as challenging in what he had to say. On this occasion his topic was 'Education and Modern Needs', and his talk epitomised the new understanding that was already spreading across the country that the war could and must be a preparation for peace, a peace in which life for everyone would be altogether better, and a peace in which that betterment of life would come about through education:

> As long as the mind of the average human being is so badly educated as to make him subject to the deceits of other men, there will be no lasting hope of peace in this world.... Education ought not to stop at fourteen years of age.... We are aiming not at defeating the German nation; we are aiming for a better nation on our side – a nation fitter than now to undertake the task of world leadership towards a world commonwealth.[2]

Sometimes even his letters to his sister would take on the same rhetorical tone, a tone which shows a certain naivety and optimism (disguised as cynical pessimism) at the same time as it reveals a deep and heart-tearing sincerity, as in this message to Nana at Christmas 1940:

> From somewhere about 1932 I stopped living.... I saw society decay. I got to know practically every distressed area in Britain. As a social servant I got on speaking terms with a million out of Britain's two million pre-war unemployed. And the few millimetres of my mind and heart that had not been Bolshevised by the Rhondda and the inherent decency of my being turned scarlet.... I became so calloused by the spectacle of misery liberally administered and patiently, enduringly borne I became something of a John the Baptist. I sensed that a terrible vengeance would come upon the agents and the victims of such inhumanity. But not even J the Bap could have foretold a vengeance quite as horrible as the one that the joint Imperialisms of Germany and Britain are now pouring nightly and daily from the skies of Europe. Men asked for this by their refusal to be decent. In odd corners, in the unemployed clubs of our great land, I preached the gospel of dignity and brotherliness. But the corners were too odd and too dark and my voice and all the voices like mine were as whispers compared with the roar of the tool-makers and the lie-makers who were forging the new instruments of force and injustice.

It was a time of death, natural as well as unnatural, all unacceptable, all adding to the pain which made Gwyn increasingly long to escape back to his home, somehow or other to get back to Wales. In 1940

Lyn's mother, still quite young, suddenly fell ill and died; and news came from Cymmer that Walter senior, the father whom his children in their mixture of irritation and affection had come to call 'the Jake', had died too. Such times of loss come to all, but double and unexpected blows are hard to bear. Gwyn felt the loss of his father, whom he had come to know and understand a little better during the past few years, more deeply than he expected to; in many writings about him in later years he gave the old man a sort of immortality a little like that given by D.H. Lawrence to his unsatisfactory but misunderstood father, or perhaps even more like that given by Clarence Day in America to his wholly satisfactory parent.

When Gwyn and Lyn heard that their friend, Leslie Smith, the handsome RAF pilot, had been killed in aerial combat, their misery was complete. And then the war's toll acted in their favour. So many teachers were leaving their classrooms to put on uniforms that vacancies became available in a way that had not been seen for many years. In the late summer of 1940 Gwyn learned of a vacancy in the languages department at the County School in Cardigan and wrote to the headmaster, Mr Tom Evans. Very quickly a meeting in Liverpool was arranged; the headmaster from west Wales decided that he liked what he saw in the visage of the applicant; and Gwyn was on his way to engage in what he later described as 'a weird traffic between one who never wished to tell and those who had never wished to know'.

Cardigan is a small fishing port at the mouth of the River Teifi, which flows into the Irish Sea between Fishguard and Aberystwyth on the western coast of Wales. An attractive township consisting of little more than a main street, a ruined castle, a river frontage and a small harbour, it gave its name not only to the whole hinterland which used to be known as Cardiganshire (until recent reorganisation renamed the entire south-western promontory as Dyfed) but also to the great bay formed by the arms of St David's Head to the south and the Lleyn peninsula far away to the north. It was in 1940 a remote, quiet rural community, with an economy based on agriculture and fishing, hardly known to the rest of the world except perhaps through the folk wisdom that said that Cardigan people (Cardis) were hard and mean, puritanical and ungenerous, and the infamous stories of Caradoc Evans which seemed to confirm this. It is a beautiful and peaceful place and must have seemed to Gwyn and Lyn when they arrived in September 1940 the most complete antithesis possible to the noisy, dirty, populous Lancashire that they were leaving behind.

For a while they had to be content with living in rather cramped accommodation in a couple of rented rooms, but so great was their initial delight with their return to Wales and the satisfactions of a job in teaching at last that they were very content. Gwyn, unlike his brother Eddie and his friend Wynne Roberts, had not done a teacher-training course, but he was sure that his natural instincts would allow him to pick up the essentials without difficulty. A widespread belief in the value of a university degree as a teaching qualification in those days meant that most graduate entrants to the profession were untrained in the arts of the classroom. Some would argue that they were none the worse for it. Schools were judged by their examination results, and by that criterion their teachers were often superb.

The Cardigan County School took in boys and girls from a large area round the town, many of them bussed in from the farms and outlying villages in ancient yellowish vehicles which Gwyn called the 'coffee-pots'. From the first moment he felt he was in his element; the company of the teachers in the staff-room and that of the children in the class-room were equally delightful to him. In both he found ready-made and admiring audiences for his humour which, in the light of this pleasant and glowing encouragement, grew rapidly more expansive and, in time, increasingly mellow. He seemed a wonderfully exotic bloom to the dourer Cardis as well as to the children who found his mild eccentricities much to their taste. For some time he had allowed his pleasure in films to affect his taste in dress and manners, not much, but quite enough to seem somewhat strange and dashing to a community that in many ways was moving relatively slowly and cautiously through the changes wrought by the twentieth century. He wore most notably a slouch hat pulled low over the brow and a raincoat with the collar turned up; and his speech, especially when he was being funny, tended to be clipped in utterance and modern in vocabulary, so much so that there were some who thought of him as being almost American rather than a fellow Welshman from just over the other side of the Preseli mountains. Lyn, too, was thought to be the last word in modern smartness, and some heads were shaken rather sadly as she was seen marching into town actually wearing trousers.

It was additionally odd in the bilingual community of Cardigan that the new couple were not Welsh speakers and that they did not appear the least bit interested in the Welsh language. It was put down to their being from the Rhondda, and no offence was taken; indeed there were those who found his attitude illuminating. One of his former pupils said that while there was no sense in which they felt that Gwyn was proselytising for English, his attitudes generally helped them widen their horizons in significant ways. And his energies and enthusiasms were inspiring. It was a delight to the children to find in Gwyn a teacher who was an avid reader and who loved to share with anyone who would listen to his latest discoveries, or who would even borrow from them their own favourite books, no matter how childish or, as it seemed to them, daring, and enjoy reading them. They enjoyed his uninhibited response to what he found funny, and liked to observe the way some of the other teachers would look askance at their new colleague as he did or said something unexpected or out of keeping with the solemnity of his role as teacher. He had, for instance, no time whatever for sport, and often said so in ringing tones. This was not well received in all quarters of a school that prided itself upon its rugby team and general achievements in athletics, except among those who saw the provocative humour which led to his more outrageous pronouncements. Among these was a sports master called Hunt, who would calmly say, 'Don't be so bloody silly, Gwyn, mun, there's more to life than just study', a reply which endeared them both to the boys who were party to their discussions.

His personality drew people to him as much as if not more than his skills as a teacher, about which there was some debate from the earliest days. When in his enthusiasm he started a series of extra Spanish classes there were as many present who wanted to hear his wonderful stories of bull-fighting and banditry as wanted to improve their language skills for the examination. Some felt that his ability to teach French to the fifth form was quite dubious, and wondered how they managed to pass the exams; but they would not have missed the pleasure of his classes for anything. Sometimes he was moody, and his temper was uncertain, but that just made things all the more entertaining, for when his wrath was roused his invective would include such comic hyperboles that the whole class, even the victim, would soon be laughing, and the laughter would restore the sunniest of smiles to their teacher's face.

More importantly, they realised very soon that he was fanatical about fairness and justice. More than once he showed himself willing in the matter of summary punishment or unnecessary violence, if necessary to outface even the headmaster, a great believer in the salutary effects of a stiff caning, and he was known to have spoken up for a colleague who was catching the rough end of the headmaster's tongue even though no other member of the staff would have dared interrupt the great man's flow. His special skill was to deflect anger with humour, but in the phrase of the boys, he 'didn't give a toss' about authority if he felt that some principle of justice was being ignored.

Despite this independence of mind and occasional truculence of spirit, he seemed to remain in the headmaster's good books. Mr Evans was a strong and aggressive man, used always to getting his own way, quite unused to opposition of any sort from anybody. Known as 'Tom Pop' (because the best-known fizzy lemonade of the time was made by a firm called Thomas & Evans), he was not well loved by all, but Gwyn had a curious regard for him and, many years later at the old man's retirement dinner, spoke of him with affection and respect:

> When I met him I found him to be the sort of man I had expected from his letter to me: very Welsh, very charming, charged with an almost overpowering vigour of mind, imagination and tongue; a man capable of living intensely on so many levels of life as to make the average schoolman seem a monkish drab. I have known no headmaster so aware of the whole society in which he lived, so capable of infusing his school with a sense of his own crusading enthusiasm.[3]

Distance perhaps had lent enchantment to the view, but it seems likely that the two men recognised in each other a particular vitality which made them overlook their differences in a way not so easy for lesser mortals.

In his first term Gwyn teamed up with a music-loving colleague, Leslie Wynne Evans, to produce as the school's Christmas entertainment *The Mikado*. 'It was acclaimed a tremendous success,' Gwyn wrote to Nana. 'My talents amaze me.' The editors of the school magazine said that it was undoubtedly the School's greatest achievement yet in social life. For Gwyn and Lyn the most important consequence lay in the meeting it brought them with a local married couple, Melville and Elsa Johns, amateur singers of renown who took leading roles in the production. These two took to the Thomases and invited them to their home; when, a little later, they went away to serve in the war, they let their pleasant house in Greenland Meadows to their new friends, and Gwyn and Lyn were more comfortably established than they had ever been before.

They had now been married for over two years and might conceivably have decided at this point to start a family. That they did not was a deliberate and already established choice. There were many reasons for their attitude: they did not feel that they would make particularly good parents; they did not want to prevent Lyn from taking her secretarial jobs whenever they turned up, thus helping out the not very great income of a schoolmaster; they wanted to live their lives as fully as possible without the hindrances that children would inevitably constitute, especially as they still had the largest hopes for Gwyn's future as a writer. So they rationalised the matter, and defended themselves against selfishness when reproached by other members of the family. At a deeper level there must have been the ghost of Gwyn's sense of rejection by his own mother, and of his appalled experience of being so small a part of so large and pullulating a family. Deeper still there may have been the insoluble problem of Gwyn's essential disappointment with life itself. Was this absurd and terrible world truly one into which one would willingly bring more sacrificial victims? In any case, they never did have children, and even now, when Lyn is left alone and lonely, she expresses no more than the faintest whisper of regret that there are no children and grandchildren to comfort her.

If things started well in Cardigan, however, it was not very long before Gwyn's restlessness again began to manifest itself. Though fully occupied with teaching and talking – delivering lectures to servicemen at a nearby training camp as well as to more sophisticated audiences at the university college at Aberystwyth from time to time – he still felt too far from home. When an opportunity presented itself for him to join his brother Walt on the staff of the grammar school at Neath he went with high hopes to the interview. Unfortunately the night he stayed at Bryncoch with Walt and Nest turned out to be the first night of the Germans' horrific bombing raids on nearby Swansea, and Gwyn could not bear it. Saying he might as well have stayed in Manchester if death by alien explosion was to be his destiny he returned to peaceful Cardigan.

Destiny was about to call him home, however, and it came in the form of Gwyn's old friend, E.T. Griffiths, his former headmaster at Porth. Griffiths had been since 1933 head of the boys' County School at Barry. During the winter of 1941 Gwyn had at last begun to pay off his long-standing debt to E T and in doing so had opened what proved to be a pleasant correspondence. Needing a replacement teacher of languages suddenly in 1942, E T looked first to Porth, hoping to persuade his original discovery, Rochat the Swiss, to come and join him in his school on the coast. When Rochat declined, feeling himself to have become inseparable from his adopted valley, E T asked Gwyn whether he would like the post. It was no sooner proposed than accepted, and in October 1942 Gwyn and Lyn came to begin their life in Barry.

Barry is a seaside town about eight miles west of Cardiff and twenty miles south of the Rhondda. A hundred years ago it was no more than one of the villages on the edge of the Vale of Glamorgan. With the coming of the coal trade and a quarrel between magnates over the use of the docks in Cardiff all was changed. Rival docks were built at Barry, a railway link to the valleys was established, and the town exploded into life. Within a few years it had become the greatest coal-exporting port in the world. As the new town grew on a strip of the coast blessed with fine beaches and lay partly on a near-island which had its own magnificent sandy beach, it rapidly became also the mecca of those seeking relief from the noise, dirt and squalor which went with the industrial prosperity of the developed hinterland. With over thirty thousand inhabitants when Gwyn arrived there it had also established a considerable sense of civic pride, and boasted, among other things, a teachers' training college and two county schools, one for boys and one for girls, with fine reputations.

The task of settling into yet another location was made easier for Gwyn and Lyn by E T and his wife who went out of their way to be friendly and helpful to the young couple. They found themselves rooms once more on the top floor of a large terraced house in Gladstone Road. While in this respect the change from Cardigan was not for the better, it was only temporary, they hoped, and the school was a splendid place to work. Gwyn once again went through the stages of shedding his shyness and adapting to a new environment with some difficulty, but soon the new life became as busy as and even more fulfilling than the old. E T maintained his support strongly, and it became their custom to go every Sunday to have tea with the headmaster and his wife. Introductions were made, invitations followed, and soon Gwyn was again in demand as a speaker at local functions. As new routines became established, he began to relax.

He taught at Barry County School for the next twenty years. In his autobiography he gave as many pages to the period. There is little about himself in it, and what there is is presented comically and quasi-fictionally. The focus is mostly on some of the masters who crossed his path, the characteristics of two or three of the more eccentric of them being subsumed into a portrait of 'Mr Walford'. He did draw in various ways on the experience of teaching in his writings later, and it is clear that being a schoolmaster meant a great deal to him. He was, if his pupils were bright, well motivated and interested, an effective schoolmaster. It would perhaps be quite difficult not to be successful in such circumstances, though there are those who are not. With boys who needed pushing he was not so good, for his own interest in languages, especially as means of speaking to one another, was less than fanatical. His teaching was remembered though by almost all who encountered him for its human challenges, for the great waves of laughter caused by his wit and his interest in the bizarre, for the continuous sparkle of ideas and notions that sprang out of him when he found people prepared to discuss great matters like the meaning of art, the practice of government or the future of mankind.

When he came to Barry he was still obsessed with alternating belief in and doubts about himself as a writer and human being generally. Writing to Nana at Christmas 1942 he said:

> You will have to put up with my handwriting. It is the writing of a man who writes much and fast and would, if submitted to an expert in graphology, yield the following analysis:
>
> 'Profoundly intuitive but criminally unreliable. Will leave his life unfinished as he does with half the letters in every word he writes. Will write novels while thinking it an unseemly labour to write a letter. Potentially a saint and virtually a heel.... He is an error wrapped round a phoney gland.'

Although he had sent nothing off to a publisher since his failure with Gollancz four years earlier, Gwyn was still writing furiously in all his spare minutes and was thinking more seriously about what he was doing. Of his intentions in a grand way there was no doubt at all. He affirmed to Nana:

> I am glad my Conservative masters found that I was below the physical calibre required to strike a physical blow for God and Empah and to defend the vital interests of these obese and leering wretches of the Right wing who plank their fleshy backsides down on every measure of social betterment that has been presented to the British parliament during the past twelve years. It gives me leisure to prepare my brain, my tongue and my pen for what I conceive to be the essential purpose of my existence on this earth: to stir up a wave of malevolent and unforgiving hatred against our lords and masters that will make them sorry they were ever born.

What was less certain was that the manner he had adopted would ever secure him a hearing. His stories had aimed at a melodramatic but essentially realistic portrayal of the suffering and misery of the poor and exploited sections of society; they made uncomfortable reading and offered the reader little reward. It was in fact taking him a long time to learn the lesson pointed by Norman Collins' letter of four years before, that his work needed to entertain as well as to open the eyes of his public, and that bludgeoning them with unpalatable facts and unpleasant emotions would frighten off even sympathetic readers.

He had been coming slowly to grips with the problem, but it was only now that a suitable solution, that had never been very far away, dawned fully on him. Perhaps it was the immense success of his humour in the classrooms of Barry County School that ultimately brought it home to him that he had hardly been tapping his greatest attribute, his capacity for provoking laughter. Quite deliberately he began to let the comic view inform his narratives, not just in the sort of bleak irony or grimly macabre turn that had appeared in *Sorrow For Thy Sons* and *Abel*, but more in the refreshing bursts of verbal humour and farcical jest of which he was a master in the classroom and the pub. Fastening on his memories of the fun and wit that had somehow characterised the responses to painful circumstance of his family and his often sardonic friends in the Rhondda of his youth, he now wrote stories that tried to capture the resigned courage as well as the abject misery of the people under pressure, expressed in terms of their verbal resourcefulness and his own tumbling, cascading, hilarious metaphors. Every day when he came home from school he would, after a cup of tea with Lyn, take up his pen and start to scribble with a new will. Still he did nothing with the sheaves of paper that mounted up except let Lyn tidy them away, but she began to wonder about stories with titles such as 'Oscar' and 'Simeon' which seemed to her very strange and funny and true. Over-aware of her lack of a literary education, she did not know what to think. Feeling ignorant, she said nothing but took care not to lose them.

More important to Gwyn as the war wore on was his determination that afterwards there should be a lasting and decent peace in which the people should seize the opportunity to rebuild the world into a better place. When Nana begged him to harp less on political matters in his letters he said that he would try but that family gossip was as nothing to him compared with the need to argue out all the ways and means of forwarding the needs of the proletariat and sinking the forces of capitalism once and for all. Anyway, families themselves were horribly difficult to deal with:

> You see, even in the heart of one's own family where the jungle of conflicting wills and attitudes should to a certain point have been cleared by common membership of a blood group, the road is as dark, tortuous and as little to be prophesied as would be the road to an understanding of an outcast member of an aboriginal group in Papua. 'Life is a jungle of differences.' A German anarchist said that about a hundred years ago and I still rank it as one of the nattiest expressions of a complete philosophy that I have caught up with in my reading.

He had, he said, taken pains to be less explosive in the expression of his socialist sentiments, to modify in the presence of those who might be offended by his forthrightness the extremes of his wrath:

> But there has been no more calming down in me than you would find in a self-respecting volcano. I still boil with my old, accustomed ease. To express my anger frequently and to come into conflict with my neighbours drains off what little strength I have left over from my Graves' disease, so by arrangement with Graves I agree vigorously with one and all. Even if there are two people arguing at cross purposes in the same room I agree generously with both.

In July 1943 he had a birthday of some significance, saying to Nana:

> That makes me thirty. It feels like the end of an epoch. I seem to have been a hell of a time getting through the twenties. The world and I have changed but little in the interim. It is still on the foul side and I still remain a rather bewildered spectator of its capers and tantrums, shrinking back for preference into the shadow of the wings, and beguile myself with a soft sinister laughter at the incredible antics of the fools who stand in the full light of public view.

A marked change in Gwyn's fortunes was, however, not so far off even as he wrote. Taking his schoolteaching as seriously as he could he continued to win friends in the staffroom and in the town. His contributions to school activities like the debating and literary societies became high points in the calendar. In the town and round-about he became increasingly known as a reliably entertaining and provocative speaker. At the same time he was working that 'soft sinister laughter' at the absurdities of the world as he perceived it into new fictions, learning to use a technique which he later called 'a sort of sidling, malicious obliquity'. The results seemed to him more satisfactory, and when Lyn spoke of typing some of his stories up and seeing what could be done with them he made no objection. He began trying some out on friends with encouraging responses. Wynne Roberts, who had married his sweetheart Nansi Jones and had gone to teach in Yorkshire in 1942, returned to join the staff of the County School in Ebbw Vale in 1944. When Gwyn went to visit them in their digs there he had with him the manuscript of a novel which he now called *Passion Under The Ninth Rib*, but which seems to have been the story later entitled *The Alone to the Alone*. The visit was an endless outpouring of laughter, and Nansi remembers with delight Gwyn's sonorous reading of his own words. Once, hearing strangulated noises coming from Gwyn's bedroom, she looked in to find him choking with laughter at some revision he was making to the text.

The day was coming when those words in his letter to Nana on his thirtieth birthday might be made to seem more than somewhat ironical. Fate was moving him ever closer to being himself condemned by some of the more jealous of his family and friends for joining in with 'the incredible antics of the fools who stand in the full light of public view'. Of that he could have had little presentiment as the war came to an end, but Lyn, looking through the manuscripts of which she was mistress and convinced there was money in them if only it could be tapped, was almost on the point of beginning the process. She made up some parcels and sat at her typewriter to compose a covering letter or two.

7

Bursting onto the Scene

The war ended without any further cost to the Thomas family. John came home if not fit at least alive. He decided to take advantage of the scheme by which ex-servicemen could do emergency training to become teachers, and might have been happy at last; but Gwen was taken suddenly ill, and her unexpected and tragic death dealt John a blow from which he was unable to recover. Nana's husband Bill returned to his wife and little son David in Wells ready to take up life where he had left it. And Eddie, who had rather enjoyed his war service in foreign places and come back bronzed and fit to civilian life, looked with reluctance towards the classroom. Just before the war he had been hoping to launch out on a singing career; he had made some studio recordings to demonstrate his fine baritone voice, and had been just on the edge of opportunity, or so he hoped. Now he thought again about an invitation that had come his way to join the chorus at Covent Garden as a first step to greater things, and was tempted to take it even though he could see how such a decision would not make particularly easy the return to domesticity with his wife, Nancy, and the three children she had borne him.

In Barry Gwyn greeted the end of the war with the utmost relief. The nearest he had come to action was in helping to man the firewatch in the Guildhall 'in a team of four', he told Nana, 'whose average age even including my relative youthfulness was seventy-three'. It was a risible experience upon which he was able to embroider very satisfactorily for comic business in *A Frost On My Frolic*, as were the occasions when he found himself 'scheduled to promote the war by taking a band of the cannibals whom I teach in term-time to harvest the crops for a month or so', as he did each summer during the war.

The realities and horrors of the war had troubled him deeply, to a great extent because he was not convinced that they were necessary:

> One per cent of this war may be being waged with a genuine desire to preserve certain types of freedom from the Nazis. The rest is a grisly conspiracy on the part of the wealthy who are securely enthroned in power on this curious island to use the war to tie the hands of the common people tightly behind their backs and then slog the lights out of them. That is the precise function of Conservatism: to ensure that those who have always sat on velvet shall continue to sit thereon and that those who have always got it in the neck shall continue unremittingly to get it therein.

So he had written to Nana in 1943. Now that the conflict was over, and the General Election of the summer of 1945 presented the people with an opportunity to throw off the old yoke and institute a new age of socialist justice, he worked as hard as he knew how in the local constituency to ensure that this would come about. Political canvassing he found on the whole frustrating and disappointing, for except where their own personal interests were very closely touched upon most people did not seem to share his interest in the grand general debate in the same way as his cronies in the Rhondda clubs and institutes had done in the 1930s. After three years of living in wartime Barry, moreover, he was less fond of the town as a place to live than he had been, perhaps because the pressure on rented places was so acute that they still had not been able to find a more comfortable alternative to the top-floor rooms in Gladstone Road. In a letter to John he spoke of their slim hopes of finding 'some dwelling in the Rhoose area', a pleasant village a couple of miles west along the coast from Barry itself; he had even thought of a more dramatic translation altogether:

> There may be the chance of going to some other part of the world for a change and that would please me. I find the average sample of life in Britain insufferably tedious and trivial. I would not like to be a permanent exile; a few years abroad, in Mexico for example, would give a little agreeable colour to one's antics on earth.

The election over, and a Labour Government with a powerful majority and a strong mandate in office, life reverted to the ordinary. Gwyn continued to teach, to write in the evenings before going out with Lyn for a stroll that would include a visit to one of the little pubs out in the Vale or on one of Barry's steep hills, and to lecture to any institution that cared to ask him. He explained to Nana:

> I run two classes for the County Council on Current Affairs and twice weekly I have to appear before two wise and mature groups of citizens trying to explain to them the long delays which attend our advance to the New Jerusalem. Still, I enjoy it, I suppose, or I would not be such a sucker as to tolerate such a drain on my time for so little money. There is a strong preaching impulse in every Celt which must find a vent one way or another.

Instead of moving to Mexico, or even to Rhoose, they jumped at an opportunity to move to a more convenient flat less than half a mile away in Broad Street; Gwyn had a little further to walk to school, but they were closer to a pleasant shopping area and the Barry Town railway station was just a short walk down the road. They did not go off to see their many relatives as often as they might have liked, but they visited Eddie and his family in Chinnor early in 1946, and were called on from time to time by representatives of the newly expanding family from their various scattered settlements. Gwyn told John: 'I must say that I get a profound pleasure from studying the habits and outlook of the children of my brothers and sisters when I get around to seeing them', but part of the pleasure undoubtedly consisted in being able to walk away and return to the peaceful childless state as soon as he wanted to. After the visit to Eddie he confessed to Nana that he had 'found the atmosphere rather too dominated by the three children' for his entire comfort.

All in all, despite his lengthy experience of teaching and despite his usually generous and interested attitude towards his nephews and nieces, it may be doubted whether he was ever entirely comfortable with the very young. It would be wrong to judge too much from the entries he made in his notebooks from time to time, perhaps, but many of them suggest a degree of cynicism and impatience with a role in which to some extent he felt himself trapped. In a school vocabulary book which he was using as a notebook at this time, for instance, there is the following item:

> Myself to 4C: I take as my text today the apothegm of Aldous Huxley, 'Most ignorances are curable'. I will now proceed, using you as my main illustration, to dispute that thesis.

At school the boys who benefited most from the acquaintance with him were those who were clever and mature, boys who could be treated as young men with a literate turn of mind and at least the beginnings of a political consciousness. Those whom he most appreciated, among the boys as well as among the staff, were the genuine originals, those who provided some of the inspiration for the delightful eccentrics who inhabit his stories.

He was writing so fluently and so confidently, and the reactions to his pieces by those friends privileged to hear them read were so complimentary, that Lyn's determination to make some use of her husband's obvious talents came to a head. One day early in 1946 she found in the library a copy of a useful-looking directory called *The Writers' & Artists' Year Book* and thumbed through its pages seeking advice. Because Gwyn's manuscripts seemed not to conform with the requirements of the great publishers whose names she recognised, she looked with particular interest at the brief descriptions of some smaller firms, one of which actually mentioned that items of non-standard length might prove acceptable. Seized with enthusiasm she sorted through the stories she had already typed, made up three parcels and, unaware of matters like contract and copyright, addressed them to three different publishing houses. The response was more than she had bargained for, for letters arrived during the following weeks from all three houses, each accepting what had been submitted and undertaking to publish within a year.

As pleased as Lyn with the prospect of recognition at last, and quite as ignorant as she was about publishing protocol, Gwyn signed the offered contracts without noticing such details in the smaller print as those giving the firm in question the option on his next book. Without realising that they were in a kind of race to be the first to publish a new and unknown writer, the firms of Dennis Dobson, Nicholson & Watson and the Progress Publishing Company each set the processes in motion.

In August 1946 Gwyn off-handedly but with a quiet sense of triumph sent to Nana a copy of a brand-new book, saying, 'The third item in this tripartite effort will probably interest you.' Called *Triad One*, the book was the first in a series planned by Dobson; under the editorship of Jack Aistrop the enterprise was designed, as preliminary advertising promised, to provide an outlet for material that is not of standard length, such as the short novel or play, the small collection of stories or poems, the long essay. The volumes will be known as 'Triads' and each will present the work of three writers.

In *Triad One* the featured writers were James Gordon with some short stories, Elizabeth Berridge with a handful of poems, and Gwyn Thomas with a long short story or short novel entitled *The Dark Philosophers*. 'I think you'll like this novel,' he commented hopefully at the end of his letter to Nana, adding casually:

> I have some more coming out this year but with the printing trade in its present state one can never tell. Still, this is the beginning, the first of a series of literary kicks in the social and political pants that this slow corrupt old world will not swiftly forget. Also, some laughter will be caused, and that is never in too great supply. Hope you like it.

The Dark Philosophers made an immediate impression. Lionel Hale in the *Observer* declared that *Triad One* was chiefly remarkable for Gwyn's contribution, and admired his 'most persuasive flavour of comic bitterness'. Others agreed that what made the story work so well was the way in which a sense of the deep and brooding bitterness and disillusion of Gwyn's miner-narrators was always leavened with 'a pugnacious humanity and a crackling sense of humour', as Allen Hutt put it. David Martin thought it was, since Jack Jones's *Rhondda Roundabout*, 'the most interesting novel to have come out of that bleak vale'.

Three months later the Progress Publishing Company reminded the public of Gwyn's arrival on the scene by issuing *Where Did I Put My Pity?*, a collection of six short stories including two novellas, 'Oscar' and 'Simeon', which seemed to their readers particularly powerful. Arthur Calder Marshall was rather cool, suggesting that Gwyn's purpose was less certain than that of Howard Fast, whose *Freedom Road* had just come out:

> But Gwyn Thomas does not accept the limitations of his mannerisms and adventures into passions which his style cannot support. The result is not a social indictment, as one suspects the author intends, but a casebook of unemployment frustration, hopeless, negative and wildly improbable.

In the *Daily Worker* Allen Hutt took a view which suggested that he, unlike Calder Marshall, had been able to read the stories as their author intended:

> The book is appropriately sub-titled 'Folk Tales from the Modern Welsh'. The laughter and the tears, the high comedy and the stark tragedy of the valleys are all here.... The longest of these tales, nearly a short novel, depicts the monstrous life and violent death of the mountainous Oscar; it is a Hogarthian cartoon of a local kulak.

In a sense this divided approach was typical of the criticism that attended all Gwyn's writing; for numerous reasons he turned out to be a writer who attracted a devoted and passionately partisan following among those who understood his thrust and savoured his manner, while leaving decidedly cool many otherwise sensitive readers who were outraged by his non-conforming individuality or who found his densely packed method intractable. The main problem for his readers is rooted in the matter of realism and probability, as is evident in the too limiting and unimaginative Calder Marshall remarks. Gwyn was not and never became a realistic writer in the sense of being the careful craftsman of the Arnold Bennett stamp whose aim was to produce a credible imitation of real life and by that method bring the reader to reflection and perception. For Gwyn life was in many ways a nightmare, and his writing set out to explore the nightmarish, allowing his fantasy freedom to exaggerate either the dark and the monstrous or the comic by way of compensation. *The Dark Philosophers* and *Where Did I Put My Pity?* would more appropriately have been published in the opposite order and with a greater length of time between them, for, although the stories in *Where Did I Put My Pity?* have their humour (none more so than 'Dust in the Lonely Wind', the story of Uncle Gomer under the influence of the cinema), they are not so subtle in their combination of despair and resignation as *The Dark Philosophers*, which also marks Gwyn's advance towards the adoption of the curious, anonymous and almost unique 'we' narrator seen to its best advantage in the book properly published third in order.

Nicholson & Watson were much slower in preparing *The Alone to the Alone* for the press, partly for internal reasons and partly because of the contractual mess which ensued when they noticed books by their new author being published by other houses. It was not until the middle of 1947 that things were sorted out. Meanwhile, in the year which elapsed after the appearance of the book of short stories, life became more exciting for Gwyn than he expected when professional assistance was offered by the Curtis Brown literary agency.

The introduction was made when Gwyn and Lyn, invited to a literary party in London when the growing reputation of *The Dark Philosophers* brought them their first taste of modest fame, found themselves telling the story of their tangled contracts to a sympathetic listener whose wife, it turned out, was an agent with Curtis Brown. Lyn, to whom Gwyn left all arrangements without demur, leapt at the chance of receiving guidance from people who knew what they were about, and Curtis Brown acted for Gwyn for the rest of his life. Their first problem was to placate the three publishers who already thought they had Gwyn Thomas on their books. With skilful diplomacy that matter was resolved, Nicholson & Watson emerging as victors with the options on Gwyn's subsequent work. In the meantime the agency looked also to its contacts in the United States and very quickly found interest in *The Dark Philosophers* at Little, Brown & Company in Boston.

Fortunately the timing was not too late to catch the postwar burst of radical idealism in America before it began to succumb to the overwhelming conservative backlash which manifested itself as McCarthyism. When *The Dark Philosophers* came out in the United States in May 1947 it received a tremendously encouraging welcome. In the *New York Herald Tribune* Lewis Gannett summed up:

> 'A marvellous mixture of Bunyan and Runyon' is what James Hilton calls Gwyn Thomas's novelette, but John Bunyan lacked the dark humor of Gwyn Thomas's men of the Welsh coal-mining valley and Damon Runyon, not being a Welshman, didn't sing. Walter Edmonds said it was as if Thomas Hardy met Damon Runyon over a loving cup of small beer. The fact is this son of the Rhondda Valley writes with an accent all his own.

Just as Gannett drew attention to the 'doctrine of Karl Marx in the rarefied form once known as Christian Socialism' which vitalised the story, Hilton had recognised with approval the political subtext of *The Dark Philosophers*, commenting:

> He tells a bitter story, but he tells it uproariously, and if the underlying philosophy is Marxian, it is not only Marx without tears but also that even more remarkable phenomenon, Marx with laughs.[1]

It was the successful young novelist Howard Fast, however, whose praises rang loudest for 'a masterpiece, a warm, beautiful, splendid book that sets a new standard in proletarian literature, a book at once a prose poem and a testimony to the dignity and worth of all men'.[2] Fast understood as did few others at the time that America was on the lip of a slippery descent into a new rightist era, where any artist of left-wing or even liberal tendency would be persecuted and if possible obliterated, though even he could not at that stage have seen that his opposition to the authoritarian state would land him in prison before the decade was out. Thanks to Howard Fast's convictions about the book it was made a choice of the Liberty Book Club and circulated the more effectively for it.

By the summer of 1947 Nicholson & Watson were ready to publish *The Alone to the Alone*, and it came out in July. The *Western Mail* welcomed 'yet another accomplished Welsh writer' and saw the book as 'a significant, competent piece of work that warrants a hope for much from Gwyn Thomas'; the reviewer was clearly a little perturbed however by the further evidence offered by this story that Gwyn was quite unconventional in his management of his tale, especially in the matter of speech: 'The author has a remarkable flow of language and he must know that inhabitants of the Terraces would not converse like university dons.' It was only the earliest of many similarly expressed comments about Gwyn's practice throughout his writing career, and shows the same failure to recognise that he was not attempting to write in a conventional realistic mode that has already been noted. Whenever anyone tackled him on this question of his refusal to allot speeches to his characters in differentiated and appropriate idioms, making the ignorant speak ignorantly and the posh poshly, he always made the same reply: it was his duty as he saw it not simply to mirror life but to make a comment about life that would be powerful and memorable, and to this end he always did his characters the courtesy of making them as eloquent as he was capable of being himself.

P.H. Newby in the *Listener* said he thought the book 'wise, real and good' and commended 'the joyful exuberance of invention, the disdain of self-pity and above all the deep love for suffering humanity' to be found in it, and Gwyn Jones in the *Welsh Review*, though finding faults in the 'deliberate greyness and shroudlike texture' and 'the refusal to differentiate character other than by externals', recognised the appearance of a new ironic humorist of immense potential:

> The merits are the consistent vision, the power of creating the writer's own world, the power and compression of the style at its best, and the humour. If the short sketch of Tiger Watts and his wife does not appear in all future anthologies of British humour it will be because the editors don't know their business.

It was a hopeful beginning, reinforced by the information that Little, Brown were going to publish it in the United States as well. In the school summer holiday, basking in the glow of American approval for his first novel and some encouraging local response to his second, Gwyn took Lyn to Spain so that he could revisit some of the places that had stayed in his mind from the time spent there as a student fourteen years before. In the Asturias they actually succeeded in finding some friends that Gwyn had briefly made all that time before, and old thoughts and hopes were strongly revived in him as he listened to the stories of danger, survival and new Francovian oppression which they had to tell. The holiday was not wholly delightful for Lyn who felt increasingly frightened as she saw the significant looks which were sometimes exchanged when Gwyn mentioned the names of old acquaintances whom he hoped to see, or the furtive way in which some of the books Gwyn wanted to buy were brought out from back rooms. They spent so much on books that by the end of the holiday they had hardly any money left for food and their meals grew more and more meagre. At their last restaurant call Gwyn took all the remaining money from various pockets and asked the waiter what they could have, only to see him shake his head sadly. The thought of the proscribed books in their luggage quite terrified Lyn as they passed through Customs for the return journey and underwent the scrutiny of stern-faced and suspicious officials. Reminded of his love for Spain by this new experience of its magnificent landscapes and cultural glories, Gwyn felt recharged with the old anger against restrictive and repressive government; he remembered with pain the high hopes of the republic as he had known them in the university at Madrid; and he began turning over in his mind some ways in which he might write about the country and its history.

The journey home in the postwar conditions was not quite as

dreadful as the one he made in 1933, but it still entailed two sleepless days and nights and he was exhausted when he came to take up his chalk again in the school at Barry at the beginning of a new academic year. If teaching had begun to pall after seven years of constant hewing at the coalface of ignorance – to use a phrase which was a favourite of his own to describe the work of a schoolmaster – he was now additionally affected by being a published author whose writing career seemed promising and needed time and energy to develop. Showing considerable realism and not inconsiderable courage he continued to apply himself with animation and commitment to the school and the job of teaching for a long time, though the new opportunities which came his way with increasing recognition of his talent threw an ever greater burden upon him. Partly from a sense of loyalty to the school and to staff and students whose company he enjoyed, partly because after the precariousness of his younger days he could not relinquish the security which went with the job, he remained in the classroom to the delight of many generations of new boys but perhaps at greater cost to his vitality than he understood.

Ever an avid reader of the political press, he began to notice with increasing concern the reports from the United States of the great new fears of communism which seemed to be sweeping the nation. Even decent, moderate people seemed to be getting caught up in warlike attitudes towards the Soviet Union and in collateral policies of repression towards domestic left-wingers and freethinkers. Among those whose names were known to Gwyn was Howard Fast, an outspoken novelist and film-script writer whose protests in defence of individual freedom and the cause of world peace brought him into the headlines. Late in 1947 Fast was indicted, together with a number of similar protesters who held membership of or who were associated with the American Communist Party, on some rather vague charges which together amounted virtually to an action for treasonable conduct. Gwyn, moved not only by the highly complimentary review of *The Dark Philosophers* which Fast had written but also by a great surcharge of distress and anger at what he saw happening in America, wrote to him, thanking him for the review and declaring himself at one with his general political aims:

The miners here, especially the older ones who are veterans of the Syndicalist and I W W phases of our advance, are passionately interested in the American struggle and are still stirred to their very roots by the poetry of international solidarity....

For myself, I am trying to do for certain aspects of the contemporary British experience, albeit on a lower plane of mastery and significance, what you are doing for the whole broad canvas of American development. Your word of praise makes up for a lot of setbacks. From the critics of this green and Social-Democratic land I get a fairly thin time. The Tories say nothing until they can serve me with a police-notice. The 'Third Force' boys who are going all the way to hell with Bevin and read only when they can get the stars out of their eyes regard as quaintly vulgar anyone who goes raking up the facts of social and industrial decay in the basic 'black areas' that made up the life-view of those who now make up the vanguard of the British Labour movement.

The acute disillusionment which Gwyn was already feeling about the conduct of Attlee's Labour government became more and more marked during these days and his disgust with Bevin and Cripps in particular found powerful expression in his letters. For a while he threw himself with great vigour into a correspondence with Fast, allowing him to publish several of his letters more or less verbatim in the American *Daily Worker* and in the left-wing journal *Mainstream and Masses*. It was almost as if his frustration with the British situation made him take more interest in the American, where for some reason he was able to make his voice heard in a way not open to him at home. That was partly because, as a teacher who wished to hold on to his job, he understood that there were limits to the amount of overt political expression he could give vent to. It was also probably due to some extent to his realistic assessment of his talents and of the time available to him. In the time he could take for himself after school duties he wanted to function as the artist he felt himself to be, and despite the force of his political feelings he knew that it was through his art that he must express them. He simply did not feel capable of being a politician directly, knowing himself to be lacking in organisational and practical skills, and doubting his ability to draw as politicans often must upon funds of insincerity, compromise and plain untruth.

Even as he first wrote to Howard Fast in January 1948 his *The Alone to the Alone* was published in the United States by Little,

Brown. Not much impressed by Gwyn's title, they had insisted on something more attractive and less gloomy, and had come up ingeniously with the title *Venus and the Voters*. Pleasantly alliterative, it underscored the rather cynical love-theme with which the story is introduced and at the same time exploited an aspect of Gwyn's peculiar lexis in which his people are referred to as 'elements' or 'voters'. It was really very well received, though not extensively reviewed immediately; indeed, some reviews were still appearing more than a year after its date of publication as readers gradually came to recognise its value. James Hilton was pleased to find confirmation of Gwyn's 'unquenchable comic spirit'; Nelson Algren found it 'a timely tale with the light Welsh touch and the most genuine sort of understanding'; and Isabelle Mallet in the *New York Times Book Review* wrote of it most perceptively:

> Why should we laugh unrestrainedly over the goings-on of four scarecrows perched on the edge of a pallid wilderness? And why should beauty and tenderness seem to rest so confidingly in the grasp of these human outcasts? The answer lies in the spirit of the dark philosophers, a secret weapon forged of humor, integrity, wisdom and endurance.

In his development of the odd 'group narration' of the story, in which Walter, Ben, Arthur and 'I' become essentially a kind of 'we' as observer-commentator-manipulator, Gwyn was following a path almost all his own. Perhaps he remembered the oddly shifting narratorial standpoint of Conrad's *The Nigger of the Narcissus* where the story is told by an undefined 'I' who becomes 'we' before reverting to 'I'. Perhaps he was simply writing out of his youthful experience of group membership at school and among the young Rhondda unemployed where individuality could be largely secondary to a group identity. In a sketch for a play in one of his notebooks of the mid-1930s he was already toying with the idea of having as his protagonists a couple of down-and-outs whose discussions and adventures threw light on the political themes that so obsessed him. It begins:

> *Steve and Mahony sitting on a wall, gazing at a house behind trees, a rich house.*
> STEVE: Why do we have to sit on walls? I ask. I've got a right to know.
> MAHONY: The wall's got a right to know why we're sitting on it. But

it's unlikely that anybody'll ever write out a book of answers for the wall.

STEVE (*plucking off a bit of lichen and crumbling it in his hand*): This moss is soft and wet. It leaves a green mark on your hand.

MAHONY: You find entertainment in a lot of things. Could you find something to eat as well, for the sake of balance? It's one thing to be thrilled to death by moss....

STEVE: And another to be worn down to your last bone by hunger? Should I die first, my last bone is yours to keep on living as long as you can.[3]

The two tramps discuss the world and its mysteries in oblique terms for several pages, being joined by an eccentric rich man who parries their arguments. The item peters out in the notebook after fourteen pages, and at the end a scribbled comment shows Gwyn's state of mind: 'Rotten. Rotten. There's no shape at all about what I do.' While it is possible to hear in their dialogue and predicament a kind of pre-echo of what Beckett was so successfully to put onto the stage some fifteen years later in *Waiting for Godot*, it may also be felt that the wall on which Steve and Mahony are sitting is the same one as that occupied by Walter, Ben, Arthur and the narrator in *The Dark Philosophers* and *The Alone to the Alone*, and that these discontented figures are early precursors of the eloquent, mischievous anti-heroes of Gwyn's two first short novels.

Despite their modest success he did not use them again. Still refining his technique, he wrote in the autumn term of 1947 a novel with a clearly defined first-person narrator, Stobo Wilkie, an ambitious shop assistant whose designs are frustrated by an assortment of comic circumstances including a treacherous cat of a girlfriend and a hopelessly impractical and unaggressive father, the local milkman. Entitled *The Thinker and the Thrush*, after the name of the pub favoured by most of the characters, especially those who like to thrash out political philosophy against a background of wheeling and dealing, it was sent off to Nicholson & Watson who again undertook to publish it. Without a moment's delay he began another undertaking, this one about the largest of his life.

He had long been fascinated by some of the nineteenth-century Welsh heroes and martyrs who figured in the stories told by his father, and had more than once contemplated in the 1930s some forms of writing about them. With his brother Walt he had discussed

10 The ancient graveyard into which Gwyn gazed from his room (top left window) in St Edmund Hall in his final year at Oxford

11 The Brynffynon Arms ('Tavern of the Fountain', as Gwyn called it) in the tiny village of Llanwonno

12 Gwyn with Lyn (*l*) in 1937, with Lyn's sister-in-law Norma

13 Snapshot of Gwyn returning home from school about 1955, wearing his gangster-style slouch hat

the possibility of writing about Dr William Price, the eccentric philosopher of Llantrisant famous for instituting cremation as a legitimate means of dealing with the bodies of the dead, or Guto Nyth Brân, the fabulous runner, or Dic Penderyn, executed for his part in the Merthyr Rising of 1833. Suddenly decision hardened; the apprentice work had been done; now was the time to write the big one, the important work that would make his name. And the subject would be that heart-stirring attempt at revolution whose hero was Dic Penderyn, a revolution of which the people of Britain in the grim days of disappointment and betrayal of the late 1940s (as Gwyn saw them) needed to be reminded.

In the words of Lyn, in a letter to Nana in March 1948, he worked 'like a maniac' at the new novel throughout the winter. Three hundred pages were already done; about the same had yet to be completed; he was feeling very weary and tired. He was not too tired, however, to write again to Howard Fast with huge indignation when word came that he had lost his appeal and, with his dozen colleagues, would have to go to jail. 'You and Tom Paine are twin symbols of the rebellious honesty and common sense which will yet put paid to the Tory humbugs,' Gwyn declared. As the world drifted dangerously close again to war he, like Fast in America, was sure that common sense would win through in the end, although:

> The crooks and the nitwits are staging their biggest drive ever, with us as with you, to turn their world into the desired cross between thieves' kitchen and prayer-meeting. The priest-racketeer axis has never been so startlingly clear as it is in Western Europe today. Under the anti-communist canopy we see characters coming up out of the drains that we never thought to see alive on this earth again. The military maniacs with their hundredweights of medals are off on their biggest drool since the Dreyfus affair.... And every step taken by the monstrous oafs and sextons of the Right merely reveals the more clearly the terrible betrayals of principle and trust that have been nibbling at the guts of our Left wing for the past half-century.

By the summer of 1948, with the new book almost finished, Gwyn had every reason to be pleased with the way life was going despite his anxiety over the great political and military events in the world at large. The publication of his first three books in so short a time had drawn him to the attention both of the public and of the literary figures in the Welsh establishment, and suddenly there were invitations from and contacts with all sorts of new people. Particularly there was a formidable trio of Joneses: Jack, the miner-turned-novelist whose *Rhondda Roundabout* and *Off to Philadelphia in the Morning* had made him a world-famous figure; Gwyn, professor of English at Aberystwyth, novelist, critic and editor, doyen of the Welsh literary scene; and Glyn, teacher, short-story writer, and poet. Glyn Jones, the kindliest of men and Gwyn's nearest neighbour of the three, made haste to congratulate him on his achievement when he first became known. In a letter to Glyn in June Gwyn confessed that trying to keep going as a teacher while driven by an inner demon to write was almost more than he could bear. He and Lyn had earlier in the year moved house once more, this time to a flat in Porthkerry Road, halfway up the steep hill behind their Broad Street home and that much closer to the school buildings at the top of the hill, but again he was feeling unsettled and discontented:

> I'm a bit itchy about Barry, too. I think I'd like to shift. I've been here for what strikes me as a tediously long time. I'm going up to Cumberland for the summer holiday and if the place suits me and I see a really fine opportunity I might try to sink a root there. I seem to have reached the tether's end here, to have signed a kind of sinister pact with the pupils to denounce Spanish with equal vehemence. When the first abundant vigour is gone, teaching becomes incompatible with even the most tenuous intention of doing original literary work. Under the burden of this horrible and exhausting double-life one finds it less and less easy to keep away from the sharp-toothed mouth of one's own deadly mannerisms.

He could not resist adding, however, some details of his life as a schoolmaster of the kind that he later recalled and used with great delight as a story-teller of the school scene:

> My mood is complicated by a chill I picked up being a Steward at the County Sports at Tonypandy. I was so stupefied by the experience of waving flags and blowing whistles without properly understanding what exactly was being conveyed by either act I lay down on the wet grass for five minutes without being conscious of doing so and would have kept lying had it not been for some record-breaking jumper flying well beyond the limits of the sandpit and landing on my face. It was a dark and terrible day. I have been sighing and sneezing ever since. The climax came when I approached the Chief Starter (a fussy monomaniac with the

longest and loudest pistol I have ever seen) and told him that if he couldn't find another steward to deputise for me he would have a madman as well as an athletic programme on his hands. The man could not hear a word of what I was saying for he had long been deafened by the racket he was making with his weapon. He called me Major Bevan, took me with a chuckle into his crazy confidence, put his pistol arm around my neck and wagged his gun as he complained about the number of stewards who were not steady under fire. I asked him if the gun were loaded. He said No, and a second later the thing went off and as I sent groups of boys around the field to look for the blackened ear of the Starter's Steward he kept laughing and explaining to me about his hair trigger.

As the summer term ended and he and Lyn prepared for their holiday in the Lake District, word came from Curtis Brown that the new novel was to be published by Michael Joseph, who was most impressed and had the highest hopes for it. It had been a long time coming, but Gwyn had finally arrived upon the scene in an explosion of texts. As they set off for the north he was already planning in his mind another novel. This time he would write one set in that Spain about which he had read so much, and of whose glories he had been reminded by their holiday the previous year. Despite the problems, life was not so bad.

8

Rising Novelist

The Lake District in the summer of 1948 offered Gwyn just the soothing period of relaxation and reflection for which he was craving, though even here he was unable to forget politics and merely enjoy the tranquil beauty of the place. He wrote to Howard Fast:

> Currently I am on the shores of Lake Windermere meditating on the great intellectual drama of the Lake Poets and the bitter loneliness in which Hazlitt walked when the other members of his group scampered away from the principles of the French Revolution and took their hearts and souls to market. Looking at the surroundings of Wordsworth's cottage at Grasmere — the last word in serene and opiate beauty — one understands a little more of the forces that are socially operative in making a man a monkey.

It is difficult to read these words forty years after they were written without recognising a certain unconscious irony in them, for there were to be those who would accuse Gwyn too of having taken his heart and soul to market in the decades to follow. At the time he was still heart and soul committed to a position on the extreme left of the political spectrum, and there he would effectively stay in theory as long as his life lasted. In practice he was soon to begin to mellow for a whole crop of irresistible reasons. In August 1948 only the earliest signs of the process could have been detected, and they would not have been found in the project which he outlined to Fast:

> I am preparing a lecture for various progressive societies over here next winter: 'Gorki and Fast: The Novel in the Service of the People'.... I can think of no single topic that better contains within itself the materials of a full answer to the wicked absurdity of trying to persuade people, as

our press is trying to persuade us, that America and Russia are doomed and polar opposites.

The holiday in Cumberland was prolonged a little when Lyn suffered a slight accident while sliding down a goat path to the edge of a tarn among the Ennerdale fells. Her ankle was broken, and Gwyn told Fast 'I worked harder getting her down than I had done since those bitter winters of the 1920s when my brothers and I went up on to the frozen refuse tips on the surrounding hills and scratched around for ribblings of coal to keep the family warm'. It was some time before she could do more than hobble about again, and for a while they were deprived of the long walks into the Vale which they had been used to taking as their staple exercise. Never one to miss an opportunity to write, Gwyn took advantage of the extra hours at home to work on *The Dark Neighbour*, the long novel of Spain under the Moorish domination which he had begun in the summer.

The school to which Gwyn returned as the Christmas term began was never again to be quite the same as it had been during the six years he had already spent there. The well-disposed, eccentric and arts-minded E T, anxious to devote his energies to something new after his services to education, was about to retire. During the war his (as some would say) Cardiganshire-bred interest in money had led to his spending a great deal of time in the development of a factory specialising in the production of noodles and other rice-substitutes. Now he gave up what was left of his devotion to the cause of education and turned his mind to leisure. Gwyn told Nana:

> Griffiths is leaving us at the end of this year. Their daughter Nan is already out in Australia and they are selling their house in Barry and everything in it except the crockery and are clearing off to Melbourne themselves in January. That macaroni factory which they were running here nearly finished off Mrs G. By last summer she had grown to look like one of her own shorter noodles.

E T's successor at Barry County School was a man of a different stamp, and the changes he brought with him were not congenial as far as Gwyn was concerned.

The new headmaster's sympathies were scientific and technical. A stickler for order and propriety, a disciplinarian prepared to be seen as a martinet if that was what it took, a man naturally drawn to the detailed trappings of smoothly ordered routine, he was almost from the day of his arival in the school in January 1949 suspicious of a teacher like Gwyn who, his nose told him, was likely to be trouble. His outside interests, his recent success and the accompanying notoriety, the very fact of his being a novelist, a creative artist, and a somewhat uninhibited speaker of his radical opinions, all served as a warning to the newcomer that here was someone to be watched and perhaps brought into line as soon as possible.

Gwyn was already wondering whether some escape from the school treadmill might be possible even while working under the amiable and tolerant supervision of E.T. Griffiths. Had he known how soon and how considerably things were, from his point of view, to worsen, his return to school for the autumn term of 1948 would have been even more reluctant. There were promises in the air to keep him cheerful, however, and requests were beginning to come in from various sources for stories and reviews, so that he could feel that his talent was no longer out in the cold, neglected and unfulfilled. He returned to the coal-face with some resolution.

Teaching, after all, although it brought him into contact with a good deal of reluctant and even hostile response, had its very great rewards in the character and ability of some of the boys whom he encountered in the classrooms. At the time these included mature and clever lads such as Keith Thomas, later to be renowned as a historian, Keith Baxter-Wright, who would one day so build on his youthful experience in school plays as to become an actor of international reputation, and Edwin Brooks, whose fierce socialist beliefs took him in due course into Parliament and who always acknowledged that Gwyn had been one of the inspirations of his life.

Many others went on to distinguished careers especially in education; none of them ever forgot their contact with their strange, voluble, withdrawn but jovial teacher, not so much for what he taught them about Spanish as for what they learned from him about life in much more general terms. They called him 'Killer', partly perhaps because he did have a quick temper which could be triggered at times by what seemed to them to be the slightest matter, but which probably seemed to him like the last straw of warning that his lessons were getting out of control. More probably the name derived from the peculiar way in which he presented himself, looking, as several of his pupils recall, like a gangster with his slouch hat and raincoat with upturned collar, reinforced by his tendency when in a good humour to speak film Americanisms out of the side of his mouth. When Robert Morley asked him in his television programme *One Pair of Eyes*: 'Why do they call you "Killer"?', Gwyn shrugged and replied that he was the mildest of men; and so he was in terms at least of physical violence. He would no more have raised a hand to a boy than he would have bitten off his ear. His wit could be deadly, but more often the boys were won over with a more farcical brand of humour, or with the kind of wordplay by which, for instance, he gave a frequently swearing caretaker the unforgettable sobriquet, 'Lord Effingham'.

He was, in his way, a considerable contributor to the life of the school, supporting especially literary and debating events with his presence and with frequent contributions of his own. A lecture which he gave to the Literary Society was such a high point that it became an annual event keenly anticipated by both staff and boys. And on the retirement in 1950 of his colleague, J.H. Francis, who had edited the school magazine since the First World War and had built it up to be a periodical of some quality, Gwyn allowed himself to be persuaded to take on the editorship and to do the extra work involved for years to come.

It was sustaining to Gwyn that the staff included among its usual mixture of excellent and not-so-excellent masters several eccentrics, with some of whom he became very friendly. When he later wrote about his school experiences he inevitably drew on these acquaintances for the characters of his stories, but always, whether writing fiction or autobiography, he disguised and modified them so much that few could identify themselves with any certainty. The chief device was to mix characteristics and plots from several different sources and then to add something completely from his imagination, and it worked very well. The 'Mr Walford' who appears in *A Few Selected Exits* is a compound of memories from both the schools in which Gwyn taught; the 'Mr Rawlins' of *A Frost On My Frolic* and many short stories has touches of those who taught Gwyn at Porth but is also based on a Cardigan teacher and in addition is, in his ability to tell a story and in many of his wry reflections on life in and after school, quite palpably a projection of Gwyn himself.

Among his particular cronies on the staff was Sidney Jones, who taught English and Welsh; a real old bachelor, he was bald and, wearing spectacles with lenses of immense thickness, was known to the boys as Tojo. He had a great facility with verse in Welsh and English, and could produce a lyric using the Welsh form called *cynghanedd* at the drop of a hat. Like Gwyn he could not drive, but unlike Gwyn he set his hand to learning how to do so after his fiftieth birthday and became something of a terror on the local roads. A WEA lecturer during a seven-year period of unemployment in the 1930s, a communist, like his brother Arthur who later became a Communist Party councillor in Merthyr Tydfil, and a great lover of words, he admired Gwyn's work and became very attached to him.

For the most part, Gwyn's friendships, though most cordial, were not deep. There was something ultimately unfindable about his essential self, some unapproachable depths which remained a mystery even to those who thought very well of him. One colleague who walked along Jenner Road with him to and from school every day for fifteen years was Teifion Phillips, later to become headmaster of the school; he recognised that Gwyn was a man of great heart, but felt he could not claim to *know* him.

The autumn term of 1948 unfolded as any other except that in his heart Gwyn was sure that with the new novel that Michael Joseph was to bring out within the next few months he had done something rather special. Meanwhile he was beginning to worry about the fate of *Another Night, Another Day* (his revised title for *The Thinker and the Thrush*) which was still with Nicholson & Watson. He realised that there were difficulties in the postwar publishing business but it seemed that they were taking an unconscionably long time to bring it out. When it became obvious that it would not appear in time for Christmas, his advisers at Curtis Brown, fearing that it might be launched in 1949 to coincide with the publication by Michael Joseph of *My Root On Earth*, prompted Gwyn to take steps to delay it. In the event, taking advantage of a clause in the contract for *Another Night, Another Day* stipulating that it should be published within a year of its acceptance, Curtis Brown withdrew it from Nicholson & Watson altogether and finished Gwyn's association with them. They could not have realised that the effect of this would be to ensure that in the end it never was published at all. The last public vestige of it was in a joke which Gwyn liked to tell, in which a reporter, mishearing the title of the book during an interview, reports it in the local paper as *Another Night in Aberdare*.

If it had finally been published it might well have ended up with such a title, for Gwyn fiddled with his titles in the most extraordinary way. He was clearly fascinated with titles almost for themselves, and used to generate possible ones by the score. On his shelves after his death Lyn found several books into the endpapers and margins of which Gwyn had at various times scribbled innumerable titles, perhaps as a sort of game, perhaps as an *aide-mémoire* (for one can see how any one of those titles might have turned into a book if he had only had the time to follow up the implications and possibilities they offered), perhaps as just an outlet for his almost neurotic need to be writing something. On the title page of *Philip II of Spain* by Sir Charles Petrie, for instance, Gwyn's small neat print flows like a tide across all the paper left white by Eyre & Spottiswoode:

> *Outside, Laughing; The Sinister Branch; The Mood for Miracles; The Place for the Ladies; The Lapsed Mass; The Reality Set; The Fault of the Careless People; Reversible Reversions; The Legions of Equality; It Hurts, It Hurts; The Torn Strip; The Man is Everything. . . .*

and that's only the inch and a half at the top of the page, above the name of the author. In keeping with this obsession he finally informed Michael Joseph that *My Root On Earth* was to be re-titled *All Things Betray Thee*, and so it was scheduled to appear.

In November Gwyn wrote to Howard Fast to congratulate him on his latest novel, *My Glorious Brothers*:

> It's a grand and lovely book. . . . The theme, and the way of its telling, will have a deep interest for the people of these mining valleys. . . . The Scriptures have been grafted into the marrow of their revolutionary tradition as intimately as the words of Marx, Keir Hardie and Lewis Jones. (This last you may not have heard of. I'll tell you about him one day. An authentic Maccabee of the fight against finance capitalism, a miner of genius who turned out to be one of the great proletarian teachers and died woefully young.) One of my friends told me he was reminded of Lewis when reading your sentence: 'And then I went back to weep with my brothers; and above the sound of the rain I could hear the people weeping.' Those words could mount on every wind that blows out of the Rhondda.

Fast, delighted with Gwyn's letter, replied quickly with the news that he and his colleagues were still not in jail:

> For the first time in American history you have a group of people who have been indicted, tried, condemned, sentenced — and yet remain at

107

liberty.... The probable reason for this lies in the enticing contradictions of the whole case. Eleven men and women, on the one hand, are sentenced to prison without having committed any crime under the written or unwritten laws of the land. On the other hand, to make the real cream of the jest, the chairman of this obscene unamerican committee which originally framed us, Mr Parnell Thomas, representative from New Jersey, has just been indicted himself on the charge of defrauding his employees.

It could only be a temporary reprieve, for Fast and all in his position were already aware of the work against them of Senator Joseph McCarthy and others of his persuasion, though he could hardly at that point have anticipated McCarthy's astonishing emergence into prominence in 1950 and the hardening of the campaign in America against everyone having even the slightest sympathy with the left. No more could Gwyn have foreseen that his championship of Fast and his friends, as revealed to all by the publication in their communist and socialist journals of some of his letters to Fast as well as other pieces, would lead as it did before long to his own disbarment in the United States. Even if such a consequence had been obvious, it would have made no difference, for Gwyn's heart was in the struggle and, when he was sure what the truth was, nothing else would do for him.

Working hard throughout the Christmas term, Gwyn had by the early stages of the new year completed his large historical novel with a Spanish theme and sent it off to Michael Joseph with a considerable sense of achievement. For a long time no word came from them. Then, early in 1949, the Thomas family was severely rocked when the widowed John was himself admitted to hospital, his leukaemia at an advanced stage. Gwyn was too upset after visiting his brother to write to Nana, but Lyn told her that after the first shock of seeing the invalid, pale, emaciated and looking like a corpse, they had been given reason to believe he would get better. It was soon plain, however, that their hopes were not well grounded, and Gwyn could not bear it. After John's death, which came to cast a dreadful pall over the publication in May of *All Things Betray Thee*, Lyn told Nana:

Gwyn is not very well these days.... He hasn't felt the same since John went. I think that only you, Nana, could imagine what a blow it was to Gwyn. I shall never forget the way he sobbed every time he came back from the hospital.... He was feeling very sad when sending the books

108

out to the family. It's the first time that one was not sent to John, and Gwyn had looked forward to John reading this one more than any of the others.

There were other worries in the family, too, for rumours were coming to them from various directions that all was not well with Eddie's marriage. Letters flew from one member of the family to another, but neither Eddie nor Nancy was answering inquiries addressed to them and speculation was rife. Gwyn had little to say about the matter, for he was concerned with disappointments much closer to home. *All Things Betray Thee*, which he regarded as by far the most important thing he had done, was receiving something of a mixed reception; the reviews were in his estimation missing the point of much of what he had been trying to say and he fretted continually.

In his book he had departed significantly from the method established by his first successes. Instead of retaining his well-established group of narrators with their anarchic and comic view of more or less contemporary circumstances, he had placed a single, clearly characterised narrator in a story set early in the nineteenth century, a story of historical significance in the process of social and political revolution from capitalism, and had developed his theme in a style and with a proliferation of detail that he felt quite eclipsed the earlier books. Many of the reviewers seemed to be reading it as a mere historical romance in a high poetic style, and it infuriated Gwyn that they could write about it with so little perception. Locally he fared no better. The *Western Mail* hailed him in its headline as 'A Major Welsh Novelist' but reviewer Brian Evans in a brief report spoke rather vaguely of 'splendid but difficult stuff' and concluded that Mr Thomas should beware lest, with his too dense and complex sentences, readers might come to ask, like his character Lemuel, 'Are you saying something?'

When Henry Treece wrote with greater understanding of the real thrust of the novel, Gwyn was so relieved that he wrote to thank him:

Your review came like a benediction to stay and solace me. During the last fortnight I have read so many frankly moronic sentences about the book, such a stream of stupid and malicious chatter in some cases, that I could have sat down and wept my thanks all the way to you at Burton on Humber at finding in your paragraphs a fragrance of the same joy as went into the book's making.

Glyn Jones too was generally enthusiastic if critical of some aspects of the book. In order to secure a greater universality for it Gwyn had not simply told the story of Dic Penderyn in Merthyr Tydfil in 1833 with a wealth of solidly researched background detail as another man might have done (as several men have done, in fact, one way or another). In Gwyn's book the revolution takes place in a town called Moonlea, the hero is called John Simon Adams and the narrator, an outside observer, a travelling musician who against his will becomes drawn into the action, has a name (Alan Leigh) but is more generally referred to throughout as the Harpist. Inspired by the happenings in Merthyr but not a record of them, *All Things Betray Thee* attempted to explore the involvement of individuals in a revolutionary situation in a general way, free from the constraints of accurate historiography. Glyn Jones recognised something of Gwyn's intentions, but was still perturbed by what he felt were omissions and diversions. Explaining that Michael Joseph's editors had cut almost two hundred pages from the original manuscript in order to reduce it to publishable size, Gwyn told Glyn Jones:

> Without the scene of the trial and several other incidents and characters that were winnowed, the book has never possessed the balance that it struck me as having when the last page came out of the typewriter. Still, books come, books go. And no one six months after, least of all the writer, gives a damn.

In fact he gave quite a bit more than a damn, but was learning to conceal it. Besides, the reviews were not really as hostile as he imputed; many were complimentary, some were highly enthusiastic, and as time went on his book sold steadily. In any case the onward rush of events did not leave him much time to ruminate on past troubles. No sooner was *All Things Betray Thee* safely published than Michael Joseph finally delivered Gwyn a bombshell that he had pessimistically begun to expect. He complained to Glyn Jones:

> The novel which is now with the publishers is having a pretty bleak time and as far as I can see is not likely to emerge into the light of day. I am in no mood to go bargaining and cutting. They probably sense in me a potentially best-selling two-rapes-a-chapter man and if that's what they want, that's what they'll get, with the rate being jacked up to three

in any novel appearing in time for the Christmas rush. My raw material in this line is inexhaustible. I was not President of the Bird Watchers' League (Lower Trebanog Branch) for nothing.

He was pulling the leg of a man whom he knew to be both pure and a little puritanical, but his remark is more pregnant than it seems. He was joking to cover his fury at Michael Joseph's virtual rejection of *The Dark Neighbour*; genuinely not in a mood to temporise, he asked Curtis Brown after a few more months of skirmishing to find him a publisher who would better appreciate his work, because he was damned if he was going to allow Michael Joseph to push him about.

There was more yet to his comment, for the fact was that he could have written sexy bestsellers without the least difficulty. Deep within himself he was torn and disturbed by the upsurges of sexual feeling that seemed to require more exciting adventures than marriage offered; yet, shy as he was of the world and its dangers, and devoted as he was to a wife whose practical skills underlined his own helplessness in practical matters, and disgusted as he was in a puritanical sort of way by the processes of the human body, there was no answer for him but a sublimation of those urges. He could not even write about them directly and publicly, and though sensitive readers may detect a considerable erotic charge in a good deal of his writing, his books never dealt in any real or extensive way with human sexuality or amorousness and he rarely wrote about women characters with any serious intention of allowing them to develop or become important. Perhaps he could not have done, for his understanding of women was limited by rather meagre experience of them as sexual beings; he seemed indeed to ignore the sexual difference and treat men and women much alike, with the only criteria of eligibility for tolerance being those of character and intellect. That he might, on the other hand, have exploited his imaginative and verbal facilities to write shockingly and saleably about sexual goings-on is attested by notebooks that he kept in later years, which he did not show to his wife and into which he sometimes wrote extended sexual fantasies provoked by some story in the *News of the World*; here the writing makes up for what it lacks in tenderness by a sort of wild and jolly enthusiasm, a frank specificity of forbidden terms; but the effect is sad, for it suggests a man of passion whose life has been considerably frustrated by social mores and personal inhibition.

In early novellas such as 'Oscar' and 'Simeon' a strong interest in sexual matters is manifest, but the opening words of *The Alone to the Alone* indicate the more distanced stance he later took towards passion and the flesh:

> In the Terraces, we never opposed love. The way we viewed this question was that love must be pretty deeply rooted to have gone on for so long. One would have to be very deep to tinker with so deep a root, deeper than we were. Also, love passes on the time. That is a prime feature in any place where there is a scarcity of work for the local men and women to do, a state which prevailed on a high plane indeed during the years now being spoken of. Also, love, properly used, keeps people warm.

Even at his most romantic, in for instance the relationships between the Harpist and Helen Penbury in *All Things Betray Thee* or that between Gustioz and Miriam in *The Dark Neighbour*, the sexual component is regarded with the coolest of eyes. In later stories the whole business is usually regarded as material for a joking, casual side-issue at most; usually it has no place at all. In the stories which he wrote for *Coal* and *Modern Reading* immediately after *Where Did I Put My Pity?* ushered him onto the scene there is no sexual interest. He was developing with huge gusto the kind of story for which he may in the end be best remembered, stories such as 'Dust In The Lonely Wind' in *Where Did I Put My Pity?* or 'As It Was In The Beginning' in *Coal*. In these, drawing deeply on the comic side of the life of his valley people, he presents to readers a world of absurd misfortune in which a group of unsinkable and highly loquacious individuals lead their petty lives with unquenchable optimism or constant rueful pessimism. Inhabited by characters such as Teilo Topliss, Milton Nicholas the socialist dreamer, Theo Morgan the Monologue, Edwin Pugh the Pang, Gomer Gough the Gavel, Luther Cann the Col (manager of the cinema) and others, the stories turn on the slightest of incidents in the political, social or commercial life of Windy Way or Meadow Prospect or Belmont or nearby Birchtown (Pontypridd). They are about a world much loved by its creator, who partly remembered it, partly invented it. More important in them than almost anything else is the talk which they report, in the stuff of which may be seen the seeds of the dialogue skills that inevitably

112

drew him in due course towards the theatre.

If Gwyn had some reason in the summer of 1949 to be a little depressed about his writing after the enthusiastic early reception, there were compensations. Another American novelist, Jay Williams, the author of several highly successful historical romances, wrote to say that he was 'knocked over' by *The Dark Philosophers* and wanted to come and visit Gwyn when on holiday in Europe later in the summer. Again from America came a letter from Norman Rosten, poet and novelist, full of praise for *Venus and the Voters*, 'a honey of a novel ... a tragi-comic cocktail that modern literature is starving for lack of – a kind of folk-mythology, of everyday working people'. Rosten thought it should be made into a film or play, and offered himself as dramatiser, saying he was a pretty good (if unfamous) playwright. And Howard Fast wrote with great enthusiasm about *Leaves in the Wind* when in July *All Things Betray Thee* was published under that title in the United States:

> It is not only a beautiful and proud and gentle book – a book that affirms all things men live for and hope for – but it is in a very real sense a new type of book. It blazes new paths and sets new goals and it marks for me a new level in the truest kind of socialist realism and humanism.... Here in this book you have put in the mouths of your characters, in a singing, beautiful, Celtic cadence, not what they probably said to each other but what they would have said had they been able to voice their dreams, the wholeness of their fears and hopes, their passions and even the force of our splendid historical destiny.

To his expression of gratitude he was able to add the news that the Liberty Book Club had chosen *Leaves in the Wind* as its July book, thus guaranteeing a sale for it of at least six thousand copies over and above whatever Little, Brown might achieve. In his gratified reply Gwyn explained why the Dic Penderyn story, as told to him and his brothers by their father, meant so much:

> When I was a small boy there was a fine, ancient worker, a neighbour of ours, who could remember following, dragged by his father's hand, the procession which followed Dic Penderyn's body down into the Afan valley. He could still recall the songs of wrath and compassion that the people sang. The old man wept each time he told the tale and he had to tell it often, for there was no leaf of our class tradition that filled us with more pity and wonder.

113

The harpist of my novel was an elusive figure called Lewis the Huntsman. He was given a pardon and went to America. Legend says that he returned and was often seen wandering among the hills around Merthyr, drawn back by who knows what wound of unfulfilment and shame. Penderyn's death was a common enough incident in the proletarian march. The history books closed their iron doors on him. Yet there was something about this man in which the people found a dignity and wholeness which were still fragmentary in themselves; he implanted a love and a serenity of step in those who were moving forward to take the height at which he had pointed.

As 1949 drew towards its close Gwyn felt under great stress, a good deal of it perhaps attributable to an internal dichotomy which can be perceived only with the benefit of hindsight. Externally there were problems for him about which he could do nothing. He was still a very poor man. A schoolmaster's salary in the late 1940s hardly justified having a bank account, and the boosts which his income was receiving from the sale of occasional stories were minimal. The novels made his name but not his fortune. Neither he nor Lyn was satisfied with the rooms in which they were living in the terraced house in Porthkerry Road, and they were not, he claimed, much encouraged by learning that they were number 2981 on the local housing list. 'At the present rate of building, the very best Aneurin can do, we will be housed in the third decade of the next century,' he told Fast. Buying a house at that stage was out of the question.

As if that were not enough he was being made more than a little uncomfortable at school by frequent confrontations with the new headmaster, who was determined that all his staff would fall into the lines he wanted to lay down. As he was a head who practised a generally rather rigid authoritarian approach to the boys and who believed in the use of the cane, he was unlikely to find an ally in a man like Gwyn. Once, observing the headmaster talking civilly in the playground to his deputy just after a session in which he had been applying the cane, Gwyn said to a colleague: 'Look at that criminal *smiling*.' Another time, telling of some dictat which had come from the headmaster, Gwyn said: 'A man would have to creep under the linoleum to get any lower than that.' But E T had not disdained the use of the cane – Gwyn's account of being on the receiving end of that implement in *A Few Selected Exits* is unforgettable – and there is evidently something much deeper in Gwyn's antipathy for the new

14 The staff of Barry Grammar School in 1949; on the left of the front row is Sidney Jones, and fourth from the left is 'Pop' Lennox, the venerable classics master; immediately behind him is D. J. P. Richards, celebrated athlete; second from left in the second row is Digby Lloyd, and Gwyn is second from the right; on the right of the back row, Teifion Phillips, later headmaster of the school

15 At an Oxford Union debate in 1955: in the front row guests of honour Kingsley Amis and Gwyn Thomas, with Union President Desmond Watkins and his fiancée between them; on the right of the row, Michael Heseltine

16 A portrait in oils of Gwyn in the mid 1950s by the young Mollie Parkin, whose family lived nearby in Barry

17 Hewison includes Gwyn in his gallery of 'Novel Faces' in *Punch* in 1958

XXXV—GWYN THOMAS

With fiction more convincing than reality Thomas delights to tease the Principality.

man. At any rate, there was no love lost between them, and Gwyn's sense that the school was being turned from a place of cultural freedom into an automated science factory gave him constant and increasing pain.

Internally there was being waged another battle, that between his politically left-wing disposition and his developing artistry. Even as in his letters to Fast he raged against the Labour Government's weaknesses he was working on a new novel in which his fateful sense of humour and his mellowing personality were combining to undermine the force of the political statement he intended. To Fast he wrote, as the time for a new General Election approached:

> This gang here, Churchill, Macmillan and company, after the latest appalling displays by Cripps and Bevin, are confident that the field is open to them for a straight run to power. The Labour leaders, I feel convinced, are now in a mood for surrender or coalition. There is not the vestige of a working-class principle left among them.

At the same time he was writing:

> If life, as they say, is an ever-rolling stream, that stream has a bed and there are voters who fit into it more cosily than others. Take Omri Hemlock. Omri was a small, likeable man who often sat with us over a glass of cordial in Orlando's Chip and Coffee Bar. Even when Omri tried to get into the second tenor section of Meadow Prospect Orpheans, the male voice party in which we sang, Mathew Sewell the Sotto, our conductor and a lover of the headvoice, said he had never heard a dimmer, more negative sound in his life than that which came out of Omri.

The opening words of *The World Cannot Hear You*, they signal a distinct movement in Gwyn's fiction towards the very funny books of the 1950s by which he became best known. It is not an abrupt change; the tone is still reminiscent of the two short novels in which his 'sidling obliquity' of approach first became apparent; the narration proceeds from a story-teller who has no perceptible identity other than that of the group with which he associates; the setting is still the Rhondda of the 1930s tartly and tenderly recalled. While there is still a sadness and occasionally a distinct bleakness in the back-ground to the tale, however, there is now a good deal of farcical incident, a wealth of comical dialogue, a cast of characters like those in the recent short stories with funny Welsh identifiers tagged to their names, in short, an upwelling of infectious good humour.

Not that this new venture proceeded far as the year ran down, however. By Christmas Gwyn was telling Nana:

> I don't think I have ever reached such a low ebb of vitality. It was hurrying to get that novel finished during the summer and then going back to one of the toughest terms I have ever known since starting to teach.

He was depressed, too, by the final breakdown of Eddie's marriage, telling Nana that it had contributed to the general sadness of the spirit in which he had been enveloped for weeks past. 'Some human beings would give the skin off their bodies for just one chance of happiness. Others are equally strenuous in chucking it down the drain. I've not heard from Eddie and he must have interpreted from my silence what my thoughts are about him. There is no question but that what men spend most time and care in making is their own misery,' he wrote. What he did not say to Nana, but recognised sooner than the other members of the family, was that Eddie, in acknowledging that a dead marriage can be worse for the children than a clean split, might have been showing more courage and sense than his family allowed. While regretting that Nancy had been made unhappy and that the children would have to finish their growing up without the constant presence of their father, Gwyn could not in the end begrudge his brother a second bite at the cherry of happiness. In the event Eddie's subsequent marriage, to Irene Thomas, proved to be not only lasting, stable and rewarding, but also life-saving, for with her help he was able to steady up and defeat the alcoholism that threatened at one stage to overwhelm him. When Eddie sought to be accepted again by his family – not such a little matter at a time when divorce was felt to be disgraceful and often unforgivable – it was Gwyn and Lyn who gave him and his new wife a welcome while some of the brothers and sisters maintained the cold shoulder for decades to come.

One of the more encouraging features of the time was Gwyn's growing friendship with Glyn Jones, who now invited him to take part in a series of broadcasts on 'Why I Write' which were going to go out on the BBC Welsh Home Service. 'It seems', Gwyn told Nana not without some pride, 'that I am now regarded as one of Wales's five premier writers together with Richard Hughes, Dylan Thomas,

Rhys Davies and Gwyn Jones.'

> It should be a very interesting series, especially the part dealing with the role played by a writer's early past in the way he writes and the purpose he has in writing. I wish I could illustrate what I will have to say with sound-records of the life we lived at Cymmer, the great lovable tumult of it all, the song, the laughter, the argument and, above all, the genius and affection you gave to create the road along which we all came. There is so little of what one really wants to say that one can say, so little of what is really important in a man's heart that can really be said.

Buoyed up by preparations for the broadcast, with its implications about his status, he was further raised in the new year by Howard Fast's generous and enthusiastic assessment of his work in a critical book, *Literature and Reality*. He told Fast:

> I cannot describe to you the delight, the sensible, unconceited delight, with which I read the pages you devoted to myself. You have made plain my innermost aims and convictions about how our class, its life and viewpoint, should be expressed in literature, better than I, with my perverse shynesses, could ever have dreamed of doing.

Fast later tempered his comments somewhat in a letter in which he pointed out that, while his positive remarks in the book had really been less than Gwyn's potential merited, there was one strong criticism which needed to be made:

> You are going to fall short of the job you set out to do until you can conceive the story emerging head and shoulders over the verbal contest of ideas. There is your greatest weakness – the one which, I think, needs to be overcome for you to step onto a new level of work creativity.
>
> The essence of the ideas we stand for is contained in the struggle of men, and the literary reflection must carry the story and the excitement of that struggle.... You must fight with yourself to tell stories as well as to project ideas.... I think it is important for you to think about this because I know of no one in Great Britain who carries the same potential as you do for beautiful and splendid writing.

Praise from such quarters however was not doing him any good with Michael Joseph, who still refused to accept *The Dark Neighbour* without extensive revisions and considerable cutting. Finally Gwyn carried out his threat and told Curtis Brown that he wasn't going to do it. He was not, moreover, interested in offering Michael Joseph his next book, either, nor any other book he might ever write.

Anticipating this conclusion to a difficult period of negotiation, Curtis Brown had already put out some feelers on Gwyn's behalf, and now Victor Gollancz, reminded of how nearly he had become Gwyn's publisher a decade earlier, entered into promising talks.

It was a great while before all was settled, and there was disappointment for Gwyn in that in the end Gollancz was not prepared to take on *The Dark Neighbour* as he did not want a historical novel. Neither was the Stobo Wilkie novel (*Another Night, Another Day*) thought to be the best work with which to introduce Gwyn as a Gollancz author, perhaps because it made most commercial sense to begin with the Omri Hemlock story they knew Gwyn was currently working on. Deeply disturbed by the intervening uncertainty, Gwyn languished for months, unable to return to his writing with his usual confidence. *The Dark Neighbour*, all 180,000 words of it, and *The Thinker and the Thrush* were set aside, to lie undisturbed alongside the yellowing typescript of *Sorrow For Thy Sons* for the rest of their author's life.

The spring of 1950 brought new strains when first, as Lyn described to Nana, 'they had an army of inspectors at the school and this has meant an enormous amount of extra work for Gwyn. He had to bring home a pile of books for marking every night and he has been driven nearly mad'. No doubt there were those among his colleagues who thought that it was about time Gwyn should be given a prod in the matter of marking exercises more regularly, for some claimed that his pupils saw no red ink from him from one end of term to another. Equally one may doubt whether the frantic carrying of schoolbooks homeward for nightly attention lasted much beyond the end of the inspection. Much more exhausting were the calls upon his time in the General Election hoardings which dominated the mid-term period; despite his doubts about the Labour leadership at the top, he flung himself willingly into the campaign of support for Mrs Dorothy Rees in the Barry constituency and almost wore himself out with public speaking. After a stiff fight Mrs Rees won the seat, and Barry remained a little while longer in socialist hands, though the returned government with its tiny majority could not expect to retain power for long.

Immediately after the excitement of the election there was a different experience in store for Gwyn when he made his first broadcast in interview with Glyn Jones. It was something he greatly enjoyed for despite his shyness he loved to perform. His voice proved to be ideal for radio, with its rich timbre and his highly individual delivery, and he was able to overcome his initial nervousness, as he told Nana, by imagining himself at home:

As I spoke through the microphone I focused my senses on the mental picture of a small special audience who would understand without fail what I had to say: you and a few others. It made me cool as a brick. If the BBC had wished I could have gone on to lead you all in community singing.

The programme allowed him to speak with great feeling about his writing and his sense of himself as a writer. 'I enjoy writing very much,' he said.

In fact I seem to get completely absorbed in the enthusiasm of the chase after words and ideas. No part of me moves except my hand – and incidentally I feel sure that no writer has suffered from writers' cramp in more places than I have. When I'm in this state, I'm inclined to think that even if a slate fell on my head I would just reach out quietly and go on writing on the fragments of it.

He answered the criticism that all his characters spoke alike with a shrug, acknowledging the truth of the observation but saying that he simply didn't see it as a flaw, for: 'The literary convention that insists that poverty of pocket must be matched with poverty of speech has never made the slightest sense to me. Some of the most magnificent speech I've ever heard has come from the plainest and commonest people.' He confessed that he was not much interested in the externals of things: 'Of life as I go through it I tend to be very unobservant. In fact, picturesque happenings could be pelting around me as fast as hail now and they would move me to do no more than open my umbrella.' What emerged most signally from his broadcast was his devotion to his origins:

It seems to me that the limits of one's activity as a writer are fixed by the imaginative antics of boyhood.... I'm seldom conscious of an audience. Not in any solemn sense, anyway. If at all, I like to imagine I am writing for one of those groups I loved as a boy, a circle of fruity, excitable characters sitting around me on the hillside at dusk, moved to a particular tolerance, perhaps, by a session of good harmonious singing, or a cash windfall which enabled us all to buy a bagful of well-salted chips apiece.... Those Rhondda days are, for me, for ever bathed in a

119

brilliant light; the tumult of political enthusiasms, the white-hot oratory of the people's paladins; the festivals of folk-singing and hymn-singing in the vast chapels, moving groups on the hillsides at night ... their echoes can still fill my mind with an intense creative excitement. Then the hill-walks across to Llanwonno, or over to Dimbath, the Beacons to the north, pulling us towards an even wilder solitude than we had ever known; and the Vale of Glamorgan to the south, tempting us with an ordered placidity which it would benefit our souls to cultivate. And between these two poles of attraction, the fermenting disquiet of the valley streets, ringing with every note of pain and laughter contrived since man's beginning.

Being asked to do the broadcast seemed to confirm that he had indeed arrived, and he returned to his work on *The World Cannot Hear You* with renewed confidence. It was a book, after all, in which he was exploring and rendering just that Rhondda ambience of which he had spoken so glowingly in the programme, and no project could have made him happier. Although he continued in his letters to Howard Fast to demonstrate his political anger, writing sometimes with venomous force about what was happening in Britain, in the United States and in the world at large, his tone generally became more constantly humorous. As he launched himself into the 1950s and the ever-increasing flood of opportunities which the decade brought him, it was clear that a new phase of his life was beginning.

9

Lure of the Air Waves

The world moved frighteningly back towards widespread war in 1950, and had Gwyn not been so deeply involved in the problems of his own life – the unremitting grind of school and the constant difficulties with his publishers (or lack of them) – he might have found the stress unbearable. As it was he did all in his power to warn people of the dangerous and cruel irresponsibility, as he saw it, of a British Labour government that seemed no more peace-loving than a Tory administration would have been. He spoke at many local meetings and involved himself with the national and international Peace Movements of the time, constantly attacking all those interests which seemed bent on unleashing new tides of violence across the globe. The fighting in Korea and the British attempts to deal with communist guerrilla opposition in Malaya were equally odious to him, both being, as far as he could make out, examples of old-style tyrannical colonialism in not very new dress and with no greater justification. To Howard Fast he complained:

> Herbert Morrison and Winston Churchill sum up between them the fearful erosion of character that is taking place in this community as we prepare to abandon the opportunities of social change presented to us by the war's end and to come to terms with the most monstrous presumptions of our imperial outlook.

There is no doubting his sincerity, though it is possible that the friendship with and constant challenge to support Fast in his revolutionary struggle in the States intensified his feelings and promoted a heightened expression of them. This was aggravated moreover when in April the United States government finally turned down the appeal made on behalf of Fast and the other Hollywood writers sentenced with him and committed them to jail. Alarmed and saddened by the news, Gwyn wrote to Fast:

> There is a special poignancy in this act of tragic folly which is to make convicts of men whose names and work have done so much to inspire us in Europe with affection for America and its people, its great affirmation of faith in the common man.... Those born with intelligence on the wrong side of the tracks have come to regard it as a vocational risk that they will lose their freedom when society finds itself running short of wit and patience in its argument against them. But this barbarous shutting away of writers whose only crime has been to defend the dignity of their craft, to claim the right of differing on some points from the delighted satisfaction of those who see the Ark of the Covenant in every banking-house, this is a monstrous development ...
>
> The writers and thinkers are the people's tongue. Let that tongue be ripped out and the people can rest assured that the amputation will not stop there. The legs and arms of all their fundamental freedoms will follow and the dumb and helpless trunk of a community enslaved will be used, as it was by Hitler in 1939, to fuel whatever fire is needed to warm and solace the terrible, freezing minds of those who cannot visualise or accept life without a proper measure of hatred and butchery.

Such rhetorical ammunition was irresistible to Fast who made sure through his contacts that it was published in several outlets as soon as possible; letters like Gwyn's from foreign sources were, he assured Gwyn, hitting home like bursting shells in their bid to expose to the world the 'Truman–Acheson gang's mythical rosy picture of American democracy'.

With his friend in prison and the wars in the East threatening all kinds of consequences for those who prized peace above all, Gwyn's anger was high for two years or more yet, but, as the reference to Hitler in his message to Fast suggests, he was just beginning to move from the marked innocence of his left-wing position. Ten years earlier he had been as steadfastly opposed in principle to a war against Hitler as he now was to any talk of war against Russia, but he no longer denied the lessons of experience which demonstrated that Hitler could not have been allowed to go on. While he hated and deplored the use of violent means to settle an argument, he had to admit that he did not know what alternative there was in the last resort. Both he and Fast were clinging to a belief or at least a hope that the Russians and their eastern allies in communism were basically well intentioned, that they must be talked to rather than threatened, and that eventually a greater good for all mankind would emerge from the philosophy they were trying to enact. So naive were they both that Gwyn did not protest when, a few months later, Fast complained of the hysterical uproar in America when the USSR 'so innocently' exploded an atom bomb to demonstrate their possession of the ultimate weapon. Neither man was a fool, and the events of the next five or six years modified the attitudes of both of them. As long as Fast remained in prison, however, Gwyn continued to write the most powerful accusatory letters he could, and several of them were published in newspapers across the States. It was a brave gesture, the only consequence of which was to make his books unpublishable on that side of the Atlantic.

He became less keen to accept the many calls on him to speak at political protest meetings, though some were important enough to make him change personal plans. He could not visit Wells at Whit, he told Nana, because he would be 'hog-tied', having promised to speak at a rally on Sunday and a conference on Monday: 'I have been swearing to keep free of these entanglements for years past but they keep creeping up on me. They bore me or they make me ill but the cause this time is good: Peace.'

What was worrying him almost as much as the breakdown of the peace was the matter of his future as a writer. He had put the unhappy business of *The Dark Neighbour* and *Another Night, Another Day* behind him and was working on *The World Cannot Hear You*, but without any clear idea of what was going to happen to it he found writing his novel far from the usually easy and delightful task. 'It's become impossible to do any good continuous literary work after coming home from school,' he told Nana. 'A day's teaching and I am able to exchange a simple greeting like 'Hullo' and that is the end of my tether.' To Glyn Jones he wrote:

> My nerves have been literally on the bounce, tamping like rubber balls all the way down Wenvoe Terrace to the Docks.... If I were a cannibal and with everything off points I would have tinned publisher on the table for every meal. I can think of no bitch bad enough for them to be the son of. But I am majestically defiant after the fashion of Henley but with a touch of diabolism that would have left that old master respectful. One day I will get hold of the two poles between which it is black as

the pit and what I do with them will leave those marble-topped inepts in Paternoster Row and Bedford Square wondering why their seats are so far away from the chair.

When at last Victor Gollancz agreed to publish *The World Cannot Hear You*, Gwyn was greatly relieved. As he told Nana, Gollancz was a good publisher who advertised well, but he had recently seemed as wary of publishing anything with a vaguely socialist ring to it as any other publisher:

> I will make no more money with him than with the other people, because if one writes frankly and honestly these days one is lucky to be printed at all. The tide of panic prejudice against writers of the left is getting almost as bad here as in the States and I was surprised that Gollancz, who for the past ten years has been trying to bury his pro-communist past by bringing out a spate of anti-communist stuff, should have taken my book.

Given new encouragement by the Gollancz contract, Gwyn was further lifted in October by the release of Howard Fast from the term of imprisonment which he had spent breaking stones in a labour camp in the mountains of West Virginia. Exchanging letters in which each described with disgust the state of his country ('We now live in a fascist country. The madmen scream that those who talk of peace should be rewarded with the death sentence,' said Fast), Gwyn confessed that there had been in Britain no very considerable revulsion of opinion against the danger of world war brought on by the Korean conflict:

> We are cursed by the fact that the sending out of troops to discipline 'lesser breeds' has always been endemic in British history. The butchering of whole nations in the Far East who are trying to usher in a new epoch in human organisation will mean very little to people put fast asleep by a Press which has presented this war as just another police operation against a covey of insubordinate riff-raff.

Although his sympathies would never fail to be with the underdog, the tyrannised, the little, the poor, the working-class, and although intellectually he never for a moment forsook the ideas of democratic socialism, Gwyn could not and did not much longer maintain his unquestioning fealty to communism as, during the 1950s, it became clearer how far from the road of human decency totalitarian governments of any kind could stray. Perhaps it made some difference too that gradually he became, while never wealthy, at least comfortably provided for as a result of his strenuous labours during the next decade. It is hard to see things in quite the same light when one is no longer penurious oneself.

It is also not quite so easy to dislike the rich quite so thoroughly after one has had the opportunity to meet some of them and discover that they are people too, decent, good-hearted human beings as often as not with worries just like anyone else. Gwyn clearly had more than an inkling of this when he depicted Richard Penbury in *All Things Betray Thee* – the oppressor of the people is far from simply the class-enemy, but rather a tortured, mysterious, cultured man moved from his humanity by greater social forces than he can master. When *The World Cannot Hear You* was launched at last in June 1951 by Victor Gollancz, opportunities almost unthought-of before began to come Gwyn's way to discover whether his intolerance of the wealthy would stand the test of coming to know them as individuals. In July the celebrations of the twenty-fifth year of the house of Gollancz included a memorable party where Gwyn was fêted as one of the most recent and promising acquisitions to the firm's list. 'Daphne du Maurier was there,' Lyn told Nana delightedly, 'looking very beautiful in a wonderful gown that must have cost plenty. The Lord Chancellor and Viscountess Jowitt, Prince and Princess Frederick of Prussia, the Askwiths and also the Asquiths were there and the most brilliant gathering of famous literary figures in the world.'

While Gwyn was less breathlessly transported by the company than Lyn was, he found it possible to bear it. Spencer Curtis Brown, owner of the agency looking after Gwyn's interests, invited them to come to his country home in Suffolk for a weekend in August, and that too proved a revealing experience which Lyn described to Nana with enthusiasm:

> They gave us a magnificent time. What a *house!* It was a new experience for me to actually see how the rich live. An abundance of everything. The house was like something you see on films, a poem of delight, and the company was really friendly and most charming. The cellar would have delighted Bill and made him gasp with amazement at the amount some people spend on wines and spirits.

Gwyn's cynicism about riches was not to be so easily disarmed, but it pleased him to see Lyn happy and he encouraged her to enjoy it as much as possible while she had the chance. Something of a contrast with the country house life followed when they went on to spend a couple of weeks in London with Eddie and his new wife Irene. Their flat in Chiswick was too small to accommodate visitors so Gwyn and Lyn put up at a cheap boarding house nearby. It was a pleasant holiday as they recalled their impoverished days in London in the 1930s and enjoyed their small lease of the new prosperity. As became the pattern of their visits to London, their mornings were spent in visiting art galleries, their evenings at the theatre. Most delightful were the hours spent at the opera. Eddie and Irene had met while singing in the chorus at Covent Garden, and to Gwyn no sound was sweeter than that of fine voices raised in some great aria, duet or quartet. They went to all they could afford, and then, the summer holiday over, returned to Barry and to what Gwyn now called 'that damned school'.

Critical response to *The World Cannot Hear You* was very encouraging from the first day. Gwyn had created in the world of inoffensive, charming little Omri Hemlock and his *bête-noire*, Picton Gethin the go-getter, a place both real and fantastic, the Rhondda seen through the transforming eyes of one who loved it dearly. Many of the reviewers appreciated that it was not presented as a factual, documentary account of Welsh village life and allowed it its right to be *sui generis*. They praised its vigour, its gusto, its overflowing humour, its tenderness, its compassion and the wild poetry of its language. Sensing its political charge, one wrote:

> Mr Thomas has emerged from the same drear valleys as Aneurin Bevan, and the two Welshmen appear politically akin. . . . But where the politician roars into the fray, searing his foes with the flame-thrower of invective, the writer comes armed with a smiling irony, which deepens pleasantly into the belly-laughs of sheer good fun.[1]

C.P. Snow, Fred Urquhart, Lionel Hale and others added their nods of approval. Several of them invoked the names of Runyon, Shaw and Rabelais to make comparisons, deeply impressing and gratifying Lyn who told Nana quite simply that she had long known she was married to a genius and that she was glad the proper acknowledgements were now being made. In Wales a reviewer commented: 'If there is such a thing as Anglo-Welsh literature, then this should live in its history as a brilliant page of adult Welsh wit.'[2] Pleased with the reception, Gwyn was even better satisfied when he heard that, despite his fears that he might no longer be acceptable in the United States, Little, Brown & Company had decided to publish the novel there. This time they weren't going to change his title, either. Lyn began to get excited about the possibility that they might be on the verge of hitting the jackpot and making some real money, but Gwyn was less sanguine and proved to be right.

Although the reviews were on the whole as enthusiastic as he could have hoped for, the book sold in its thousands rather than its tens of thousands. A circle of Gwyn Thomas devotees began to grow and spread its ripples far across the world, but to some extent it was a specialised audience rather than a popular one and money failed to flow spectacularly into his coffers. As Gwyn pointed out to Wynne Roberts, the translations which were beginning to be made of some of his books into Norwegian, Italian, Russian, Hungarian and Polish were noteworthy rather for the honour it did him to be read abroad than for any consequent enrichment of his bank balance; the fees were small and the little money owing to him as a result of translation agreements was more often than not unforthcoming anyway, stuck behind the iron curtain and likely to remain there. The delight in his work expressed in English-speaking countries resulted in rewards more verbal than financial. The problem lay perhaps in his uncompromising determination to write only what he wanted to write. This, for readers mentally alert and verbally sophisticated, meant a reading experience full of poetic pleasure and uplifting comedy as well as provocative philosophy; but for many it presented an unexpectedly dense and difficult texture, a tenuous story, characters who seemed to do nothing but talk, and a lack of the kind of evocative pictorial writing or event-filled simple narrative that might have drawn them in.

Gwyn did not recognise any difficulty in the challenge he presented a reader. In a letter to Wynne he wrote:

I'm glad you liked the Omri book. He moved so easily out of the essence of the valley as we knew it, it was a simple and joyful book to write. I used up some ripe little legends of our early years in it: the succouring of the flooded by Dan Jones and his fleet of leaking boats from Porth Square; the Shanley bathing costumes that floated right off the body of the user on Barry Island; the great elegiac tale of Tod Jones the tenor who retired to penurious exile in Carmarthenshire and came home with the prize of a sausage which he ate only to die of the resulting congestion. The trouble is that life yields to a man only a limited number of such nourishing ingots. I dread the day when I might have to inhabit some room of grinning unsupported fantasy as I grow too sullen or too tired to go out and find the flesh and blood of lived humour.[3]

The flesh and blood of lived humour remained the staple of Gwyn's diet for the rest of his life. Never until the very end was he too tired or sullen to go out and gather it where he knew it waited unfailingly to be harvested: in the lounges and saloon bars of pubs wherever he found himself, in Barry and the Vale, in Cardiff, in his travels later on all over Wales and England, and most rewardingly of all in the valleys of the Rhondda. In time, perhaps fearful that his memory was no longer as retentive as it had been, he took to keeping much more regularly and even feverishly a notebook into which he jotted the bare bones of hundreds of conversations and story ideas picked up from friends or casual acquaintances in this pub or that. Near his home in Barry were two ports of call where he was often to be found, the Park Hotel and the R A F A Club. Here he enjoyed the company of non-literary friends, down-to-earth working men of the world whose opinions were forcefully expressed and whose yarns and gossip he drank as eagerly as the pints of ale that helped lubricate the speaking parts and warmed the atmosphere as the evening wore on. Among them was Leslie Robinson, hairdresser and master-barber, who became a particular crony. The Robinson family, whose boys went to the County School, was later struck by tragedy when the elder son, on the eve of going to university, was killed in an accident. Brought together even more by the grief of that loss, the Robinsons and the Thomases were sustained by the strong bonds of a friendship that yielded mutual comfort.

Fierce though the drive within him was to write works that delivered a political and social thump to the solar plexus of an insufficiently caring society, Gwyn realised that much of his own pleasure lay in story for its own sake, story as part of the great realm of gossip and nostalgic reminiscence, story for the laughter it offered as a contrast and alternative to the tears of experience. It was this facility of his for recreating so vividly and so comically the life of ordinary people in less than glamorous circumstances that led perhaps

inevitably towards the invitation which now set in motion a transformation in his life.

Among his unknown contemporaries at Oxford had been Elwyn
Evans, another Valley boy, a son of a former Welsh Archdruid known
as Wil Ifan. Evans was now working with the BBC in Wales.
Recognising the potential of Gwyn's stories, he approached him
through Glyn Jones early in 1951 with a suggestion that he might
like to think about writing for radio. Gwyn's first response to Glyn
Jones was cautious:

> I am afraid I have been somewhat vitiated by too much novel-writing
> in a vein where I have been able to say practically everything I wanted.
> After years of being able, in utter indifference to the scruples of publishers'
> readers, some of whom must sidle up to the ammonia-flask as soon as a
> new MS of mine steams up, to work off as much Radical wise-cracking
> and buttonless lubricity as I fancied, it would be hard to submit to the
> urgent discipline of word and impulses necessary to the broadcaster.

He was clearly drawn to the idea, confessing: 'there must be some
themes to which even a loose-lipped Dionysian like myself might
bring a fresh and useful nib'. It was plain that some additional fame
gained through the radio would probably not harm the sales of his
books; and he had rather enjoyed the one occasion when he had been
on the air. In consultation with Elwyn Evans during the following
weeks he took a short piece of Rhondda reminiscence which he had
drafted for *Coal* and began to turn it into a radio play.

Then Came We Singing recalled the wonderful summer of 1926
when, as children witnessing without full comprehension the conduct
and effects of the General Strike and the long-drawn-out miners'
strike which followed it, Gwyn and his friends had lived for the
carnivals and jazz-band processions with which the mining towns
enlivened their idleness. Out of these memories now came a radio
piece about which Evans became very excited. Re-titled simply
Gazooka (after the tinny instruments which created the curious
buzzing tunefulness for the marchers), it was broadcast on the BBC
Welsh Home Service in January 1952 to widespread acclaim. Elwyn
Evans immediately negotiated with Gwyn to supply a further three
or four scripts in a similar vein, a task willingly undertaken.

As he later re-worked his first radio play into a long short story,
it is possible to catch the flavour of the broadcast still. Between its

evocative, scene-setting opening and its elegiac close, the sad-comic world of 1926 Rhondda is warmly and skilfully presented; the conversations and characters are lively, nonsensical, pathetic and amusing, and it is not hard to imagine what the use of stirring and touching music could have given to the story of desperate rivalry between the marching bands dressed in their different fantastic ways, like Cynlais Coleman's Whirling Dervishes and Georgie Young's Boys from Dixie. A new audience was won for Gwyn's peculiar world, a new generation of devotees for his unexpected and hyperbolically developed metaphors, or for his individual nomenclature based on the old Welsh habit of identifying people by their job or trade (Evans the Milk, Sioni Winions (Johnny Onions), Williams the Post, and so on) but taking it to new heights of inventiveness: Erasmus John, the Going-Gone (the local auctioneer), for instance, or Georgie Young the Further-Flung (because he had fought in some of our African wars at the limits of Empire).

When Gwyn's second play, *The Orpheans*, again about singers and their troubles in a Rhondda town, was broadcast seven months later in September 1952, he had already begun work on a third for the Welsh Home Service. The plays were heard and appreciated in England too, and a request came before the year was out from Denis Mitchell in Manchester that he should write something for the Northern Region. In January 1953 a new production of *Gazooka* went out from London on the BBC Third Programme and attracted very complimentary reviews from commentators such as Lionel Hale ('Dear Corporation, if you love us as a mother loves her little children, I implore you to give us more of Mr Gwyn Thomas'), J.C. Trewin ('Once heard, this will revive itself often in the grateful memory') and Maurice Wiggin ('A fine narrative compulsion, wit, insight, tenderness. And with all that a hilarious bit of fun. It made most of the English programmes sound forced, poverty-stricken, lame'). Unencumbered apparently by the kind of problem that Equity might throw in his path today, Gwyn himself played the role of Milton Nicholas, one of the thoughtful elements in Meadow Prospect, and enjoyed himself thoroughly. He told Nana:

The experience of radio acting I found tiring but stimulating. After a strictly lonely and·private job like novel-writing, being mixed up in a tropically hot studio with a bunch of gifted clowns is most odd. But I am glad that I accepted Elwyn Evans's invitation to take part because you learn more about the tricks of the radio-broadcasting trade in an hour around a microphone than you do in a year of thinking about it.

Though his new career seemed to have got off to a good start, and was very time-consuming, Gwyn still did no more about giving up teaching than think longingly about the day when he might be able to afford to do so. As he was simultaneously working on a second novel for Gollancz it is rather difficult to see how he could find time to do his teaching, but somehow he did, though its insidious drain on his energy and health could not be altogether denied. Fortunate in that he could rely on Lyn to do everything for him in the line of running the home and looking after him with devotion and skill, he was also able to call on her secretarial abilities more and more, and she joined in with a will. They made a good team, she thought; proud as could be of every honour and commission that came his way, she helped him to take it on with encouragement and organising ability that saved the day for him. She did what she could to protect his health, though stopping short of any suggestion that he might reject a commission, for to her fell the duty of managing all their financial affairs and the little bits of extra money that began to come their way were never too much. Tensions and strains showed themselves from time to time in, for instance, an unpleasant attack of shingles which made him miserable in the spring of 1952, but for the most part life seemed to be getting better for them and Lyn felt very happy.

One of the effects of the constant demands on Gwyn was that he sat longer at the table where he wrote and consequently walked rather less; with less exercise and increasingly more to eat and drink he began to put on weight. This became more noticeable after he woke up one morning in 1953 on a day when he had undertaken to give a talk at a businessmen's lunch, reached for his cigarettes as usual, and found after a puff or two that his voice would not come. Learning that the temporary loss of voice was probably, like some of his other ailments, due to his smoking, and considering that his voice was one of the most precious elements in his equipment especially now that broadcasting might help make his fortune, he there and then gave up the habit. Going from being a heavy smoker to a non-smoker overnight suggests a powerful will; certainly he never smoked again. As an inevitable consequence he found, as smokers do when they abandon the habit, that his weight and girth began to increase more rapidly than it usually does in middle age, so that over the next few years his appearance was considerably transformed. The thin and rather drawn young man of the late 1940s had by the end of the decade ripened into the burly, thickset, chubby-cheeked figure familiar to those who knew him at the height of his fame.

While his venture into radio-writing was in its early stages his Omri Hemlock book came out in the United States in March 1952; two months later Gollancz published *Now Lead Us Home*, a new novel that he had been working on during the previous winter. American reactions to *The World Cannot Hear You* were not at first discouraging but, as Gwyn had feared might happen, the book received much less coverage than it might have had if its author was not known to be a communist sympathiser. In the end it sank from sight, and Little, Brown lost interest for a while in Gwyn's work, though the subject of his new story, which was about an American millionaire who buys a castle in South Wales and brings his influence to bear upon the life of the locality, might have seemed attractive.

In Britain *Now Lead Us Home* was accorded favourable reviews on its appearance in May. Inspired as it obviously was by the purchase by William Randolph Hearst of St Donat's Castle on the Glamorgan coast, the novel explores the reactions to such an event of a Welsh township in the grip of unemployment. Ferncleft seems indistinguishable from Meadow Prospect in most ways; it is only three miles from the sea and its inhabitants have different names, but the concerns and institutions are all the same and the characteristics of the people are markedly similar. The time is still the 1930s. The narration is again accomplished by a minor character who reports as from a group point of view, 'we' rather than 'I'. Using a method characteristically his own and now just about perfected, Gwyn with this book reached his apogee as far as reception as a novelist was concerned. The reviewers used their superlatives unsparingly. The book was 'irresistible, exuberant fun' (John Connell, London *Evening News*); 'hysterically funny and tragic in the same breath', it contained 'satire of a ferocity that makes Evelyn Waugh seem by comparison a cooing dove' (Frederick Laws, *News Chronicle*); it had 'a poet's imagination as well as a proletarian's humour' (*Yorkshire Post*). Rupert

Croft-Cooke was reminded of Dylan Thomas and John Cowper Powys:

> His seemingly effortless rhetoric never flags; it rises at times to real beauty and at others to loud and ribald laughter. It is euphuistic and full of far-fetched metaphor and it works on the reader like some abracadabra, forcing him to listen to its rhythms and drum-beats. (*Daily Sketch*)

In the *Daily Worker* Alison Macleod pointed out perceptively how:

> The theme of the book repeats the theme of earlier Gwyn Thomas novels... The American millionaire, with his plan for permanent war, is a more highly developed version of the self-made men who are the villains of earlier books, cheating and trampling their way to power.

Norman Shrapnel in the *Manchester Guardian* discussed the 'exuberant but haunted spirit' behind Gwyn's jokes; he noted how others had compared Gwyn's work with that of Rabelais, Runyon, Peacock, Chaucer and Bernard Shaw, and said he was tempted to add Joyce Cary, Christopher Fry and John Bunyan to the list. Both Pamela Hansford Johnson (in *John O'London's Weekly*) and R.C. Churchill (*Birmingham Post*) found parallels with James Joyce, the former on the grounds of the difficulties to be found in the text: '*Ulysses* is a lazy garden-hammock reading to this book', while Churchill said: '*Ulysses* has been irreverently compared with a giant pub-crawl, and the novels of Mr Thomas give us a similar feeling of attending a crowded session in some pub on the Celtic fringe.'

This time quite pleased with the coverage and reception his book had received, Gwyn was neither surprised nor particularly discouraged when, three or four months later, Juliet O'Hea (who at Curtis Brown had taken over as Gwyn's agent) had to pass on the news from Gollancz that *Now Lead Us Home*, though doing reasonably well, was not exactly a best-seller. By then he was too much involved in his radio-writing and in yet another new novel to have time to reflect on past endeavours. It having occurred to him that his teaching career had yielded a more than sufficient number of incidents and characters out of which he could fashion another story, he had started writing a book about school life. Since his own work as a schoolmaster had begun at the beginning of the war, and many of the incidents he wanted to use were inextricably associated in his mind with the Cardigan years, he set his story firmly in war-time, incidentally moving forward for the first time from the 1930s in which some accused him of being time-trapped.

Thoroughly enjoying the writing of *A Frost On My Frolic*, his first thought when Denis Mitchell asked for a play for the Northern Region of the BBC was to continue in the same vein. The result was *Forenoon*, billed in the *Radio Times* as 'Impressions of the tug-of-war between teachers and taught'. Essentially a conversation in a staff-room among a number of older and younger hands at the teaching game, it had little plot but much entertainment value and was a great success. Gilbert Harding, Esmé Percy and James Donald were in the cast, together with the young Jeremy Spenser as a representative of the taught, and the broadcast in January 1953 was treated to some very complimentary reviews. Using the radio medium with great confidence after his relatively short apprenticeship, Gwyn devised a means by which the listener was taken immediately into the mind of Mr Walford (the first appearance of this character who later took over the teaching-days section of Gwyn's autobiography) and then allowed to eavesdrop on the school day and its happenings through Walford's responses to it. The man's musings, interspersed with his exchanges with boys and staff during the school morning, proved irresistible. Here he is thinking to himself as he first walks into the school:

WALFORD: The life of the young is a dream, with touches of nightmare added for flavour. But here's the school, and this is my entrance door. Just inside are the junior classrooms. I generally have a look in here as I pass, just to see what's ...

GRAMS: *Tumult. Cries of boys.*

WALFORD: H'm. If jungle warfare is any worse than this, I'll eat my gown. There's a strong pattern of affection and violence in the lives of those juniors who hang their coats up here. Look at *that* boy, now. Seager. Physique of a gorilla and a grin so broad it would wear out a weaker boy. He'll kill someone with that satchel. (*He shouts*) Now then, Seager, what kind of setting-up exercise is this, boy? If you feel you must beat Wickow's brains out, do it on neutral premises and select a boy with some to spare. And you there, Arundel, stop crouching up there on the lockers like a death watch beetle. In what cathedral rafters did you spend the long vacation? Come down from there. You are less of a menace at sea level.

GRAMS: *Some laughter from the boys.*

WALFORD: Cooped up every day with five hundred walking bombs, these small jokes somehow ease the tension, shatter the glumness of the contract that pins a master and his pupils to the society that begets them.[4]

With great good humour, scalding wit and some pathos, the play explored the world of the ordinary secondary school and gave the listening public plenty to enjoy and plenty to think about on topics of perennial interest for every generation. Although Gilbert Harding received a good deal of praise for his venture into acting in the role of the maths teacher, he was replaced in the cast by the more experienced Howard Marion Crawford when the play was given a new production in April on the Home Service. Hugh Burden took over from James Donald as the narrating Mr Walford, and the broadcast was saluted as a gem.

Gwyn was clearly established as a most promising new writer for radio, and requests and contracts began to flood in. He was asked not only to write scripts but also to record his own stories and to consider taking part in discussion programmes. A new world was opening up to him and he liked the view. New acquaintances and talents were like food to him. Telling Nana how gruelling it was to settle to making recordings where he was on his own with the microphone, he showed what pleasure there came from mixing with the actors and producers who came together for his plays: 'On that last show, if there had been someone with a recording tape to take down the session of talk between Meredith Edwards, Basil Jones, W.P. ('Tommy Trouble') Thomas and myself, we would have had a second and bigger show.' As gradually he added to his circle of acquaintance people with local and then national fame, like Wynford Vaughan Thomas, Richard Burton and his brothers, Stanley Baker, Donald and Glyn Houston, Harry Secombe and so on, his cup began to fill. There were inevitable consequences, of course. Some members of his own family were not without a modicum of jealousy of their brother's new-found fame; not all felt it was properly merited, and it was thought unfair that the youngest and most spoiled lad should be receiving such attention when other brothers, infinitely more gifted if only their luck were better and their talent could be recognised, were ignored; and some felt it unreasonable that he should claim to be so busy that he hardly ever visited them any more. At school too there was in some quarters a degree of dismay at Gwyn's success, which

135

was held to be preventing him from functioning with full effectiveness as a colleague or subordinate. Whatever he thought of all this, he soldiered on, and perhaps it did not greatly trouble him.

The immediate future, as he sat down to polish up the script of another radio piece, *Festival*, in February 1953, looked about as full as it could get, but the demands on his time and talent were only just beginning. In the wings a curious, hunched, hook-nosed, cackling fellow was waiting to make his entry into the play of Gwyn Thomas's life and add one more dimension.

10

Recruit to Mr Punch

It was a measure of Gwyn's newly expanding fame as a literary personality that in October 1953 *John O'London's Weekly* carried on its front page a full-scale article about him by Mimi Josephson. 'Gwyn Thomas is acknowledged by literary critics and discerning readers', she wrote, 'to be one of the foremost humorous writers of the day.' Earlier in the year there was another indication of this respect for his talent as a laughter-maker when Malcolm Muggeridge, newly ensconced as editor of *Punch*, asked Gwyn whether he would like to contribute some pieces. At first Gwyn was surprised by the invitation and extremely tentative about accepting it. *Punch* had always seemed to him, when he gave it any thought at all, at about the opposite end of the political spectrum to his own. Breaking the news to Nana, he wrote: '*Punch*, which is now trying to model itself on the *New Yorker*, has asked me to do a series of short pieces for them. I have reservations about this particular assignment because I have a feeling that the average reader of *Punch* would in no way consider me funny; or at least, about as funny as I would consider him.'

Muggeridge was persuasive, however, even suggesting that the magazine would, under its new editorship, soon be perceived to be moving from its occupancy of the right wing and becoming much more liberal. Never one to turn an invitation down, Gwyn allowed himself to be convinced and within a few weeks had sent in some trial stories. It was the beginning of a long and fruitful association; during the years that followed, while first Muggeridge and then for fifteen years Bernard Hollowood sat in the editorial chair, about a hundred and thirty Gwyn Thomas stories and reflective pieces were published in *Punch*'s pages.

From the start he wrote exactly the same for *Punch* as he would have for any other publication, as he did for the mining magazine *Coal* for instance, and as he did later for *Vogue* and various American and Canadian magazines. He wrote about his Wales, the gallery of characters who inhabited the Meadow Prospect and Belmont of his novels and their richly embroidered petty adventures in personal rivalry and civic management. The *Punch* readership rapidly became enamoured of Gwyn's world and looked forward eagerly to new revelations about Teilo Topliss, Theo Morgan the Monologue, Jason Grace the town publicist, Ogley Floyd who fell under the influence of parsnip wine while conducting an anti-drink campaign, Kitchener Bowen the irrepressible opportunist and many others. Sometimes the stories were more overtly autobiographical, drawing on his reminiscences of school both as a teacher and as one of the taught; occasionally they took the form of travel or diary essays, thoughts and perceptions with just a core of anecdote. Whatever he offered was promptly accepted, and so one more straw was added to the burden of work he already carried.

Among his earliest *Punch* stories was 'That Vanished Canaan', in which the character Mr Rawlins, schoolmaster, figures as narrator of reminiscences about schoolboys and mouthpiece of opinions about education and morality in his addresses to the sixth form. 'There is still a vicious vacuum in the lives of the young,' he announces, and goes on to warn his charges against the influence of the cinema with an account of the oafish behaviour of a local juvenile delinquent who has learnt his approach to life from the pictures. Mr Rawlins lived on in many subsequent tales, most memorably of all perhaps in 'O Brother Man', an amusing story about a boy who steals a euphonium, but he is enshrined also in the novel, *A Frost On My Frolic*, which was published by Gollancz in July 1953. The *Punch* story was originally a part of *A Frost On My Frolic* which had had to be edited out because the manuscript was far too long; during the years that followed very little that Gwyn wrote went to waste, for if it couldn't be used in one form he could very often adapt it to another without much difficulty. At least that partly reduced the pressure on him as he tried to fulfil all his commitments.

The setting of *A Frost On My Frolic* is a town called Mynydd Coch (Red Mountain), but it hardly seems a different place from Meadow Prospect or Belmont. Someone who wanted to draw a map of the

Gwyn Thomas country – in the way that people have done detailed cartographic expositions of Middle-Earth for instance – would have a hard time of it. There are relatively few details of landscape or topographical interest in Gwyn's books, and those that do exist tend to contradict each other. Townships merge, shift about, acquire new names. Always, underneath the fiction, they are Cymmer, Porth, and nearby Pontypridd. If the reader wants to get his/her bearings it would be best to look at the Ordnance Survey map of the Rhondda and then put the imagination to work with what clues can be found in the text. The problem is that to the untutored eye one Rhondda community looks physically almost indistinguishable from another; a narrow valley, a dirty river at its bottom; rows of terraced houses snaking their way along the contours of the hills on either side; small pubs and clubs at frequent intervals; bleak, uncompromising chapel buildings interrupting the rooflines with their larger bulk at even more frequent intervals; the steel tower and winding wheels of a colliery near the bed of the valley or a little way up the side of the hill, surrounded by outbuildings and dumps of coal and hoppers and engine-houses, and with a trail of wires leading away up the hill to where vast quantities of spoil have been thrown to cover the natural mountain and change its hollows and plateaux to black, angular, brooding shapes. Though Gwyn made little attempt to capture this kind of landscape in his writing, it looms always behind his most surreal joke, and his assumption is that it seeps unmistakably through the narrative, leaving the writer no need to harp on it. Under the comedy of his surface there lay always an admiration and a fierce compassion for the people who lived in such places.

A Frost On My Frolic is about a secondary school and the community it serves during the Second World War. The narrator is one of a group of schoolboys, and his account of events in 1944 is presented unusually for Gwyn in present-tense narration. The vision both of the school and of the township is sharp-eyed, sardonic, sometimes a little cruel and always very funny. After a long and leisurely survey of the life of the place a story begins to develop when the boys are taken, as Gwyn more than once took groups of his own pupils, to a summer farming camp where they are expected to help with the harvest. Here they encounter a rural community and are required by some more sinister events to revalue aspects of their own life. Though no one would suppose that Gwyn's portrait of schoolmasters and their charges was intended to be a photographic reproduction of real life, it is more true to the general experience than many a solemn documentary could be.

His new novel was widely reviewed and very frequently with enthusiasm; but notes of adverse criticism were creeping in. Some reviewers felt unhappy about the episodic nature of the narrative and warned Gwyn to watch his plot management; some again and more loudly declared themselves against his refusal to give characters appropriate language, objecting that nobody ever spoke like these people; and some Welsh critics felt insulted by the picture of Welsh life offered by the book. 'In a book whose overtones are humorous, savagery has no place,' declared the *Western Mail*; and the *South Wales Evening Post* in its efforts to put Gwyn in his place remarked: 'Both Gwyn Thomas and Jack Jones are strictly regional. They write of the Rhondda and Cardiff in language and plots which do not suggest a universal application.' Gwyn grumbled to Glyn Jones:

> This last novel of mine is gathering a wreath of picturesquely black reviews. Trying to be a bright-minded clown puts a man in trickier spots than a curriculum of adulteries.... Yes, my frolic is truly a-shiver. The High Church boys are really letting me have it. You can hear the rattle of flung censers from here to Bengazi. It's enough to drive an ignorant novelist to drink.

Chief among his detractors was David Paul in the *Observer*, who said: 'It may be that I am allergic to this kind of Welsh wizardry, but much of the writing gave me a feeling of listening to a breathless comedian rushing his script. The style degenerates into a kind of patter.' Observations of that kind stick in the mind long after one has forgotten the more generous praises even of a multitude of others, and Gwyn against his will was downcast by them until the demands of his busy life forced them into the background. A letter of thanks for the enormous pleasure she had got from reading the book came from Naomi Mitchison, and that helped to compensate. Lettice Cooper, Pamela Hansford Johnson, Rupert Croft-Cooke, R.G.G. Price, R.C. Churchill, Richard Church, John Connell, John Heath-Stubbs and others were in print loud in praise of *A Frost On My Frolic*, and if good reviews produced large numbers of buyers Gwyn's fortune would have been made. As it was it sold quite steadily and for a year or two grew in reputation, but not all Gollancz's supportive advertising and enthusiastic marketing could lift it into the best-sellerdom they had hoped for it.

With all the extra pennies coming in from this source and that, Lyn began to feel during the spring of 1953 that they might at last be able to afford their own house. After some searching they found a new housing development under way on farmland just behind Pontypridd Road on the plateau at the top of the hills on whose sides sloping down to the sea Barry had been built. A bungalow at what was to be 8 Lidmore Road caught Lyn's fancy and, though it meant virtually going to live on a building site, they moved into their new home in October. 'The painters are still working on the front of the house,' Lyn told Nana, 'and they are making a concrete path for us to walk on in the front. . . . I am still waiting for my dining stuff and we are eating in the kitchen until it arrives. . . . We do need the money that the BBC scripts bring in. This house is terrifyingly expensive and the bills we have to meet are really enormous.'

She had to manage everything more or less on her own, for Gwyn was far too busy with his writing. He would have been of little use about the house or garden anyway, having neither the ability nor the energy to be bothered with practical things. His work for the BBC was involving him in more travel than ever before. Catching buses and trains was time-consuming and worrying, but there was no hope yet of getting a car; there was not sufficient money, neither of them could drive, and in 1953 it was anyway still very rare for people of what they thought of as their sort to have a car.

One of his further away destinations was Pontefract where for the Northern Region he had been invited to write and narrate a programme 'on liquorice, of all things,' he informed Nana. 'Reading that I would say that's the biggest whopper even I've told. But I'll prove it to you.' *The Deep Sweet Roots* went out in November, while on the Welsh Home Service a programme of reminiscences called *Our Outings* was a signal success. Throughout the winter he was working on numerous scripts while at the same time trying hard to finish another novel for Gollancz. It was with the greatest relief he was able to send off the typescript in January 1954 and return to his ideas for radio plays.

His work was now interrupted, pleasurably enough, by increasing numbers of visitors. As Lyn imposed some sort of order on the inside of the house and the tide of builders receded a little from their immediate area she began to look forward to receiving guests occasionally and soon had her wish. Jay Williams, the American novelist, arrived with his family at half-term, and Juliet O'Hea, Gwyn's agent, came over for a weekend. But the main thrust of life was Gwyn's ceaseless work. Another novel was already taking shape in his mind and on paper; he began to take part in broadcast discussions and talks as well as writing more plays and features for the radio; pieces for *Punch* were produced with increasing confidence. At school he continued to make his contributions with unaffected energy, delivering comical though scrupulously fair judgements at the traditional St David's Day Eisteddfod and taking seriously his responsibilities as editor of the *Barrian*, the school's annual magazine. For the Whitsun break they made a quick dash to London to escape for a few hours from the chaotic builders' gavotte at the centre of which lay their attempt at an island of domestic harmony; Gwyn had a broadcast to record, and lunched splendidly with Gollancz, so did not regret the time away from his writing table. A week or two later a letter followed him home; Rayner Heppenstall, whom he had met at the BBC, had forgotten to tell him something and now wanted to repair the omission:

> The last coherent exchange I had with Dylan Thomas was about you and took the following form:
> Me: I was just reading a book by *Gwyn* Thomas. Have you ever tried him?
> Dylan: Oh, yes.
> Me: What do you think?
> Dylan: Oh, I think he's *great*. Mind you, I am very chary of using words like 'great' ... and words like 'chary'.

Gwyn, who had met Dylan Thomas several times since emerging from obscurity and who greatly admired the work of his late and troubled compatriot, appreciated Heppenstall's gesture. He had noted with some irony the tendency of unthinking commentators to compare his work with Dylan's; it was pleasant to hear that Dylan had appreciated his work. Speaking to an audience in Barry earlier in 1954 Gwyn, thinking perhaps of how he, like his namesake, had come under attack for his adherence to English, had commented:

> I say to all patriots who maintain that a Welshman without the language is not a Welshman that it is one of the glories of our times that one of

them, Dylan Thomas, with his unique gift of patriotic expression, was capable in a dozen English words of causing the whole natural landscape to flare up like flames from a fire.

It was one of the earliest shots in what turned out to be a running and occasionally bitter battle between Gwyn, staunchly, wittily and sometimes very caustically defending the right of a Welshman to think in English, and representatives of the increasingly influential Welsh-language advocates who were offended by his position.

He was busy not only with writing, performing and school-teaching but also with the kind of public duty that came his way as a literary figure of consequence within the Welsh community. Since his radio interview with Glyn Jones and being featured the following year in a major exhibition of Contemporary Anglo-Welsh Writers at the Cardiff Central Library, he had been involved in, for instance, the campaign to secure a pension for the poet Huw Menai. Though not fitted by reason of his conspicuously un-solemn nature to become a portentous establishment figure, laden with honours, Gwyn worked hard and generously for the cause of literature and literary people when moved to it. At the same time, a kind of shift in his attitude towards life's more dark and serious face was undoubtedly taking place. As the ominous overtones of global war slowly faded, and in America McCarthy's noxious career came to its sudden end, and in the Rhondda and such places something remarkably like full employment returned, the political passions that had motivated Gwyn retreated from the foreground of his vision. The correspondence with Fast faded away and they became just literary friends. A certain disillusion set in as it became evident to Gwyn both that the world was not going to be improved by revolution yet for a while and that for himself, as for the Rhondda people enjoying a slowly improving standard of living, comparative prosperity and the less vital energies of middle age were combining to make him accept the status quo. In a letter to Nana he actually declared: 'Now, having ripened in my view of my fellow men, I have embraced with a desperate completeness the doctrine that above all a man must live easily. To the devil with the creed of living with sombre earnestness and integrity.' And he added, his comic tone typically tinged with an underlying hurt: 'Look at Wynne Roberts. The integrity of a rock and even less hair, poor schmoll' – for Wynne, suffering from an attack of alopecia areata, had become completely bald. The cause of alopecia not being known, it was generous of Gwyn to attribute it in Wynne's case to integrity just as he felt he was somehow surrendering his own.

Midsummer saw the publication of *The Stranger At My Side*. 'It had a good review in the *Sunday Times*,' Gwyn told Nana, 'and it will probably have the same *pianissimo* success as the others had. It's a very funny book. If you get a few laughs out of it, I shall be well pleased.' The appearance of a Gwyn Thomas novel more or less annually was beginning to seem routine to him; his expectations of huge success were no longer high and he barely took notice of what the papers might say. Other matters were far more pressing. What the reviewers did say – and the novel was given very extensive exposure – was much as before, offering a range of responses from eager enthusiasm to quite cool dismissals. John Davenport, for instance, quoted a review of an earlier book for his opening sentence in the *Observer*: 'A comic genius who "takes you by the throat and shakes you with laughter, wonder, joy and gratitude" is an uncomfortable companion. Nobody wants to play rat to a writer's terrier.' Which was witty but unfair, showing only that the Gwyn Thomas style was a phenomenon which was either liked or disliked, thought wonderful or overdone, according to the respondent's taste. Set this time in Windy Way, above Meadow Prospect (which has Mynydd Coch and Trecysgod as neighbouring towns), *The Stranger At My Side* gives an account of how Theo Morgan masterminds a series of ploys by which his uncle, Edwin Pugh the Pang, may find compensation for the loss of that sighing sympathy for mankind which had given him his sobriquet. It is episodic in that five stages in this undertaking constitute virtually separate stories, comical adventures often farcical in essence. There is a cast of scores of characters, many of whom make but the briefest of appearances but all named and many with label as well: Teilo Dew the Doom (thinker at the Library and Institute); Paddington Pawley the Purge (puritanical chapel elder); Parr the Pittance (council official); Iorwerth Pater the Scrutator (well-known *voyeur* of the hillsides) and so on. The book was essentially criticised for lacking serious narrative thrust, for not being, in effect, the large-scale realist work that some were hoping would eventually come from Gwyn's pen.

Those who saw that there was a real book to be discovered, once one could set aside a concern to describe only its surface method, revelled in its beautiful and ironic incidents, its proliferation of witty and provocative talk. There was criticism of the Rhondda people implicit in some of the narrative, for this book is set in the relatively affluent 1950s and embodies some of Gwyn's growing disillusionment with the effects of materialism on the intellectual and artistic qualities of the community; but equally evident is his love and understanding of his people, his excited interest in their vitality, sexuality, defeated psychology and splendid individuality.

Among the responsibilities which distracted Gwyn's attention from the reviews was an undertaking which occupied him fully in July, when he made his first contribution to the Coleg Harlech summer school, lecturing on the Anglo-Welsh novel to the great delight of the students and colleagues who attended. He knew that it was placing extra strain on him for very little reward; 'they got the last farthing's worth of their tiny fee out of me at Harlech and wrung me dry,' he told Nana. But the Harlech enterprise, offering the chance of education to a high level to the working man, was one for which he had the most passionate respect and enthusiasm, and once he had begun to contribute to its work he continued for years to do so with the utmost goodwill. Besides, the company was very good; Glyn Jones, Gwyn Jones, A.G. Prys-Jones and Henry Treece were contributing; and after the summer school the Welsh novelist Richard Hughes, who had also been there, came back to Barry and 'paused in his leonine way with us for a while' as Gwyn told Nana.

Other visitors in the summer included a woman writer from South Africa who tried to persuade Gwyn that his talents were needed down there in the southern hemisphere, and an Italian who had been commissioned to translate some of Gwyn's books into his language; prudently, he wanted to discuss some of the linguistic minefields he saw lying in his path. Gwyn said to Nana that he liked having his books translated because on the proceeds he could really live it up and take Lyn twice to the Tivoli cinema down the road before Christmas.

The summer brought one other excitement in the form of Gwyn's début on television, the step from the aural medium to the visual. It was to prove of immense significance for him. Some commentators, gifted with hindsight, later saw it as a move fatal to his future as a serious creative writer, perhaps even fatal to him generally. At the time it looked like the door to a new and splendid opportunity, and

Gwyn stepped through it with his usual combination of hope and ironic self-depreciation.

There was going to be at Porthcawl as part of the season's celebrations a festival of music made by gazooka bands; it was a nostalgic look backwards towards the carnivals of the 1930s, and it was immediately evident to the programme's producer, David Thomas, that the writer of *Gazooka* should be in attendance. Together with Alun Williams, a seasoned broadcaster who would carry the main brunt of the commentary, Gwyn went to Coney Beach to appear on film for the first time. He was convinced that the piece about the gazooka bands that *Radio Times* had asked him for would turn out to be better than anything he could contribute to the programme, but it turned out very well. Getting used to the paraphernalia that surrounded a television recording as opposed to the simplicities of radio took him some time and provided him with plenty of joking comments for later, but he liked it and hoped that there would be further occasions. Like other shy men, he found that the opportunity to perform brought out something extra in him. In the supra-personal contact offered by the camera, he could respond as in a pub surrounded by strangers; the talk would begin, and the flow came on cue, witty and amusing, colourful and inventive, causing bystanders on all sides to laugh with pleasure. It was a rare gift, and Gwyn saw the sense of it when his friends urged him to turn it to financial advantage.

Several radio pieces kept the public aware of his name in the second half of 1954: he contributed for instance to a series of 'Imaginary Journeys', travelling through the eighteenth century as a bard who, seeking a haven of sensual warmth, stumbles into a nest of wreckers at Dunraven Castle on the Glamorgan coast; there was a couple of his nostalgic pieces in 'The Past Has A Beating Heart' and 'The Sweet Singers of Meadow Prospect'; and there was a portrait of his village of Cymmer which he liked so much that he recommended it to his sister. Printed as the opening essay in his *A Welsh Eye* a decade later, it provides a pleasing introduction to Gwyn's birthplace, and as it has been put on to the page exactly as he read it on the air it seems to reproduce too, for those who have heard it once, the ·exact colour and intonation of his strangely haunting and individual voice.

In 1955, while working on his fifth novel for Gollancz and continuing to broadcast whenever invited, he turned journalist at the invitation of the *Empire News* and in July contributed a series of pieces about his best summer places, Barry, Porthcawl, Aberystwyth. Popular papers thereafter continued to court him for occasional articles and series, the extra money being put very rapidly to good use by Lyn in her improvement of the Lidmore Road house. She began to think again about the desirability of acquiring a car and learning to drive it, for Gwyn's constant travelling to BBC studios in Cardiff and further afield was becoming a real problem. There was no reason why she should not become chauffeuse to him as well as everything else. They had been involved, a year or two earlier, in a rather bizarre road accident; a friend who had long been at sea in the Merchant Navy came home to live, bought a car, and insisted on demonstrating to them the vehicle's capabilities. He proceeded, according to Gwyn's account, 'to astonish the town with some of the unsteadiest driving ever seen.... The journey lasted less than a minute. The car mounted the kerb and scattered a group of elderly pedestrians. They vanished over the walls in utter disarray. The captain tried to brake but put his foot with fanatical force on the wrong pedal. One could hear the speedometer gasp with shock as we shot up into the Mille Miglia class. Then, just as the car whizzed back onto the road, I heard him say something about taking to the lifeboats. The car turned over four or five times and came to rest on its roof.'[1] Lyn and the driver struggled out, relieved to find that they were not seriously hurt. Gwyn, who had been sitting in the back, was found crumpled forward, but as they nervously got the door open it appeared that he was groping around for something. 'Where's my bloody hat?' he asked. Bruised and rather frightened as they both were by the incident, Lyn was nevertheless undeterred from her idea that only a car of their own could solve their transport problems.

She proceeded to make the necessary arrangements. Driving, she found, was something she could do without difficulty, despite Gwyn's looks askance as she got behind the wheel alongside her instructor. Furnished in due course with a licence, she bought a car, little expecting the problem she was going to have in getting Gwyn into it with her as chauffeuse. Their first trip in to the BBC's studio in Broadway in Cardiff was not, fortunately, typical of all the many rides they had together in the years which followed. At first Gwyn refused pointblank to get into the car when she brought it to the front door, and it was only with the soothing help and reassurances of their friend Edna Robinson that he was persuaded that all would be well. As Lyn drove she could see Gwyn's knuckles white as his hand gripped the door-hold fiercely, and his sharp intakes of breath and agonised mutterings were a sore affliction. Arriving at Broadway without mishap, Gwyn could not wait to get out of the vehicle and into the bar, where he drained a tankard before the colour came back into his face. He was never a perfect passenger, having a strong tendency to berate other road-users as they went along, sometimes shaking his fist and shouting, 'Assassin!' at anyone who seemed to come too close; unable to drive himself, he was not shy of giving Lyn hints and instructions often at the most inconvenient moments; but as time went on he found it invaluable that Lyn had taken over the matter of getting him from place to place, and she went everywhere with him.

Gwyn's play *Vive l'Oompa*, about a Meadow Prospect brass band that goes to Paris, was produced by Peter Duval-Smith for the Third Programme in August, and *Up the Handling Code* went out to a delighted Welsh audience on the eve of an international match at Cardiff Arms Park in November. No particular fan of rugby but an untiring observer of the manners of his countrymen, Gwyn got the idea for this play from a memory of witnessing in a Port Talbot pub an argument of shocking violence about exactly how the winning try had been scored in Wales's notable defeat of New Zealand's All-Blacks in 1905. Since none of the men involved had even been born when that match took place, it seems symptomatic of a real fever in the Welsh blood. In his play the 'immortal voters of Meadow Prospect' (as the *Radio Times* put it) try to resuscitate the rugby team that once brought fame to the village and carry the ball as far as Cardiff to play another historic match.

Whenever he recalled his miserable days at Oxford Gwyn always said that he could not imagine ever going back there, but one day his mind was changed when a young man called Desmond Watkins came to call:

> I met Gwyn Thomas by walking up to his front door and ringing the bell. A strip of the door opened and the author's face peered out as from the inside dust cover of a book. I introduced myself, then my fiancée, and said I wanted to invite him to speak in a debate at the Oxford Union. Gwyn looked at us and then up and down the road, as though

this might be a ruse to sell encyclopaedias or brushes or fiancées, and then said, 'You'd better come in.' It was a weekday and, so that we could catch him after he returned from school, we had called at five-thirty. We left some time around three in the morning, exhilarated rather than tired, but aching with having repeatedly fallen out of our chairs with helpless laughter.[2]

It was the beginning of a lifelong friendship. The debate, in which Gwyn opposed Kingsley Amis, was broadcast in Wales, where it was considered that Gwyn had won hands down. More importantly, in giving Gwyn an opportunity to spend a couple of days in Oxford, in the company of a President of the Union who clearly idolised him, it helped him to modify the bitterness with which he recalled his university days and see them with a greater sense of proportion. He did not go back to his old college, but subsequently accepted invitations to Oxford from time to time and enjoyed his visits there.

He was heavily engaged in broadcasting throughout the winter, appearing among other things in an experimental radio magazine called *Highlight*, the brainchild of the young Donald Baverstock; editing a series of programmes called *Present Indicative*; and taking his place for the first time in January 1956 on the panel of *The Brains Trust*, a venture which filled him with alternating amusement and panic. Never one to over-estimate himself, it had not occurred to him to equate himself with the articulate polymaths who filled the air with propositions and counter-arguments so impressively on this programme. When persuaded to take part he acquitted himself well, bringing a welcome charge of comic extravagance to a programme that often took itself a little too seriously. The audience liked him, and at frequent intervals during the next five years he returned to the programme, both on radio and television. Never afraid to let laughter creep in, he sometimes became enmeshed in such intricate responses to the questions that no one knew what he had said. Members of the family shook their heads as he 'put himself on show' and 'made a fool of himself', especially when they detected that in his attempts to be fair he had turned his argument round in mid-stream and was now proceeding in the opposite direction to that in which he had started, but many fan letters suggested that his combination of wit and wisdom was found very satisfactory.

He had during the previous summer succeeded in completing another novel, which was duly published in March 1956. *A Point of*

Order was again widely reviewed, the reviewers being more notably than ever divided in their opinions. Almost all of them pointed out that the novel lacked plot, or 'architectonics' as the *Western Mail* solemnly put it. To some this did not matter; the theme gave the series of episodes a sufficient unity and coherence. To others it was a fatal flaw, as were the facts that Gwyn was still writing about little Welsh towns and ignoring the great wide world, or that his verbal flow was, as they felt, undisciplined and overwhelming. Alexander Baron, confessing himself an addict, insisted that it was a mystery that Gwyn Thomas's name was not better known among socialists: 'By common consent of a large body of critics he is one of the most important British writers today. Certainly he is the funniest.... He is more than a humorist. His work is given depth by its concern with the tragic essence of things.[3] In Canada Robertson Davies attributed Gwyn's failure to capture a large popular audience to his prose which 'every two or three pages rises to a splendidly poetic level.... But there is a catch in the poetry of Mr Thomas, and it is this: it is wildly and extravagantly comic.... This characteristic – rather I should say this superb gift – and the fact that Mr Thomas is careless about plot makes his books an enthusiasm of a few, rather than bestsellers.'[4]

The book has as its central figure, linking together a number of episodes in which he is involved, one Eryl Pym, councillor for the ward of Minerva Slopes in the borough of Elmhill. Using first-person narrative, which exposes Eryl's personality mercilessly to the light, the book follows his career as a tireless worker within his community and relishes the comedy of his ups and downs. There are ironic implications about his motivation and concerns, but much of what he says and stands for throws light on Gwyn's personal perturbation as the growth of the British welfare state in the 1950s had unexpected adverse effects on the culture and aspirations of the people. Bingo came in as concerts and debates went out, and the growth of a television-watching public rendered obsolete the libraries and institutes which had, it seemed, given the people their intellectual freedom and self-respect in pre-war days. Eryl, unlike his opponents Cynddylan Bott and Cadoc Rowe, has lost the purity of his socialist enthusiasms and is increasingly pragmatic in his decision making. He is tempted by the possibilities of a successful political career, and prepared to temporise in order to secure a parliamentary nomination. This dilemma underlies a series of droll misadventures, particularly in his amorous life where his occasional pursuit of Jasmine Mort is frustrated by his own low-level sexual drive and the constant demands of his political life.

It is a novel of prodigal invention. With almost a hundred named characters, with a constant flash of imagery, much of it music-related, and with its spirited flow of comic incident, it might with better luck have become thought of as one of Gwyn's best novels. Perhaps it would have sold in larger numbers than the now expected seven or eight thousand if the public could have known that it was to be his last comic novel. As it was, Gwyn probably did not know it himself, but the pressure of his diversifying life and the constant suggestion by some critics that he was better in short takes were moving him away from the extended fiction and towards the short story in greater earnest.

By the autumn of 1956 he was becoming a nationally known figure as his appearances on *The Brains Trust* gained him a whole host of new admirers, many of whom knew nothing about him as a writer. Proud of the new eminence of their local author, papers such as the *South Wales Echo* sent reporters to interview him. 'Among the popular pundits on TV's *Brains Trust* tomorrow morning will be a squat, solemn-looking man who has only to utter six words to establish himself as Gwyn Thomas,' wrote Herbert Williams. 'His flimsiest phrase resounds with the diction of the voters of Meadow Prospect, those Rhondda layabouts who speak in his novels with the tongues of angels.' Gwyn told him that the cameras held no terrors for him. 'The best training ground for *The Brains Trust* was lecturing in the Rhondda for the WEA. Up they came with their questions – huge, fundamental things. If you've faced these and avoided extinction, Lime Grove's got nothing to worry you.' He regarded the whole exercise as a game, he said. 'The mind makes a reflex and you go chasing it like some lout who's kicked a ball on the football field.'

He was not altogether happy in his new role as a television pundit, though the new contacts he made were interesting and the hospitality of the television studio, in those days tending to be very lavish, was tempting. He told Nana:

This *Brains Trust* thing is fantastic. Once you've been on it, it's got such a huge viewing public that even dogs that watch TV stare at you. The team meets at Scott's Restaurant in Piccadilly, one of the really fancy eating spots in London. The panel is given so much to eat and drink it's a wonder they're not carried into the studio on litters. At the end of the meal which is served in a private room, when the brandy is served with the coffee, a trolley loaded with about a thousand cigars is brought in. Bronowski always picks the very biggest, a giant of a thing as long as his own torso. I take one too, same length, not to smoke, just to beat Lady Violet over the head with during her longer and sillier memoirs.

In *A Few Selected Exits* he recalled some of the more memorable of the men and women whom he joined on *Brains Trust* panels, in words not altogether complimentary: Dr Jacob Bronowski, for instance, 'one of the marvels of the contemporary mind . . . almost total intelligence', yet a man without humour, who failed to see the funny side of one of Gwyn's best loved stories, about a group of Italians who are conned into thinking that they have emigrated to America when a scrimshanking travel organiser has actually shipped them to Treorchy in the Rhondda. In a way Gwyn felt over-shadowed by the other's qualities of mind, and was a little resentful that 'I don't think that Dr Bronowski ever accorded me any clear identity ... he looked at people as if he had rejected them from a theorem.' It was more than a little comic that Bronowski twice greeted him as Dr Glyn Daniel; a mistake neatly topped when Gwyn visited a West Wales pub, much exciting the landlord who called up to his wife, 'Come down here! We've got Dr Bronowski in the bar!'

He was easily irritated by Lady Violet Bonham Carter, and sometimes by Lord David Cecil, but with Lionel Hale and John Betjeman he found a strong and rewarding accord. The programmes involved him in much travelling, sometimes to such locations as Eton or Oxford, and he found it very exhausting, especially when each invitation to reappear caused him new difficulties with a headmaster who resented his occasionally missing school.

Throughout 1957 he continued to be involved in much broadcasting both as writer and performer, while also contributing to *Punch, Ingot*, the *Times Literary Supplement* and others. This year there was no novel for Gollancz to publish, but instead they were happy to bring out in September a volume of his short stories. *Gazooka* consisted of thirteen pieces written at various times in the previous decade, some reprinted from magazines and some of them never before published. The title story, 'Gazooka', worked back into continuous prose form of novella length the highly successful radio play developed from his original short story, 'Then Came We Singing', and was the item most frequently singled out by the reviewers for praise. The collection included 'Where My Dark Lover Lies', one of Gwyn's own favourite stories, the one about the rain-beset funeral at which the mourners forgetfully left the coffin in a pub, a traditional bit of Welsh folklore; 'O Brother Man', the Mr Rawlins story about Chaplin Everest's criminal career and the matter of the stolen euphonium; 'The Pot of Gold at Fear's End', one of the semi-auto-biographical stories featuring Gwyn's father and his cronies in Meadow Prospect, first published in *Modern Reading 16* and now lengthened by the incorporation of 'The Limp in My Longing' from *Modern Reading 15*; and 'The Leaf That Hurts The Hand', a sardonic and macabre story about Willie Palmer, possessor of the most neglected garden in Ferncleft, in which is found the murdered body of his neighbour's wife. 'Little Fury', about how little Willie Nuttall's irrational anger helps bring together two teachers at his primary school, was selected by John Pudney for his *Pick of Today's Short Stories* the following year, and Alun Richards chose 'The Teacher' to represent Gwyn's output in his *Penguin Book of Welsh Short Stories* in 1976. Altogether it was a distinguished and delightful collection, offering evidence to those who wanted it that Gwyn Thomas was indeed very much at home with shorter fictions.

His most serious efforts during 1957 were devoted to the writing of a novel in which he returned to the exploration of Spanish themes, the rejection of *The Dark Neighbour* now well behind him. Gollancz, though surprised by the desertion of the Rhondda-based comic motif, liked what he was doing and accepted the typescript when it arrived at Christmas 1957 without reservation. But writing it on top of everything else had been a great strain. 'All this radio stuff is inter-esting,' he told Nana, 'but I bitterly miss the days when there were no calls on my time and I could dawdle for twelve months on end over one particular book.'

Among Gwyn's earliest serious and really perceptive critics had been two of his former pupils at Barry County School, Gwyn Ingli James and T.H. Corfe. In long letters to the *Barry Herald* in 1952 they sought to start discussion about their local literary phenomenon, Corfe with a waspish hostility ('Outwardly taking a detached, reflect-ive, amused attitude, he is in fact always narrowly and unjustly intolerant') and James with profound and extensively justified admiration. Gwyn's warm and good-natured reply, printed the following week, explained the apparent narrowness of his subject matter:

> My first ten or fifteen years, lived on the steepening and grievous slope of a crippled economy and a weirdly unlovely social context, among a people of unique passion, kindliness and wit, are the compost heap from which arose the materials I have used in my writing.... It has enabled me to assemble from quite unlikely materials a small private world of expression in which there would be room not merely for a comic vision of what men and women do but also for the anger and pity which, even in my mellowing middle-age, have not grown much less sharp.

It was his intention, he said, to continue along the same lines, notwithstanding the urgent requests of readers such as Tom Corfe for him to turn his attention to other aspects of the world or to exploit other conventions of fiction. 'Surely there is room for me to go on my own bitter-sweet eccentric way, turning my back firmly but courteously on gangsters, smugglers, spies and even, reluctantly, *femmes fatales*,' he wrote. To one of Corfe's suggestions he made no specific reference. This was: 'If Mr Thomas never succeeded in teaching us a great deal of Spanish in our schooldays, he has subsequently taught us a lot about life.... Mr Thomas knows quite a lot about Spaniards and quite a lot about schoolboys. It is time we met some of these in his novels.' Gwyn might have pointed out that he had already essayed a novel on Spanish themes which his publishers had spurned; he might have said that he was already writing a novel in which his knowledge of schoolboys was put to use. When *A Frost On My Frolic* appeared the following year, it is to be hoped that Mr Corfe was duly satisfied. Now, five years later, here was another Spanish novel, and at first sight it is as different from any of his previous books as might be imagined.

The idea had come to him to tell the Don Juan story in a completely new way. Traditionally Juan pays the price for his amours and infidelities by being stopped in his tracks at an early age and taken down into hell by the horrific apparition of a living statue. What if, thought Gwyn, that legend had superimposed itself upon a more simple truth? Suppose that Juan, aged, say, thirty-five and troubled not by apparitions but by physical and mental exhaustion after a misspent youth, were to be caught, silenced and used by the secular and ecclesiastical powers that he had put to so much trouble over the years? He found that a powerful and moving story got into its stride as he recreated the sixteenth-century Spain of the Don's exploits, and a number of themes of great significance to him were worked out in the book's pages. Proving him capable of a grander structure if it were necessary, the novel also showed him able to deploy a much less exuberant prose style. Still witty, still exploding from time to time with a fine and unexpected metaphor, the sentences are of a classical elegance and the narrative is fast and economical where it needs to be. Somehow his own sardonic voice is still unmistakably present, but in a refined and potent form. The reader may still laugh aloud from time to time, but the theme is serious and disturbing, and the final effect is lasting.

Although *The Love Man*, when it was published in June 1958, received the most glowing reviews he had had for years, and although Macmillan were sufficiently excited by it to decide to try publishing him in the States again, it was his last novel. Try as he might, he could not resist the constant influx of remunerative invitations from the BBC and the well-heeled newspapers. Ridiculous though it was, a couple of appearances on television brought in almost as much in money terms as the proceeds of a novel that had taken a year or more to germinate and get on to paper. Increasingly he contemplated giving up teaching at last, for now he was making nearly as much from his writing as he was from schoolmastering; the strain was killing; and most of the joy had gone out of teaching anyway.

IV

A SMILING PUBLIC MAN

11

Invitation to the Theatre

It was as early as June 1956 that the Artistic Director of the Royal Court Theatre, London, first made an approach to Gwyn Thomas. 'I wonder if you could find time to have lunch with me one day, as I would like to discuss with you the possibility of your writing for the theatre. As you know, it is our policy here to introduce writers to the theatre, and I would be interested to know your views on the matter,' wrote George Devine. Very doubtfully, despite the success of his radio plays, Gwyn made an appointment to see Devine later in the year. He liked the theatre and would not miss an opportunity to see a play when he could afford the time; a natural performer himself, who sometimes thought that had he followed his best instincts when young he would have become an actor, he had a perceptive eye for what others had achieved in the theatre. But instinctive appreciation of theatrical arts did not guarantee instinctive knowledge of the playwright's skills. He felt he did not have the constructional faculty that would be even more necessary to the playwright than it was to the novelist, and which, as a novelist, he had been told frequently enough he did not possess. Devine assured him, however, that producing plays was a matter of teamwork; scripts could be edited beforehand just as they would inevitably be modified in rehearsal; if Gwyn would try his hand, he might well produce something that between their efforts would be well worth while.

Gwyn allowed himself to be persuaded, and in such moments as he could tear out for himself from the rags of time left when no other commission was demanding his attentions he made a number of false starts over the following months and years. He told Nana in 1958:

159

I've got a lot of ideas that might come to life on the stage, but I can't really work up any considerable heat about working for the live theatre. It's probably having grown up as a cinema addict. I still prefer a good film to any play. And besides, the risk of total humiliation on the stage is far greater than it would be in a novel.

The Love Man began life as a possible stage play, but when he spoke to his BBC friends about it they persuaded him that the material was ideal for radio. Broadcast as *To This One Place* in November 1956, it was sufficiently well received and seemed strong enough as a story for him to go on and develop it as a novel. A later adaptation for television was undertaken not by Gwyn but by Elaine Morgan. Other attempts at writing for the stage came to nothing too, until in 1959 the outline of a play about a Welsh family was declared by Devine to be the sort of thing he was hoping for. Gwyn began to work at it more seriously, and at last, early in 1960, Devine said that it was time he put his company to work on a production.

While tinkering occasionally with ideas for a theatre play, Gwyn's round of involvement with various kinds of broadcasting showed no let-up. In a radio programme called *World of Books* he spoke to W. John Morgan about *The Love Man*, explaining how the Swiftian savage indignation of his early writing had been superseded by the 'oblique sidling approach' which won him his reputation as a humorist. But it was a terrible strain to go on writing comically about South Wales, for his novels had been written 'out of the life blood, the experience, the suffering of all the people of this community' and:

> There came a point where my stamina, my energy, had in some way to be conserved, and it simply meant a clean dramatic break-away from the valleys, and of course, where else but Spain to go? It is a country that I know a little about, and it has the same kind of ravaged beauty that I have found in the valleys.

In choosing to write about Don Juan he had not wished to examine him as the great lover, the great enjoyer of life. 'I mean, I am not very good at the confrontations of man and woman.... There is something rather banal about the usual mechanism of romance; I've never been able to take this seriously at all.... The humorist is not particularly endowed with sympathy for these terrible mutilating intimacies.' His understanding of Juan was that he had found in a kind of multiple seduction of humanity some small satisfaction for the terrible unease underlying his whole life.. The old legend of Juan's descent into hell with the statue of the *commendatore* was no longer interesting, because:

> He would only find wisdom, of course, when he had been stripped of beauty, stripped of strength. And this is what fascinates me in human life, it is the erosion of character, it is the taking away of beauty, it is the mere skeleton which is left to face life in middle and old age.... The hells that men and women create for themselves on earth are infinitely more lacerating than anything the old theologians ever conceived.

With good humour and gusto sufficient to belie any morbid tendency which might be inferred from this expression of his inmost thoughts, he wrote a radio feature about Guto Nyth Brân, the fabulous runner whose name often occurred in Gwyn's talk about the wonders of South Wales. 'I've been involved in so much talking and writing about that old hero that I keep breaking into a run every time my eyes wander to the north and see the Rhondda hills,' Gwyn confided to Nana. *The Long Run* was broadcast on the Home Service in July, and Robert Robinson remarked in the *Observer* that 'Mr Thomas is more entertaining in half an hour than others are in a month'. Talking about humour was becoming one of Gwyn's specialities as well; a recording of his address on 'Contemporary Comedy' to the Cardiff Business Club in February was broadcast to such good effect that when he was invited to speak at the Cheltenham Festival of Literature in September it was suggested that this should again be his topic.

His work on the experimental magazine programme *Highlight* had been noted, and now Donald Baverstock called upon him to contribute regularly to his new television magazine, *Tonight*. 'There is a sort of tenuous link between this Donald and ourselves,' Gwyn told Nana. 'His father was a clerk at the Senghenydd colliery at the time of the explosion. It blew him as far as Kent where he still lives.' Following up an idea that the Guto theme would make good television, Baverstock sent a camera team and producer across to South Wales to look about the locations with Gwyn and see how the land lay. The enterprise was badly timed, as Gwyn explained to Nana:

> They arrived here in the middle of a summer storm of the sort that used to send Mrs Martin of High Street whipping out her hairpins and diving into the protective shadow of the *cwtch*. A thick mist was drifting in

from the sea. The project was that we should motor along the road from Pontypridd as far as the breast of Trehafod hill and that astonishing view of the Cymmer tip and the spur of hillside on which Guto was born. Then double back to Ynysybwl and circle slowly round the mountain, taking in the new forest, and wind up at Guto's grave. The weather foxed us. We sent a scout in a fast car to see if he could find the village of Llanwonno in the middle of the mountain. He was back in a couple of hours. He couldn't find the village. He was sent forth again. The second time he couldn't find the mountain.

We may try again in the autumn.

In February 1959 *The Love Man* was published in the United States with a new title, *The Wolf at Dusk*, to a chorus of highly approving reviews led by Louis Untermeyer who said it was the best historical novel he had read for years: 'It is bitter and bawdy and beautifully written. . . . A grim and gorgeous story.'[1] The book sold quite well, and a new opportunity for the name of Gwyn Thomas to be established in the United States seemed to be presenting itself. When he turned down offers to go and promote his novel there, however, the chance faded away again.

Late in the year an American filmmaker, Richard Frank, whose credits included the film *Somebody Up There Likes Me* about the boxer Rocky Graziano, called on Gwyn to discuss the possibility of turning his early novel, *The Alone to the Alone*, into a musical. Gwyn thought the book unlikely material for such a project, but Frank was full of ideas about what could be done if a promising young composer he knew could successfully extract the flavour of some of the Welsh minor key laments and mix it up with things like the Blues and some Jewish rhythms. 'I know that your book is kind of left wing, Gwyn,' said Frank, who had himself suffered under the McCarthy purges, 'but doing it this way, the music will take the curse off it.' Very doubtfully, Gwyn gave him a copy of the Welsh Congregationalist hymnal, expecting that the odds were probably about a hundred to one against the project's getting off the ground. It would have been a safe enough bet. Quite a number of similar optimistic suggestions came up during the next few years. At one stage Gwyn became almost convinced that a Hollywood film version of *All Things Betray Thee* was actually going to be made, but although the would-be producer, George Slaff, paid a fee every year for twenty years to keep his option open, in the end it didn't happen. Gwyn resigned

18 Stars in the Welsh literary pantheon meet at Coleg Harlech for a Summer School in 1954: Gwyn, Gwyn Jones, Richard Hughes, Glyn Jones and Henry Treece

19 Gwyn presents Harry Secombe with a Littlewoods cheque for a win on the pools in a ceremony at the New Theatre, Cardiff, in 1962

20 Gwyn photographed against a
Rhondda background in 1963

21 Lyn allows herself to be
photographed in a studio in 1955

himself early to such disappointments, and treated most of such approaches as more diverting than promising.

A Russian translation of *All Things Betray Thee* was published in 1959. Sending his sister a copy at Christmas, Gwyn told her how disturbing he had found the motif of a broken harp on the book's cover. *All Things Betray Thee* had been published originally just too late for his brother John to read it. At John's funeral a wreath in the shape of a broken harp had been sent by one of the mourning families. The recurrence of the image now moved Gwyn deeply. He was at a low ebb anyway after a year of exhausting demands upon him. His appearances 'down the line' on *Tonight* had become a feature of the programme. Paul Ferris had called him 'the funniest speaker in the world' and Baverstock wanted him to go to London and become a full-time member of the team with Cliff Michelmore and Anthony Jay. But he still couldn't bring himself to finish with schoolmastering, even though new developments at Barry were beginning to look like the last straw.

The old, cramped, Victorian buildings which the school had occupied since its founding were to be abandoned and a great move was planned to a new site on the northern edge of the town. Gwyn did not see that the move was going to be for the better. He had grown used, he said, to the genial misery of the old place, falling down though it might be, and he had no wish to start again in cheap and nasty modern buildings which offered virtually no real improvement in accommodation. 'The actual teaching space will be smaller than what we had in the old ruin,' he complained to Nana. 'The only thing larger, I am told, will be the stage in the hall from which the Head and the Governors can project even more grandiose brands of bull than they did before.' He would no longer be able to walk home at lunchtime in comfort; if he did go home to lunch he would barely have time to have a fish thrown at him at the front gate, seal fashion, before having to set off on the return journey. In a broadcast talk later in the year, 'On Leaving a School', he described some aspects of the old school, his voice as usual a rare mixture of the sardonic and the sentimental:

Built in 1896, it was one of a large number of Intermediate schools erected at that time to contain the swirling intellectual gases released by the Compulsory Education Acts. It stood on a hill and overlooked the

163

sea, and these were its only intimations of dignity and grace. It belonged to what one might call the penitentiary period of municipal building. Whether you ordered a school, a library or a hospital, you got a gaol.

The corridors were narrow and the lighting neanderthal. Electricity was installed in the late 1940s. The gas fixtures which it replaced were of a sort that must have set Faraday seriously to work. During the war the natural murk was doubled by such ARP devices as webbing across the windows and sand bags piled up against most of the apertures. In some of the less fortunate rooms there was no way of knowing whether you were actually addressing a class. You advanced to the door with your arms extended. You made a sharp turn left and if your hand touched hair and flesh you started to teach.... The darker and more cunning of the pupils, between the fine quality of the shadows and the congestion caused by boys pouring down from the laboratories into corridors already crowded, could remain academically virgin for years on end.

When, in January 1960, Henry Treece asked his advice about giving up teaching to concentrate wholly on writing, Gwyn told him firmly to hang on. 'There is a lot to be said for keeping teaching as a core, provided that one makes ruthless cuts in the energy one gives to it.' The year that was just beginning, however, brought Gwyn almost to the end of his tether, and when five months later Treece told him that he had decided to make the break, Gwyn confessed that he was envious that his friend had got the teaching incubus off his back.

If it was a time of pressure, it was a time of promise too. Gollancz had agreed to accept another collection of short stories while he gathered together his energies before embarking on another novel, and as he had by then written several dozen short stories for *Punch* the material for a book was at hand. Twenty-six selected stories under the title *Ring Delirium 123* appeared in May and the new book was welcomed by critics who were able to say how well it confirmed their feelings that Gwyn's writing was most acceptable in short bursts. As the setting of the stories was in and around Meadow Prospect, 'that small but universal corner of Wales where Gwyn Thomas discovers all the tender, bawdy, furious and tragic poetry of life' as the blurb writer put it, the collection had a pleasing degree of unity. On the cover quotations from reviewers compared Gwyn with every writer of class that could be imagined: Chaucer, Dickens, Compton-Burnett, Bernard Shaw, Damon Runyon, Swift, Aristophanes, Thomas Love Peacock, Evelyn Waugh, Balzac, P.G. Wode-house, D.H. Lawrence, Rabelais, Dylan Thomas. One of Gwyn's funniest ever books, it sold as well as a collection of short stories could be expected to, and requests came from Bernard Hollowood for more and more pieces for his magazine. Ever ready to oblige, Gwyn supplied a series of nine autobiographical articles under the general title 'Gwyn Thomas's Schooldays' which were featured in *Punch* during the summer of 1960; the following year a further series of autobiographical pieces called 'The Seeding Twenties' was given pride of place.

While attending to these matters Gwyn had been writing for radio and television and appearing with increasing frequency on both media. One enterprise conducted by the B B C's Welsh Region Variety Producer, Brian Evans, was to have a series of programmes on 'How to become ...', to which Gwyn contributed plays on becoming a Welsh Headmaster and winning influence as a Committee-Man. The actor playing the Committee-Man fell ill during the recording and Donald Houston, who was in Cardiff for a television play, stepped into the breach. Giving Gwyn a lift home to Barry after the recording, Donald expressed an eagerness to have Gwyn write a comedy script for a Welsh film. He and Stanley Baker, another Rhondda boy who was doing well in films in the great world beyond Wales, and other Welsh actors would be glad of a vehicle for a new production company Baker was setting up.

Very well, said Gwyn, and the next time he was in London Baker sent a Rolls to collect him from his hotel and whisk him to the studios at Shepperton for a preliminary chat. His principal partner in the project, Baker told Gwyn, was Harry Secombe, and what they visualised was a story in which he, Houston and Secombe could play together. On a Sunday which Gwyn found most memorable he spent a day with the three principals in London. He told Nana:

> Secombe is without doubt one of the most versatile and vigorous men in the theatre today. We had a fantastic lunch in one of the tonier restaurants in Soho. We were all in good form. We laughed so much the waiters must have thought the lot of us mad. Then we went on to Stanley Baker's place in Wimbledon – a far cry from the Blaenllechau hovel he left to take his chance on the stage when he was fourteen.... The script has been started and it *may* come to something. But films are a dark forest.

After such a good start it was a pity that, as he feared, little further was heard about the idea. Gwyn became caught up in a theatrical whirlwind, and the others were so fully occupied that the opportunity to work together as they had hoped did not recur. Socially Gwyn began to encounter other actors, among them Richard Burton, whose Shakespeare seasons at the Old Vic had given Gwyn and Lyn so much pleasure on the few occasions they had been able to get to London. While visiting the Neath and Port Talbot areas in the past, calling on family or friends or going to talk to clubs and societies, Gwyn had inevitably encountered Burton's brothers and liked them greatly; when he met Burton there was an instant spark between them struck from a mutual respect for the other's verbal skills and high good humour. Reverberations from their casual early encounter later grew large in Gwyn's life.

Rooted in autobiography as so much of his fiction had been, it is not surprising that Gwyn's first play had, as he confessed in *A Few Selected Exits*, a plot which was 'a kind of extension of autobiography. It was an attempt to imagine what my family life would have been if my brothers and I had not been dispersed from our kitchen by the squalid autumn of the thirties.' Set quite specifically in 1954, *The Keep* portrayed a family called Morton living in a typical South Wales valley community. Ben, the patriarch, is a man broken by his past and little more than a papier-mâché figurehead. Mam, who would normally be the main strength and inspiration of the family, has gone away to America and died there (or so it seems), and is now just a picture on the wall. Her place has been taken by her daughter, Miriam, who has sacrificed her own chances in life to look after her father and five brothers. The eldest brother Constantine, ambitious and paternal, has been keeping the family together in what the other brothers increasingly rebel against as a prison that is somehow suffocating their own lives. The play takes us through a family crisis when the rebellion comes to a head, only to be deflated by unexpected factors, leaving life to go on not much changed by the revelations of the evening.

Allowing Gwyn to explore and play with many of his favourite themes, the play was nevertheless comparatively well disciplined after a certain amount of re-writing requested by Devine, and Gwyn began to think well of it. After he had submitted his final script there was a silence from the Royal Court so long that he almost forgot about it, but then came a proposal to give it a single Sunday evening performance. Graham Crowden was keen to direct, and Glyn Houston, Dudley Jones and Jessie Evans would play the leading roles. The tryout was scheduled for 7 August 1960.

Gwyn travelled to London by car to see the results of his labours. The journey, interrupted by stops at interesting-looking public houses so that his trepidation could be assuaged by a pint from time to time, seemed to take for ever. Black clouds ahead mounted ever higher until the whole sky loured and rumbled. The omens did not look good. As they approached London they ran into rainfall and, as Gwyn said in his autobiography, 'Every street became a river.... The car felt like a bathyscope and appeared now and then to be floating sideways. We peered out of the windows, looking for fish or Cousteau.... We moored the car in a side-street.... There were no traffic-wardens around to tell you either to burn the car or to back it down to the Devon border.' The occasion was a washout in the most literal way possible: the tremendous downpour had flooded the theatre to a depth of four feet and rendered any production impossible. The distinguished audience – when Gwyn arrived at the theatre, Meredith Edwards, Donald Houston, and Clifford Evans among others were waiting outside the Royal Court's tightly closed doors – listened gloomily to George Devine's tale of disaster and agreed to return the following Sunday. Gwyn and his party went to the pub next door and sat out a curious evening. 'I could not share the genuine grief of the actors,' wrote Gwyn in *A Few Selected Exits*. 'Their ardour and pride had been doused by dirty water. I felt no strangeness. I seek in every circumstance a bloom of absurdity and the bloom is delivered on the dot.'[2]

A second attempt the following Sunday was more rewarding. The audience laughed at the verbal fireworks and critics such as Irving Wardle and Robert Muller felt that the omens were good, both for the play and for the playwright. Devine agreed that a full production should be planned and asked Gwyn what he had in mind for a follow-up to *The Keep*.

While he was giving that some thought, the busy days of teaching and radio work resumed. Feeling that he should make some gesture towards easing the work of those who needed to be constantly in contact with him, Gwyn at last allowed Lyn to order a telephone, but could rarely bring himself to use it personally. His experience being that modern, mechanical things usually caused more trouble than they were worth, he left them alone as much as possible. Lyn came in from a shopping expedition one day when Gwyn was working at a table within two paces of the phone. 'That thing's been ringing on and off all morning,' he said. 'I wonder who it was?'

One of those who used the telephone to get in touch was an American, Harry Sions, editor of a glossy magazine called *Holiday*. Would Gwyn like to do an article about Wales for him? 'Journey Through Wales', the first of a number of such pieces which Gwyn gladly wrote for *Holiday*, was published in September 1960. He was stunned and delighted by the generosity of American rates of pay compared with British, and carried out his commissions with all his skill. Another caller was Wolf Mankowitz, who thought that it would be a great idea to turn *The Love Man* into a musical, transferring it to a Welsh setting. 'That'll be a tough one,' thought Gwyn, not too unhappy when no action in the matter ensued.

Just over a year after its single exposure, *The Keep* received a full production at the Royal Court Theatre in November 1961. With the dialogue somewhat more restrained and the structure tightened a little, and with John Dexter directing a cast which now included Mervyn Johns, Glyn Owen and Windsor Davies, it had a considerable success. J.C. Trewin, W.A. Darlington and T.C. Worsley all praised many felicities in it and agreed that a night at the theatre where one laughed so continuously and helplessly was a great blessing. Several commentators were a little uneasy about there being rather more talk than action, but, the talk being so wonderful, forbore to complain, except for Graham Samuel whose report was headlined: 'An Overweight of Wit'. Crowds continued to come to see it; a television version gave it valuable publicity and a second run followed, though not quite enough of an audience turned up to justify the move when it transferred to the comparatively large Piccadilly Theatre. For a while it was the phenomenon of the hour, and there were many who were prepared to believe that a significant new playwright had appeared on the British scene. J.C. Trewin selected *The Keep* for publication as one of his *Plays of the Year*. What with one thing and another, Gwyn had good cause to be pleased, and when George Devine repeated his request for a second play he lost no time in tackling another theme dear to his heart.

The Brains Trust was wound up towards the end of 1961, but

Gwyn was still kept busy with commissions for *Tonight* and m.
radio bits and pieces, including a series of programmes with archive
material in which he seemed to be having solemn and fascinating
discussions with people like Gilbert Murray, James Stephens, Bernard
Shaw, Hilaire Belloc and others. He wrote a long article on King
Arthur's Places for Harry Sions' *Holiday*. Approached by an aristo-
cratic and wealthy young man called Richard Rhys, he agreed to
write a play with music, to be produced by him in due course, and
quickly drafted an outline to which he gave the title *Loud Organs*.
During the winter, however, his main effort was to produce a second
playscript for Devine, and in the spring of 1962 he was able to send
off the first two acts of *Jackie the Jumper*. It is little wonder that
schoolteaching was now a positive thorn in his side, the strain of
keeping up with all his commitments making him ill. When *The Keep*
reopened at the Royal Court in February, Lyn had to see the opening
night on her own, because Gwyn had to be back at school, the half-
term holiday over. When she returned to Barry she found him not
at all well; he had picked up a virus in London, or was suffering from
overstrain, or both, and had missed several days of school. It was
difficult to see how he could keep it up much longer.

When Devine received the first part of *Jackie the Jumper* in April
he quickly signalled his delight with the new play and asked for
delivery of the third act as soon as possible, so that they could make
plans for an autumn production. It seemed to bring matters to a head.
Gwyn sat down and totalled up all the things he was supposed to
do within the next week or two. Most pressing: *Jackie*, Act Three.
Next, a request from Harold Harris at Hutchinson's that he should
write a book about his Wales to join a series begun with *Brendan
Behan's Island*. There was the ongoing concern with *Loud Organs*, for
which Richard Rhys Productions were anxiously waiting. There was
an idea for a musical play called *Sap*, about the First World War,
which had popped into his head and which he had broached to Gerry
Raffles of the Theatre Royal at Stratford East; excited by the proposal,
Raffles had already spoken to Donald Albery about it, and they were
anxious for Gwyn to sign a contract. Most exciting of all, word had
reached Richard Burton of ideas Gwyn had been airing about a play
based on the life of Aneurin Bevan, and now Gwyn learned that
Burton was interested in seeing a script, convinced that the perfect
role for himself would be in it. It was a mountain of work that lay in

Gwyn's path. Quite suddenly he realised that he was going to have to make a decision. Agonised at the thought of losing his scholmaster's pension but convinced that his future lay with the writing he seemed so full of, Gwyn did at last what perhaps he should have done at least half a decade before, but did it with a suddenness for which the school authorities were hardly prepared. He resigned. The summer was his. With a sigh of relief he put away his schoolbooks and sat at his table, finally a professional writer with no source of income to depend on but his pen. 'I hope I can do it, Lyn,' he said. 'Of course you can,' she replied. Of that she had not a shadow of doubt.

12

Television and All That

No sooner did word get out that Gwyn had finally retired from teaching than a canny executive from the local independent television company arrived on his doorstep with an offer he could not refuse. Television Wales and the West, or TWW as it was known, had, under the control of Lord Derby and Jack Hylton, established itself as a vital and enthusiastic alternative to the BBC's television channels in the area. In January 1961 Gwyn had appeared on a TWW programme called *Two's Company*, in which he and host personality Sir David Llewellyn had been seen talking together, and reactions to Gwyn's performance had been very favourable. 'Gwyn Thomas sat there like a sort of atomic pile, radiating wit, good humour and epigram,' commented Robert Graham in the *Western Mail*. Realising that the BBC, though staider in its methods, would not be slow in trying to secure Gwyn's talents, TWW offered him a contract that seemed mouth-watering in its generosity. Perhaps, had he been fully aware of just how exclusive the contract was, Gwyn might not have signed quite so readily; worried as he was by the deliberate sacrifice of his income from teaching, however, he probably would have accepted anyway.

His first task as a freelance writer was to complete the various playscripts he had undertaken, and he got down to it with a will. The third act of *Jackie the Jumper* was delivered to Devine early in June 1962, to be welcomed with a telegram: 'Marvellous third act congratulations – George.' John Dexter was happy to undertake the direction of the new play, and a production at the Royal Court was scheduled for the following February. Secondly, as soon as the finished script was received, Richard Rhys Productions set things in motion for *Loud Organs* to have a provincial tryout in the autumn. And, thirdly, Gwyn wrote to Richard Burton about his plans for a play about Aneurin Bevan:

> Theatrically I would say the strange essence of Nye finds its only perfect response in the core of your own immense talent. I wish the piece in no way to be a chronicle of things that pushed a dead man towards his end. I want to go right into the hinterland beyond Nye; all the voices in the valleys that were faintly heard but never truly sounded.... I would like to express the valour, wisdom, laughter of all the men and women in our part of Wales who thrust Aneurin like a lance at the spiteful boobs at Westminster who regarded us in their inmost thoughts as a kind of intolerable dirt. A thundering vindication of us and our kind, a salute to all the people we can recall from your boyhood and mine whose lives closed on a note of muted pathos, who had loved humanity almost to their own hurt.

He had hoped that the play would be finished by then, he said, but the last months of teaching had reduced his mind to the status of a rissole: 'The drifts of chalk-dust on the sinuses, the dandruff of the heart that comes from too long a spell of spinning tedium, had carried me to the very lip of lunacy.' But now the fog was lifting and his thoughts were marching into battle-line. He hoped to have something to show very soon.

He was able to send off a draft of the first two acts of *Return and End* to Burton in July. The actor was deeply involved just then in filming *Cleopatra* in Rome, and the loss of his heart to his co-star Elizabeth Taylor was fast becoming apparent not only to him but to a good deal of the observing world. He was not too busy with his own concerns, nevertheless, to recognise in Gwyn's script a power and force that he would like to release himself, and an invitation was extended for Gwyn to visit him at his home in Switzerland in September: DEAR GWYN READ WITH DELIGHT YOUR TWO ACTS MARVELLOUSLY ELOQUENT CREATION AND INFINITELY ACTABLE SMALL WORRY ABOUT AGE OF 51 I AM 36 BUT BOOZE AND LATE NIGHTS CAN WORK WONDERS MAD TO SEE THIRD ACT AND YOU AND MRS HERE SOON TINY CHALET APART FROM THE MAIN HOUSE SPECIALLY MADE FOR OVERWORKED WRITERS CONGRATULATIONS AND TO QUOTE YOU AN ADMIRING SHOUT FROM PONTRHYDYFEN TO PORTH — RICHARD

By early July arrangements were well under way for *Sap* to be produced at the Theatre Royal, Stratford East. John Barber, the theatrical expert looking after Gwyn's interests at Curtis Brown, sent him the contract signed by Gerry Raffles on 6 July. They were clearly delighted with the novelty of Gwyn's play, which looked at the First World War experience through a mixture of dialogue scenes and the music of the time; Raffles was very pleased with a list of suitable songs suggested by Gwyn, and was already negotiating for a West End theatre to which the musical could be transferred quickly if it was the success they expected. What happened next has never been fully explained. Gwyn's script was duly completed in November, and he visited London to be wined and dined by an enthusiastic Raffles. Time went by quickly, for there were many other projects on Gwyn's mind during the autumn and winter. History has it, as for instance in the *Penguin Dictionary of Theatre*, that:

> In 1961 Joan Littlewood left Theatre Workshop for eighteen months to work elsewhere and make a film, but returned in 1963 with *Oh! What A Lovely War*, a musical evocation and critique of the First World War, evolved collectively by her and the whole company.

How Joan Littlewood managed to take the idea over so completely when Raffles told her about it is not clear. When by early 1963 the theatre at Stratford East seemed to be very slow in taking the matter of *Sap* any further, John Barber suggested that Gwyn should show his script to Devine instead. Devine liked what he saw, but was too busy immediately to make any firm decision. The next thing they knew was that Theatre Workshop had come up with a remarkable idea for a sort of impromptu musical satire on the First World War. When he realised what was happening, Gwyn could not at first believe that anyone could act in such a way. *Oh! What A Lovely War* was not his play in the sense that he had written all the words used in the theatre, but it was his idea, his formulation, his research, that were being used, and acknowledgement even of this there was none. As the play moved on to its great success, however, Gwyn made no move to claim any rights in it. With a shrug of disgust he turned away to other things, preferring to ignore the matter and continue as before to trust those with whom he worked. The script of *Sap* went into his cupboard of rejected and abandoned work, for it would have no credibility as it stood. People would simply say he had stolen he idea from Theatre Workshop. As far as he could see there was no future for it, and he let it lie.

With no sixth sense to warn him how letdown and disappointment might be queuing up to attend more than one of his undertakings, Gwyn and Lyn flew out to Switzerland at the beginning of September 1962 to stay with Richard Burton at Celigny and to show him the now completed script of *Return and End*. Nothing could have been more pleasing than Burton's response to what he read. It was a wonderful play, he declared, and proved his interest by demonstrating a couple of days later that he already had the first act by heart. They had a wonderful holiday together, and when it was time to return to Wales Gwyn's hopes were as high as they could be.

He now took up a round of work that would have been impossible if he had still been teaching. *The Keep* had been released for repertory company production, and starting in August there were to be productions throughout the autumn in Guildford, Birmingham, Swansea, Derby, Salisbury, Lincoln, Scunthorpe – there was even one in South Africa. When possible Gwyn called in at some of these productions, though as he grew older he became even more shy of parading himself as author of his plays. One production he did not go to see was in West Germany where, at the Hamburger Kammerspiele and under the title of *Träume in der Mausefalle* (*Dreams in the Mousetrap*), it was, according to Hans Georg Heepe: 'A success.... The critics as well as the auditorium like your play. In translation from *Hamburger Abendblatt*: 'The Hamburger Kammerspiele present a writer of an overwhelming dialogue and striking wit. The audience did not stop laughing....'¹

Chief among his duties in the autumn of 1962 was involvement in a much-trumpeted series of television programmes for TWW. Called *Wales and the West*, it allowed two presenters, one from either side of the Bristol Channel which divided TWW's area in two, to take a close look on film at their territories. Gwyn, newly recruited by TWW to be one of their more charismatic presenters, was to deal with the Welsh area, and John Betjeman was to be his counterpart for the English side. Though Betjeman and Gwyn might on the face of things have seemed to have little in common, they felt an immediate rapport when they met for the first time at the Pontcanna studios, and their programmes became a considerable success.

Gwyn's pungent, witty commentaries on his journeys into the

valleys were much appreciated by many viewers, though he came in for some lively criticism from a fair number of councillors and local officials upset by those of his remarks which suggested that South Wales still had some way to go before it became a perfect paradise. 'Gwyn Thomas is a literary prostitute who has sold his country to the English public for a few cheap laughs,' exploded Welsh Nationalist Councillor Glyn James; 'These glib and fanciful pictures of Gwyn Thomas's are doing tremendous harm as far as the Rhondda is concerned,' said Alderman E.J. Williams; and Cardiff Councillor Emrys Pride, author of *Rhondda, My Valley Brave*, announced that he was sending an immediate letter of protest to the producers of the programme. They were the vanguard of a number of similar carpings from humourless viewers which were directed at Gwyn's programmes during the next few years, and the first marked notes of a vein of hostility towards him from his own people that caused him increasing pain as the years passed; always surprised that he had upset anyone with his remarks, he would try to show that no harm was intended and that all that he ever said or did about South Wales sprang from his great but realistic love of the country and its people. And he would carry on exactly as before, surely believing that the truth was what mattered and that to look at the truth armed with humour was always the best thing to do. His travels as the series went on took him further afield, one of his own particular favourites among the programmes being one made in Laugharne where he spoke memorably of Dylan Thomas's life and poetry.

Loud Organs meanwhile was on the brink of its first production, and Gwyn had profound worries about what was being done with it. Beset with difficulties over the music, which Gwyn didn't think very effective, as well as with casting, Richard Rhys had not lost his own enthusiasm for the piece and soldiered on. The first performances were in Blackpool in October, and the responses were not good; re-jigged with some rapid re-writing it opened in Cardiff on 29 October 1962. Gwyn did not send Nana and Bill tickets, explaining:

> I had the blackest doubts about the play. The production was disastrous, an expensive and unholy mess, like Skybolt. The impresario ... logged in a young composer as brash and clueless as himself. Whenever there was a funny line it was hurried to the graveyard by a blast of trombones. They had a choreographer to devise dances that left the cast too winded to speak the lines.... Altogether, one of the most significant bits of

theatre since I scored a hit as the principal camel-boy in 'Dan y Palmwydd' in Caersalem Vestry.

Better things had been hoped for the play, and in more professional hands better things might have come of it. Set in Cardiff's Tiger Bay docklands, it presented a vividly realised picture of a community damaged by early sixties decadence but still full of life and promise. A fantastic plot brings Jim Bumford, a Hollywood writer, to the docks with a mission to expose the more or less criminal activities of club-owner, pimp, and dubious businessman Wffie Morgan. Against a whirlwind of comic incidents and some very satirical song-lyrics lampooning matters (such as rugby-mania) very dear to the Welsh heart, a series of relationships is not untenderly explored. Inevitably the script bursts at the seams with Thomasisms, very funny jokes and unexpected metaphors, and it might well be argued that the structure could have been tighter; but reading the play on the page, its indifferent reception in the theatre would be hard to predict. Despite the presence in the cast of enthusiastic and talented actors such as Glyn Houston, Gerald James and Roberta D'Esti, the play could not survive its inept production, unsatisfactory 'musical' content, and hostile reception from a significant proportion of Welsh audiences that felt they were being made fun of. A further exposure in Brighton did not improve the situation. The hoped-for transfer to London in time for Christmas did not take place, and the play was not heard of again.

Hugging failures to his chest was not Gwyn's way. He put it out of his mind and hoped for better things with *Jackie the Jumper*, which was soon to go into rehearsal at the Royal Court. George Devine, John Dexter and the team who were to be responsible for the production knew their onions and would presumably be able to avoid the sort of crass mistakes which had sunk *Loud Organs*. A little uneasily, especially when he heard that there was a significant costing for musicians for the new play to be taken into account, Gwyn warned Devine against letting the small musical element he had called for take the whole thing over. John Dexter replied that Gwyn was not to worry. At the Royal Court the music would most certainly avoid the ridiculous elaborations which took place in *Loud Organs*.

Encouraged by Dexter's assurances as well as by his praise of *Sap* and *Return and End*, copies of which he said he had seen by accident,

Gwyn looked forward hopefully to the appearance of the new play. For *Jackie the Jumper* he had returned to the Dic Penderyn theme of his novel *All Things Betray Thee*, recasting it as a half-fantastic story about a legendary hero who meets his match because of the failure of faith in his supporters. Jackie is the vital man, his rebellion against society particularly symbolised by his sexual amorality, society's response essentially encoded in the puritanical ethic of the sinisterly triumphant Reverend Richie Rees. In a preface to a printed version of the play, published in *Plays and Players* accidentally the month *before* the actual production rather than after it had opened, Gwyn explained:

> After years of writing rather quiet philosophic novels featuring no weapon deadlier than the blunter sort of chip-shop fork, I had a fancy to write something gusty and rollicking, festooned with swords, horses, gibbets and mayhem in all stock sizes.... I wanted a play that would paint the full face of sensuality, rebellion and revivalism.

The transition was quite natural, he claimed, for someone brought up as he was with an addiction to grand opera 'in a social ambience so emphatically tainted with lunacy as that of a mining area moving into dereliction'. The result was a theatrical curiosity in many ways. With music by Alun Hoddinott to point the more dramatic, tender and absurd moments, and with a script of such wit and humour that not one of the actors failed to have at least one line that set the house laughing, the play nevertheless had a serious core of political rebelliousness and an uncomfortable moral which caused Milton Shulman to headline his review: 'Mr Thomas's Hard Men Triumph'.

John Dexter's direction was accorded some mixed comments in the reviews when *Jackie the Jumper* opened on 1 February 1963, but the actors won a good deal of praise, especially Ronald Lewis, Dudley Jones and Michael Gough. The play itself was criticised as having its faults but generally critical reaction was warm and welcoming and the early audiences responded with marked enthusiasm. Something went wrong, however. Perhaps it was at least something to do with the dreadful winter of that year, when snow fell heavily in January and remained on the ground, occasionally added to by fresh blizzards, for nearly two months. Whether it was the bitter cold or there was some other reason, Devine wrote sadly to Gwyn in mid-February: 'I'm afraid *Jackie* has missed it. In spite of a *lot* of good press, the public is just not coming. It is an expensive show to run – with orchestra – and we cannot afford to keep it on beyond the end of next week... It is hard to discover how the play has failed finally. Most people who come enjoy it. Unfortunately today unless you have a *hit*, you have a failure.'

Failure or not, J.C. Trewin liked it well enough to select it for Volume 26 of his *Plays of the Year*; and its run at the Royal Court was not, as it turned out, its only production.

Other aspects of the work Gwyn produced during that long, hard winter were more successful. By the end of January he had completed the book about his view of Wales commissioned by Harold Harris at Hutchinson. As he had written so much on Welsh themes at various times, putting the book together had not proved too troublesome. Some of his broadcast pieces provided an ideal foundation for the book, and with just a little polishing were ready to be put in as they stood; given such a start, the rest followed smoothly. Harris was very pleased with Gwyn's 'boisterous, witty and yet very moving picture' of *his* Wales. He was a little bothered about possible libels which would have to be looked into: 'I am thinking in particular of people like those splendid librarians Conrad and Leroy Cromwell who almost succeeded in getting books banned from the Institute.' Confidently and with typical innocence, Gwyn assured him that they need not worry about such matters: 'The only people of whom I speak in a possibly defamatory way are dead, have fled, or can't read.' Not surprisingly, Harris's concern was not quite so easily laid to rest, and the book was subjected to a very thorough check by Hutchinson's lawyers before it was allowed to go to press.

Before Gwyn's contract with TWW came into effect and prevented him from engaging in any further television work for the BBC, he had written for Gilchrist Calder a play, based on the concluding section of his novel *A Point of Order*, about how the people of Top Terrace and the Birchtown Council react when a moving mountain threatens their homes. Liking the look of it, the BBC had asked for more and Gwyn had supplied a further script for a teleplay called *The Dig*. The first of these was transmitted on 14 October 1962, the second a year later. As both of them were well spoken of and gave a great deal of pleasure, it seems surprising that TWW did not persuade Gwyn to write play scripts for them, especially as their record in the field of drama was considerably less

22 Publicity shot from *The Keep*, Royal Court Theatre, London, 1961
(*l–r*) Glyn Owen, Denys Graham, Richard Davies

23 Gwyn, during a lull in the problems besetting the production of his play
The Breakers at the Sherman Theatre, Cardiff, 1976

impressive than it was in other areas. They preferred, however, to use him as a documentary presenter or general entertainer, roles which he swiftly showed he could excel at but which, it may be thought, neglected to tap his essential talent. In the coming months TWW did show an interest in making television versions of Gwyn's stage plays, but took it no further when they found that their contract did not entitle them to these works automatically. In March 1963 a radio play, *The Walkout*, reminded listeners to the BBC Third Programme of Gwyn's successes a decade earlier, but TWW still did not take the hint.

Set in a school, *The Walkout* was a funny and disturbing play about a deputy headmaster who, asked to take over the reins for a year, is changed from a pleasant colleague into a tyrannical and puritanical dictator when his new powers go to his head. Harried beyond measure, the boys end his reign with a spontaneous mass walkout in the closing minutes. The play gave Kenneth Griffith a wonderful role as the demented teacher and he remained ever afterwards a devoted admirer of Gwyn both as a man and a writer. Rosemary Timperley, also a novelist who had been a teacher, wrote to thank Gwyn for the pleasure the play had given her, saying it was 'beautifully written – funny and terrible and true'. The response to the play was positive enough for John Griffiths, the BBC's senior features producer in Wales, to ask him for another one with a school setting, and Gwyn duly sent him *The Entrance*, which was promptly accepted but not produced until April 1964.

As the spring of 1963 continued to be held at bay by the icy winter, Gwyn became involved in the first of the many television and radio programmes in which during the next dozen or so years he helped to celebrate 1 March, St David's Day. For this programme he was to be the presenter and linker of a series of items spoken by Richard Burton in *This World of Wales*, a programme networked across the United States. TWW's producer was the young Wyn Roberts – not to be confused with Gwyn's childhood friend Wynne, this Wyn Roberts later became MP for Conway and Minister of State for Wales – and he found Gwyn so excellent a colleague that plans by which his talents could be best used began immediately to form in his mind. The programme was greatly enjoyed by most who saw it. Gwyn's television presence was well on the way to becoming a national treasure, his appearance strangely misleading in its contrast with the warmth and comicality of his utterance. He was neatly described in the *Daily Express*: 'The most mesmerising Thomas since Dylan. . . . A stocky, doom-laden figure, his black spectacle rims heavy with scepticism, scattering epigrams as he goes.'

Admiring Burton greatly as he did, and made very happy by the way Burton in his turn clearly admired him, Gwyn was also, as he introduced him on St David's Day, very hopeful for the future of *Return and End*. Plans were hardening for a production of the play, Burton having indicated that he hoped to be free to start rehearsing in April and that he envisaged a theatre run of about four and a half months. He had sounded out Peter Brook to direct, and Brook had shown enthusiasm. Telling Gwyn about these movements, Richard Rhys, who was acting as his agent in the matter, warned him that he dared not yet feel too excited, because the film world was liable to changes at short notice; but the prospects did look as bright as they had ever done. Gwyn by now knew better than to believe anything until he saw it. Telling Nana in early April of his frustrations and involvement in 'schemes that never seem to see the light' in the world of television which he had already perceived as utterly mad, he bewailed also his disappointed hopes for his last two plays: 'If this keeps up, every theatrical backer in Britain will flee to Zermatt as soon as they hear me put pen to paper. Typhus is safer.' Richard Burton's plans to start rehearsing *Return and End* had already been postponed because of 'the boy's domestic crises' and because of a commitment to film *Becket* in North Wales. The plan now was to open *Return and End* on Broadway in the autumn. 'By which time,' Gwyn said fatalistically, 'Master Burton will be filming with Miss Taylor in Tahiti or the moon and I will be wishing them the best of Welsh luck.'

In the summer of 1963 Gwyn began travelling on a scale he had never experienced before. It was quite an adventure to go to Cannes with a camera team in May to make a film about the International Film Festival. He quickly found a theme of contrasts to work when, out in the bay, they saw lying at anchor a huge American aircraft-carrier. 'This is a place where humanity sheds ugliness, work and pain,' ruminated Gwyn, as the camera panned over the beach crowded with holidaying families and beautiful girls striving to catch the attention of the film moguls; and then belied his statement by allowing the constant reminders of danger to recur in shot after shot where the military police and the sailors and the great looming ship dominated the background. Like all Gwyn's films, said Colin Voisey, one of the T W W team involved in its making, it had something different, something special about it which arose naturally from the man's penetrating vision and compassionate soul, allied to the fresh phrase-making that made his commentaries as entertaining as they were provocative.

Immediately on return from France he went to North Wales to cover the International Eisteddfod at Llangollen for T W W. 'Working conditions were pretty rough,' he told Nana. 'We recorded one show in a tent very late at night. The canvas and wet grass made the air bitterly cold. Twice I left the tent shuddering and explaining that I was Captain Oates wishful to give Captain Scott a better chance.' He shot up to Llandudno to announce and describe the arrival of the Queen at the National Eisteddfod, and half-ashamedly told his sister: 'The things one does when time, weariness and greed have rusted the hinges of one's first loves, enthusiasms and goodness.' Where was the old revolutionary socialist now, he wondered, as he 'fooled and flunkeyed on television'? But the trap had closed and he had to go on.

In the autumn he went to East Germany to film for T W W and to Wittenberg especially to write a piece on Martin Luther for *Holiday*. Far from comfortable with the excessive police and military presence behind this part of the iron curtain, Gwyn was delighted when the work was done and they were able to return home. Harry Sions, *Holiday*'s editor, then came to London with his wife Louise late in September. No sooner had Gwyn and Lyn met them for the first time, laying the foundations of a very warm friendship, than Gwyn was off to New York with Wyn Roberts to make a film there. Whisked about at breathtaking pace, he was filmed at the top of the Rockefeller Center in Manhattan and subsequently at a dozen other locations in what he called 'this incredible and fantastic city': Fifth Avenue, Grand Central Station, Central Park, the United Nations building for the grand element; and then to assorted dives and cultural landmarks: Harlem and 'Skid Row', Greenwich Village, the White Horse Tavern where Dylan Thomas used to drink, and Broadway as a brilliant finale. Although in his commentary he remained as ebullient and sardonic as ever, privately he took little pleasure in the trip. He hated being removed from Lyn, upon whose ministrations, encouragement and presence he relied greatly, and he wrote plaintively to her about the sticky heat of New York and the inefficiency of the arrangements that had been made. One thing of note had happened: 'Last night we ate at Lindy's, Runyon's famous restaurant on Broadway — the only time I've ever faced a pancake that was bigger than the table.' He had a dreadful cold, he added, and missed her beyond belief.

The nature of the pressure upon him at this time may be gathered from simply listing some of the other work he did on top of the film-making in the last two or three months of 1963. He began to be a regular member of the BBC's *Any Questions?* team; he broadcast several individual talks; he wrote a dozen stories and essays for *Punch*; the play, *The Dig*, which he had written for BBC Television before joining TWW, gained him many plaudits and led to a campaign by a number of the BBC's executives to get him back into the fold; he took part in a TWW programme celebrating the life of Dylan Thomas; he appeared at the Albert Hall in the company of Bernard Miles, John Neville, Vanessa Redgrave and others in *Please Sir*, a dramatised anthology on education produced by Michael Croft as part of the Campaign for Education of that year; he wrote a Christmas story for Reginald Collin at ABC Television and devised a St David's Day script for them; he began to contribute a fortnightly series of essays to the *Teacher* at the request of its editor, Brian Hammond; and he worked out the script for a 'Self-Interview' to be conducted on *Woman's Hour*. 'It has been a short year,' he told Nana in December. 'Here we are, the eve of Midwinter Day and the sun is blazing outside, and its only use in effect is that you can see more exactly who is freezing to death in the public highway.' He continued:

> I'm just managing to ride a thumping attack of exhaustion. Those trips abroad, France, Germany, America, were too much, too fast. Funny, the amount of time I've spent fiddling about with other people's languages, and I still hate other people's countries. The sight of a frontier guard brings me out in hate-bumps.

Adding to the general stress was a decision that Gwyn and Lyn had taken to remove themselves from Barry now that he no longer needed to be close to the school and now that they could perhaps afford somewhere a little better. Various possibilities presented themselves, one very sensible suggestion made by Herbert Davies, their BBC producer friend, being that they should buy a house that had just come on the market in Palace Road, Llandaff, a pleasant and convenient address no more than ten minutes' walk from the Pontcanna studios of TWW — and even closer to the BBC, as it happened. But Lyn was quite drawn to the idea of something a little more rural, and after some searching she found a house in Ogmore-by-Sea which she thought would be just perfect. As soon as the Christmas celebrations of 1963 were over, they began to pack up their things at Lidmore Road and said goodbye to Barry, where they had lived for twenty-two years. It was not, they realised later, the most sensible decision they had ever made.

13

A Welsh Eye

The new bungalow at 5 Sea View, Ogmore-by-Sea, to which Gwyn and Lyn moved in the spring of 1964, had seemed attractive enough when they were seeking a change from Barry, especially when they considered its remote quietness in comparison to the obtrusive hammering and bangings from new neighbours carrying out alterations at Lidmore Road. 'We were literally hammered westwards,' Gwyn explained to Nana. They had seen the new bungalows while visiting the Bryan branch of the family there and Lyn had resolved immediately that this was the haven of peace for which they had been looking. Ogmore is a small seaside town on a hillside on the eastern side of the Ogmore river's meeting with the sea. Backed by rolling miles of farmland, it has a pleasant sandy beach, over-hung to the east by high cliffs; the river cuts off access to a large area of high sand-dunes and the long stretch of sandy beach which lines the bay right round to Porthcawl, a couple of miles further west. At first Gwyn found it rather soothing. 'This is a nice, comatose place,' he confided to Teifion Phillips, with whom he had been used to walking home from school in his teaching days. 'The sheep are everywhere wandering about in juries of twelve, waiting to pass judgement on the farmers who throw them onto the diminishing resources of the common land. It must be the only place where sheep go into shops to buy sweets.'

Although the bungalows had been built closer to each other than would have suited the tastes of some people, Gwyn found that there was more than enough land attached to his, gardening not being for him a credible occupation at all. 'I am cultivating what one might call instant wilderness,' he told Nana. 'I'm putting the larger part of it under stone, leaving just a fragment of soil for me to laugh mockingly at when the fit is on me.'

The journey to Cardiff was now twenty miles rather than the eight or nine from Barry, however, and this being a period when Gwyn's broadcasting work required him to be anywhere but at home for much of the time, new strains were soon apparent. Lyn was happy to take him in to the Cardiff studios or to catch trains for London, as indeed she was happy to accompany him on as many of his assignments as possible, but the constant driving, often late at night, eventually became a greater burden than she had anticipated. They had not been residents of Ogmore for more than six months when she began looking round for somewhere rather more convenient.

Though he did not perhaps at this early stage perceive it, Gwyn was just beginning to pay the price of the decision he had made to leave school-teaching and devote himself to freelance writing and performing on radio and television. There was no slackening of his zest for performance, and the flow of language showed no sign of silting up, but already the way of life he had adopted was taking its subtle toll. He no longer had time for writing at length and with the degree of seriousness that had made him a novelist, nor was such writing economically viable. 'The novel is not dead, only the novelist,' he said to one inquirer, and though he did not publicly mourn this passing, he recognised it as a kind of death. What also began slowly to become evident was that the travelling, the stress-filled build-up to performance, the rush to meet deadlines from too many com-missions and the careless dietary and drinking habits which were consequences of the very hospitable side of his business were forming a deadly combination to undermine his never robust constitution. It was only with the greatest reluctance that he would ever say no to any request, whether lucrative commission or neighbourly favour, and for the next half-dozen years he roared around like a typhoon, concealing from himself as from all observers except his doctor the fact that he was not as healthy as his performance in public suggested.

His schedule in 1964 was no less full than that of the previous year which, as he had confessed to Nana, had almost done for him. A St David's Day script for Reginald Collin at ABC television led to a very successful *Tempo* programme in March. Called 'The Jagged Land', Gwyn's usual mixture of poetic and humorous reflections on Wales gave Ronald Lewis as the narrator a chance to make a delighted meal of the richly rhetorical lines the play provided. During the winter Gwyn turned his attention also to two more articles for *Holiday*. 'A Joyful Noise – Growing Up With Music' cost him little effort, for it was one of his favourite topics and nothing gave him greater pleasure or more surely directed his pen than the half-comic, half-sentimental glances backwards to the culture of his childhood which he was more and more frequently invited to provide. 'A Fugue of Inns', as he first called it, or 'Tranquillity and Warm Beer: A Treasury of Favorite Inns in England's Cotswold Country' as it appeared in the magazine, required him to make a foray into Oxford-shire to reconnoitre the territory, a task very much to his liking. Mixing a little anecdotal history with some pleasant topographical description and a good deal of humorous reflection, he was able to make it an essay that must have had Americans in large numbers deciding to sample the locality for themselves in subsequent summers. Of the Bull at Burford, for instance, he wrote:

> In 1649 Burford was the centre of a rumpus started by the Levellers; they were the Bolsheviks of the time, lads who had a full set of black drapes ready to hang on wealth and sensual pleasure. Oliver Cromwell marched in, locked the agitators in the church and struck a brisk, modern note by shooting three of them dead in the churchyard. It is unlikely that Oliver called in at the Bull. The business that brought him to these parts rarely included drinking. Charles II, who loved oranges and women (and especially Nell Gwyn, who sold oranges), once slept here, setting the seal of quietude and comfort on the place once more.

And on a more personal and contemporary note, he continued:

> The day I was there two lads of about twelve burst in. They were bearing between them, on a large salver, what looked like a lump of dark, gnarled wood. The boys had a picaresque look about them and I thought at first that they had torn off a piece of the inn's fabric and were now trying to sell it back to the owner. I was wrong. What they were carrying was a freshly roasted swan. They gave me a slice to taste. I learned little from the experience except that swans are better alive on water than dead on dishes.

To Jane Clapperton, associate editor of *Holiday* and a former native of south Oxfordshire, who told Gwyn what a lovely piece it was and how homesick it made her, he said that that stretch of countryside was a real pearl, and that he hoped to be able to repeat his journey for its own sake: 'The zeal of my research into the village inns of the zone almost had me canonised by the more ale-ridden of the yeomen.'

Some of the travelling he undertook a little later in the year with Wyn Roberts and Colin Voisey to make films for TWW was equally rewarding but much more exhausting. Included in these per-egrinations was a period in Venice where, accompanied by Lyn as well as the usual TWW production team, he made his contribution to a film called *The Drowning City*. When he put his commentary onto the finished film later in the year, Mike Towers, a TWW producer, was so impressed with his professionalism and the quality of his script that he invited him to travel imaginatively with him to the heart of Asia. A camera team had been to Afghanistan and come back with over two hours of film. Would Gwyn care to view the footage, help cut it and provide a commentary? Gwyn found the experience both demanding and entertaining, and the resulting film was much talked about when given air-time the following year. The local travelling within Wales to give talks or take part in programmes such as *Any Questions?* or to cover an Eisteddfod was almost more debilitating than the foreign set piece: apologising for a delayed reply to a letter from Harry Sions he said he had been 'up and down Wales like a panting Bedouin on television business'.

Between journeys he still thought of himself as a writer essentially for print and whenever he could he sat at his table, plied with tea by the attentive Lyn, scribbling stories and articles. For *Holiday* he wrote a long, scholarly, exciting and amusing account of the literature of Spain; called 'The Passionate Authors', it reviewed the whole range of narrative writing from the medieval epic of *The Song of El Cid* to Ortega y Gasset and Benito Pérez Galdós. To exemplify the Spanish delight in savagery he outlined the story told in the twelfth-century ballad of *The Knights of Lara*, remembering, perhaps, as he did so, how the plot of his unpublished novel *The Dark Neighbour* had been inspired by this same true story of medieval mayhem. Two of his keenest interests united in a passage about the writing of the Spanish Romantic period:

> The theatre of this period is a thunderclap of disillusion and revolt, a heart-cry of young protesters who had seen their dreams sold down every conceivable river, who viewed the Spain they lived in as a vile irredeemable grotto.... The Duke of Rivas's *Don Alvaro* I would name as an utterly characteristic bit of Spanish writing. Violence blows through

it like a sirocco, everybody beaten black and blue by a fate that can think up a new malignity for every minute of the day. Every line of it calls out for Verdi, and to it Verdi came. *La Forza Del Destino* is the result. The story is the ultimate manifesto of the Spanish conviction that, however high the hope you have as you approach a corner, you are going to be clobbered as soon as you turn it. It remains my favourite imbroglio, the piece I read when I have an intense wish to feel vicariously Spanish.

No matter how comically he put it, this Spanish perception about the nature of life was, as far as Gwyn was concerned, absolutely and tragically and absurdly true.

Curiously enough he had never regularised his position with *Punch*; he had taken cocktails at *Punch* headquarters, eaten lunch at *Punch*'s table, and Bernard Hollowood invited him to send further contributions, which he duly provided; but it never occurred to him to submit a piece without a prior invitation. Busy now with regular articles for the *Teacher* as well as increasingly frequent pieces in the *Western Mail* (for which he began to review books as well as to provide an occasional 'Personal Column' at this time), he sent only seven or eight pieces to *Punch* in 1964. Several of these inevitably drew on his memories and fantasies of 'Meadow Prospect', though the main source of ideas was becoming his own more recent past: immediate capitalisation on experiences like visiting the seaside or taking a trip into the countryside, or, more vitally, on his now finished career as a schoolmaster. Two or three of his stories this year dealt with 'Mr Walford', an eccentric colleague who was a composite of two or three of the men with whom he had taught. One of them, D.J.P. Richards, a former athlete and widely revered by the boys as a 'character', had been among Gwyn's closer acquaintances on the staff, a man who never ceased to surprise, irritate and delight his bump of affection for the absurd. Asked by Harry Sions, who, unexpectedly ousted from his position at *Holiday*, now became an editor at Little, Brown, whether he had any ideas for a new book in 1965, Gwyn, fresh from writing a Mr Walford story, outlined a few possibilities. Sions immediately discerned their common basis in autobiography, and in March 1965 wrote suggesting that the book Gwyn should really be writing was one which would tell the story of 'the many lives of Gwyn Thomas' – an autobiography proper.

It was clear that for some time Gwyn had been moving closer to

a directly autobiographical mode. His book on Wales, published at
last in October 1964, contained a good deal of such material, and he
had enjoyed putting it together. One of the chapters, typically
entitled 'A Clutch of Perished Bards', was made up of essays on W.H.
Davies, Dylan Thomas and Huw Menai, neatly mixing autobiographical and critical material for the last two and drawing a
special commendation from John Betjeman; it was one of the best
books even Gwyn had written, he said, and pleased him specially
because of the way it had opened the poetry of Davies to him. The
long delay in publishing had come about because of difficulties with
the artwork. Hutchinson wanted the series to consist of handsomely
produced books with a strong appeal to the eye, and for Gwyn's
Welsh volume, for which they had finally agreed on the title, *A Welsh
Eye*, they had appointed an artist called John David Evans. Highly
gifted, with a moody and expressive drawing style, Evans had proved
to be 'a veritable Gully Jimson' to deal with; a perfectionist, he had
worked painfully slowly and self-critically. Now that the book was
out, and was being welcomed with considerable warmth, the viability
of such a kind of writing could not be denied, and Gwyn considered
Sions' suggestion though not without suspicion and some awareness
of the difficulties it would cause him.

Although there were plaudits for *A Welsh Eye*, and a fair amount
of exposure in that the *Spectator* printed extracts and it was widely
and appreciatively reviewed, there were quite a few disappointments
and frustrations in 1964 which took the edge off the better moments.
After all the early hopes for *Return and End*, Richard Burton's life had
become too complicated for him to undertake it. George Devine had
waxed cold, then warm, then cool again; then the Royal Shakespeare
Company had expressed a keen interest which came to nothing. John
Barber at Curtis Brown was very puzzled; people who read the play
were loud in their enthusiasm for it; but no production was proposed.
It was suggested that the problem lay in the very topic; although
the leading character was called Simon Adams (like the doomed
protagonist of *All Things Betray Thee*), he was obviously based on
Aneurin Bevan, and it was said that some influential people did not
like Gwyn's treatment of the theme or the man. Whatever the reason,
it was hard for Gwyn to live with. In March 1964, when a suggestion
even came from Curtis Brown that Gwyn might allow the Swansea
Repertory Company a chance to try out the play, he mused sadly in

reply: 'I doubt if any piece for the theatre has created so many sardonic echoes ... Richard Burton ... The Royal Shakespeare people.... When I myself last spoke to John Neville he was in a glow of enthusiasm about it. Now we are reduced to the possibility of a deal with a repertory company. Has a play ever had a swifter declension of prestige? I will need a bit of time to decide whether to offer the thing to the Eskimos or just dump it in the bay. I would for just a few more moments like to cling to the intimations of fame and fortune that attended the first phases of this ill-starred epos.'

Hopes for *Return and End* were revived several times in the years which followed, but always it seemed to go the same way: first a surge of promise, then a silence, then a lame apology. Meanwhile in the summer of 1964 he had started another theatre project in association with Warren Jenkins for the Welsh Arts Council. But after an enthusiastic reception of Gwyn's proposal for a play of episodic structure to be called *The Ways of Ewan Probert*, Jenkins was unhappy with the draft. He proposed a lengthy postponement while first he went ahead with 'an established play'. The constant let-downs must have been affecting him, because for once Gwyn allowed a note of real bitterness to come into his reply: 'In all my depressing career of contacts with stage producers I have not met so wet a response to a bright theatrical idea. It's clear that your imagination and mine work in disastrously different ways of perception. When I heard you voice your obsession with mime, I should have been warned to pull out. One never learns.'

Despite everything, Gwyn allowed himself to glow with new hope when an American film producer, Phil Brown, wrote in November saying that he wanted to make a film of *All Things Betray Thee* and that Stanley Baker was keen to play the central role. Like other projects enthusiastically broached that year, however, this film was never made.

By the end of the year, Gwyn had become thoroughly dissatisfied with living in Ogmore. 'As far as I'm concerned, the place is an intolerable pain in the neck,' he told Nana in his Christmas letter, 'and I'll be glad to get out of it.' Lyn had already been looking hard for an alternative, and even as Gwyn wrote they were sure that she had found the right place in the Vale village of Peterston-super-Ely, just five miles or so from Cardiff. There they moved at the end of January 1965, and though there were times, especially at first, when they wondered whether they had made another mistake, Cherry Trees was Gwyn's last home. It was a spacious bungalow in a recently and rather pleasantly developed area called Wyndham Park just south of the river Ely, hardly more than a stream across the field at the bottom of the garden. Surrounded by elms and beeches, and with some fine young pines in the back garden – though only one cherry tree, as far as Gwyn could see – it was the nearest thing to a gracious country mansion that they had ever lived in. An attractive pub, the Sportsman's Rest, was no more than a quarter of a mile away, if you took the footpath over the river. There was a problem that they were not prepared for: the river tended to flood widely through the water-meadows on either side after heavy rain – of which there is no lack in Glamorgan. When this happened, as it did several times in their first year or two until measures were at last taken by the council to improve the drainage, Wyndham Park became cut off from the village, the Sportsman's Rest was under water, and irritation abounded. All in all, however, their lives now became more comfortable, and their situation was much less inconvenient.

The success of the films which Gwyn and his TWW colleagues had made about East Germany and Venice was so great when they were shown that plans were laid for another major excursion in 1965, this time to Moscow. While waiting for Wyn Roberts to sort out the details, which hung on their passing themselves off as a camera team anxious to record a football match between Wales and the USSR, Gwyn busied himself with radio programmes, an appearance on the Eamonn Andrews show and with preparations for a new chat show (though they were not then so called) of his own, *As I See It*, which was to begin in April. He wrote a play for radio called *The Bungalow*, based on the character of the ambitious local councillor who had animated his book *A Point of Order*, the man whose pure political motivation had gradually been tempered to a more pragmatic approach. Herbert Davies at the BBC immediately perceived that the new piece had distinct possibilities as a stage play and urged Gwyn to look into them. Delighted, Gwyn agreed, and further accepted Davies's suggestion that a better title for the play would be *The Alderman*. Subject to another enthusiasm, he also accepted a BBC commission for a play about Archbishop Latimer which would require a good deal of research. Where he thought he was going to find the time is a mystery, but he simply could not say no to a commission if pressed with sufficient enthusiasm.

In response to an invitation from Sam Wanamaker, he called on him to discuss some proposals for a film about the Great Train Robbers; Richard Burton, he learned, was again involved, and it looked as if the project was going to be very big indeed. Doubting somewhat but ever hopeful and ready to oblige, Gwyn took Lyn to Dublin to meet the principals and discuss the lines along which his script was to go. A few days later Sam Wanamaker sent an efficient memorandum on what had been agreed and asked for Gwyn's 'treatment, outline, or synopsis' within the next three or four weeks. Pleased to sense a certain urgency in the request, Gwyn read up on the sensational train robbery case that had so excited Britain a year or so before and worked out some initial prescriptions. He had heard nothing more about the idea of filming *All Things Betray Thee*; was his luck going to prove a little better this time?

Late in March 1965 Gwyn lunched with his publisher, Sir Robert Lusty of Hutchinson, who was visiting Cardiff, tentatively bringing the matter of autobiographies and such forms of writing into the conversation. As soon as he had returned to London, it occurred to Lusty that Gwyn's autobiography, if he could be persuaded to write it, would be a most engaging work. Letters were exchanged, Harry Sions at Little, Brown was informed, and the project was ratified. Contracts were signed in April and Gwyn found himself launched on his first real book for several years, with publication guaranteed on both sides of the Atlantic. It was a good moment, though he had as yet no idea how he would solve all the problems implicit in direct autobiography compared with the various fictional uses he had been making of autobiography for years.

The trip to Moscow inevitably proved a memorable experience. With Wyn Roberts in charge of the party, they flew out on an Ilyushin jet on Monday 24 May, arriving in the USSR approximately half full of vodka. Gwyn and Roberts found themselves sharing a room in the Ukrainya Hotel; convinced that every light fixture was fitted with a listening device, Gwyn wondered before long whether his false teeth might not have been bugged when he turned his back on them for a moment. Although Wyn Roberts was rather nervous about some aspects of the situation, they found they were well received and kindly looked after. One evening, finding themselves in the company of a group of Russians none of whom could speak

English, Gwyn found a perfect means of communication, breaking into the strains of 'Myfanwy'. The sad and beautiful melody was taken up by his companions; when they had finished, the Russians sang the 'Song of the Volga Boatmen' and a happy, well-lubricated session ensued. No difficulties were raised about their filming street scenes around Moscow, well away from the football stadium, and the cameraman, Bob Edwards, was able to capture many images that pleased him.

It was strange for Gwyn to find himself in Moscow at last, long after the days when Russia was seen both by himself and many of his friends as the Mecca of sensible socialist thinking to where all men should go. Now he looked with some sadness at the great, grey crowds, the broad streets with few cars, the shops more notable for empty shelving than saleable goods, and said to Roberts: 'These people are finding out that when you divide everything equally there's not very much to go round.' He was able to pick up and spend a few of the roubles owing to him from Russian editions of some of his early books, something he had virtually never expected to see. When he came to write his script for the film, he concentrated on the initial strangeness of this vast land and the essential ordinariness of its humanity:

> But this is a city like any other.... The multitudes of people go about their immemorial business of working, walking, talking, standing. They strike one at times as being perhaps a little more dour, a trifle more serious, but that may be due to the boredom and fear that courses through the bloodstream of all great cities. Sanity tends to shrink as size increases.
>
> Always, always we must think of the man, the woman, making their way from bed to work, work to pleasure, beginning to end. Empires may topple, dictators may wither or vanish, the human reality remains.

After the excitement of the Russian visit Gwyn returned to a more local round of broadcasting and occasional journalism which kept him very busy. Because of the developments in the Richard Burton/Elizabeth Taylor saga, there was little progress on the train robbers film, despite the efforts of Sam Wanamaker to keep things moving methodically. Gwyn made some guest appearances in a Rediffusion television programme called *Three After Six* and then began to work with John Mead at TWW on an evening satirical programme of his own scheduled to begin early in 1966. Invited to contribute some Welsh features to Border Television's *Kaleidoscope*, he did a couple of pieces which he greatly enjoyed. The first was on the Davies family of Llandinam: David Davies, the entrepreneur who had built Barry Docks and virtually created Barry Town when frustrated by his rivals for the use of the Cardiff docks; the sisters, who bequeathed their art collection to the National Museum of Wales; and their fabulous home in the house called Gregynog in mid-Wales. The second was about the young Welsh soprano, Gwyneth Jones, whose career was just bursting into grandeur; the subject was very close to Gwyn's heart, and allowed him to take a trip to Craig y Nos, the castle in the Swansea Valley to which Dame Adelina Patti had retired.

November 1965 saw the publication of an American edition of *A Welsh Eye* by the Stephen Greene Press of Vermont. Although urged very warmly by Greene to come to the States and capitalise on the publication, Gwyn could not, he said, find the time: 'I work for the regional television company as a sort of cut-rate Socrates,' he explained, 'and I have a weekly programme that will go on through the winter.' In Britain a book of articles selected from his *Teacher* contributions was published under the title *A Hatful of Humours*. Gwyn agreed to give a TWW colleague an interview about it to help promote some local sales, but he could not bring himself to face a session of public book-signing in Lear's in Cardiff; it was an experience, he said, which terrified him. He might consider doing it if the bookshop would fit him into a curtained alcove from which just his hand clutching a pen would emerge, but he was sure Lear's would not think that practicable.

He was not very well. His health, as he told Nana at Christmas, had been 'most dismally out of whack for some months past'. What he did not yet know was that he was suffering the first consequences of diabetes, the disease which was to wreck his physique and slowly undermine his whole life. Lyn, too, was not in good form. She had in the darkness tripped over a low wall while on her way to commune with her friend next door. 'The wall was taller than she thought,' Gwyn told Nana. 'She broke her arm and was lucky not to do as much for her back.' Anxious about Lyn, and missing her ability to look after him as fully as usual while under the weather herself, Gwyn found the times difficult enough.

10.42 and All That, the new weekly television programme which Gwyn began for TWW in January 1966, was so called because it began at just that time each Thursday evening. This was considered to be late enough in the evening for satire to be unconstrained; it was a live show, parts of it devoted to unscripted interchange with the studio audience when anything might happen. The format devised by the producer, John Mead, was offbeat and inventive, but relied heavily on Gwyn's impromptu performance. So good was his form as he responded to the challenges, so immediate and entertaining his outpourings in response to almost any stimulus, that not once in the season did the programme seem to falter. Gwyn himself wrote and performed in regular scripted sketches, as for instance in a series set in a pub where Ray Smith played the landlord to Gwyn's loquacious and sometimes cantankerous customer. A pretty young singer, Jenny Johnson, and Allan Smethurst, the 'Singing Postman', provided music at intervals, and other actors and comedians made appearances; John Edmunds opened the show by reading some choice news items which Gwyn would comment on. Every week the show built towards the moment when this secretive, private man stepped down among the audience and began to talk with them as if they were his oldest friends, developing an immediate and rewarding rapport. 'It is mainly a vehicle for Mr Thomas's rare ability as a commentator whose words can alternately crush like a steam-roller, cut like a bacon-slicer, or soothe like a charm,' said the *South Wales Echo*.

Although it was rather frightening and tiring to work in so exposed a way, Gwyn did it with a will because in a strange way it made him more alive than at any other time. A young actress playing in some of the sketches was rather in awe of his professionalism but found him genial and supportive. Finding her in make-up and wearing a frilly, low-cut blouse one day, he said: 'Ginny Lewis, with those breasts in that blouse you look like a throbbing doily.' Performance and its trappings gave him a lease of life in which he revelled. The ease he showed was not achieved without a drink or two, however, and for some years he had found himself drinking more and more heavily; it was socially almost unavoidable and professionally almost a necessity; it loosened his tongue, and he enjoyed it. No matter how much he drank, he never seemed the worse for it; it made him even wittier, perhaps, but never aggressive, rude or unpleasant. The trouble was that even as it opened life more easily to him, banishing his reticence and allowing him to forget his sad self-doubts for a while, it was contributing to kill him. Alcohol and diabetes are not good stable-mates.

In April 1966 Wyn Roberts and Colin Voisey took him off for another TWW film, this time to Spain. The trip started badly. Voisey ate something that disagreed with him even before they had left London. 'Trout will out,' Gwyn wrote to Lyn from the Hotel Fenix in Madrid, and he went on to explain that they were unable to start filming because of a lack of equipment:

> Tony and Brian had their cameras impounded at the frontier. The usual old racket. Some sinister official slaps a preposterous bond on them which they can't possibly pay. Then out of the shadows steps a smiling and obliging 'agent'. The sinister official's brother. And they split the take.

The delay exasperated Gwyn so much that he felt even more home-sick than usual. 'I miss you with savage insistence,' he wrote to Lyn, 'I hold my watch to my ear and savour the passage of time which will soon have me back with you.' When the third day arrived and the cameras had still not been released, he wrote: 'When I get back I will have things to tell you about the efficiency of TWW that will blacken the walls of our lovely home (O God, how I am missing every inch of them).... I am behaving with the same calculated, torpid detachment that you have come to know so well since 2 May 1937. I've been hiding in a corner of this vast hotel reading.' Once a good deal of time had been wasted and a large sum of money had eventually changed hands, they were free to start travelling about, filming in Madrid, Cuenca, and Cordoba. They met Dominic Elwes who was so delighted with Gwyn's mesmerising flow of talk that he invited them all down to his castle in the south. 'But if we go,' Gwyn winked at Voisey, 'we'll never escape.' Voisey had never seen Gwyn in better form and was amazed by his knowledge and the enthusiasm and ease with which he imparted it. It was like being constantly in the presence of a university professor of brilliance; the only problem, as far as making a film was concerned, lay in trying to harvest the gems of comment which spilled from him, in finding some means of editing the cornucopia to fit it into the time available. Yet in retrospect he seemed a good listener, too, a sympathetic and encouraging man capable of helping others to find and put to the test their own ability.

All the locations had been chosen by Gwyn in advance, and each proved a rich source of images for the cameras. One of the most memorable scenes they filmed was when they came across a religious procession in a village high up in the mountains behind Cuenca. Some of the more fanatical pilgrims were walking barefoot over broken bottles. What caught Gwyn's eye was an angelic girl of about ten who seemed to float past, borne on the wings of innocence; a moment later he was delighted to see her administer a good cuffing to one of her little boy attendants who had made some small error. A moment not recorded on film was somehow typical of Gwyn's experiences: outside a hotel in Granada he was suddenly surrounded by a party of ladies who tumbled from a coach and were anxious to speak to him – it was a party on tour from Porth, and as the Alhambra Palace gleamed whitely in the background all they wanted to do was share their thoughts about the Rhondda and the folk there they had in common. The film eventually made from the materials collected in Spain was called *The Darker Neighbour* and made a powerful impact when it was shown on television in 1967; transferred later to 35 mm stock it also enjoyed life as a cinema film.

Much of his time as the year went on was devoted to his work on the autobiography. His play *The Alderman* had received appreciative comments when broadcast on the BBC Home Service in January, and some effort in the next few months went to adapting it for stage performance, but the memories and stories that came flooding out when he began *A Few Selected Exits* took pride of place. From the first he had intended that his book should be no ordinary autobiography, no flat chronicle of names and dates and places. His tactic was one of concealment as much as revelation. No one was to be hurt by any of his remarks. A little fictionalisation here, a little compression there, a decent reticence about emotional matters, an avoidance as far as possible of anecdote about people still living who might be offended, these approaches he adopted. Shocked to hear, in August, of the early death of his old friend John Wynne Roberts, he made an exception in his case and wrote a moving page or two about him as he remembered far-off things almost forgotten. He wrote with immense gusto, putting it aside from time to time to attend to more immediate requests, returning to it with pleasure when opportunity presented itself.

In October, at Aberfan, near Merthyr Tydfil, a mountain of coal-spoil turned to slurry and slipped down to engulf the village school and a whole generation of children. Gwyn, who had in his plays *Merlin's Brow* and *The Slip* as well as in *A Point of Order* written about more minor forms of such a disaster, an ever-present danger in the steep-sided valleys of the South Wales coal-field, was, like the rest of the world, appalled and horrified. Being for many the personification of Welshness, he accepted from the BBC an invitation to talk on the radio about the catastrophe. Nothing that he ever did was more solemn, more beautiful, more tragic or more moving. Requests came in such numbers from a public that wanted to hear again the grave, compassionate voice and share the pain and the terrible anger barely hidden in his phrases, that the BBC sought Gwyn's permission to make available a tape recording of the broadcast, the proceeds to be added to the fund set up for the relief of the survivors. An expanded version of the talk was published in the *Teacher*, drawing thanks from many readers who recognised a superb and somehow comforting expression of their own inarticulate thoughts. Gwyn's words were not forgotten, and his wisdom was invoked again for a further broadcast some time later, in an attempt to still some of the sounds of argument and recrimination which shamefully began to arise over distribution of the huge amount of money which had been given to the Aberfan fund.

When the film which they had gone to Russia to make was finished and shown during the autumn, it was another considerable success. At a special showing for members of the Soviet Embassy in London, *The Growing People* was commended for its fairness; the following year it won a prize at the Prague Film Festival, and the team at TWW was cock-a-hoop. Though there was no particular television project immediately ahead for Gwyn, TWW did not hesitate to take up their option to continue his contract; he was clearly one of their treasures. At the BBC in London there were those who thought so too; Alasdair Milne no longer wrote annually asking Gwyn to consider allying himself to his department when the TWW contract finished, but tentative inquiries still came from other sources from time to time.

Throughout the winter Gwyn continued to add to his autobiography and Lyn, although having a poor time of it with bronchitis, worked valiantly to type rapidly growing piles of paper. He did a number of pieces for radio, enjoying his sessions with John Darran but becoming increasingly worried and irritated by the growth of the power and influence of the Welsh-language cohort in the BBC at Cardiff. It would not have troubled him had the Welsh speakers not been so fanatical, as it seemed to him, for their cause, and had they not early singled him out as an enemy because of his proud adherence to the English language. Hurt at the suggestion that an English-speaking Welshman is somehow a lesser breed, a less patriotic animal, an un-Welsh sort of Welshman, he was roused to the defence of his position. The results were dramatic, because there were few who could match his linguistic resources, and if self-defence required that he should attack, that is what he would do in no uncertain terms. What his opponents failed to notice was that there was no lasting malice in him, no matter how wickedly provocative his observations might seem at the time of utterance. He wanted no enemies, but he could not listen patiently to what seemed to him to be nonsense. The consequences were unhappy, for as the notion that the true Welshman speaks primarily in Welsh gained momentum and power, so the Welsh 'establishment' began to lose sight of Gwyn as one of the greatest Welshmen alive.

1967 started well enough when in February the *South Wales Echo* and *Western Mail* Television and Radio Awards ceremony gave *The Growing People* the award for Best Television Production of the year, coupling it with an award to Gwyn as Best Television Performer. A little later the post brought proposals from Maxwell Geismar, an American scholar, that there should be a new edition of *All Things Betray Thee* in the United States. Buoyed up by thoughts of a revival of interest in his novels, which might well be given a boost by the publication of his autobiography, Gwyn completed a draft of *A Few Selected Exits* by the end of May and sent it off with a sense of relief. He was not quite prepared for the reception Harold Harris gave it. He had been laughing a lot, he said, but the book was disorganised and self-indulgent and needed a lot of pruning. Ever ready to accept criticism, Gwyn replied: 'I take your points with a nod of grave approval. If I have an art, obliquity is its essence. I shall probably even go to the grave sideways.' When similar comments were received from Harry Sions at Little, Brown, Gwyn swallowed hard, picked up the bulging manuscript that represented a winter's work and began again, striking out page after page, reorganising and rewriting. 'It will give me intense pleasure to write the book you had in mind in the first place,' he told Sions, not without some irony. It took him six more months before the job was done, and even then he was able to put it from him only by ignoring several appeals from Sions to do just a little more, to put in something more, at least, about Lyn, who barely appeared in the book and then only as a casual reference to 'my wife'. He had never intended the book as a personal document, a key to the essence of Gwyn Thomas, a blow-by-blow account of domestic bliss, and he was not going to start now.

Gwyn's last major undertaking for TWW was a series of lectures to students from Swansea, Bristol and the WEA on literary topics: 'The Criminal in Literature', 'Laughter in Writing', 'Love in Literature' and so on. In each case they were followed by discussions between Gwyn and the members of the audience, and there were some lively encounters. Filmed in the early months of 1968, they were taken over in March by Harlech Television when TWW unexpectedly lost its franchise. The new regime retained the services of many of those who had worked for TWW, and renewed the contract with Gwyn, but something had gone with the departure of Lord Derby and Jack Hylton, whom Gwyn had liked tremendously. In the months which followed the changeover, he tried but failed to adapt to the new order, which didn't really seem to know what to do with Gwyn. Aled Vaughan, who had joined HTV from the BBC, was enthusiastic about a show which tried developing a format foreshadowed in *10.42 and All That*; since Gwyn was nowhere more at home than in a pub, the argument went, why not give him a pub in which to expand on television?

Free House was supposed to be set in a pub called the Bridge; members of the public came in and found Gwyn in session and responded to and enjoyed his impromptu talk; everyone was equipped with plenty to drink at the company's expense, and it was expected that it would be riotously entertaining. Some people found it so, but Gwyn was not impressed by the programme's rationale and could not feel that it was working. 'Professionally my life proceeds through the same tunnel of muted mysteries,' he confessed to Nana. 'These Harlech people seem to be dottier than the people who went before.... I've been involved in a hideous programme called *Free House* in which drunken buffoons air their views, and the air has never been the same.'

He wrote to Vaughan, bitterly deploring what he called 'this inscrutable shambles of a show'. He wanted nothing more to do with it. 'If having to perform as an undistinguished footman among the muttering rabble in that awful bar is genuinely the best thing you can think of for me, I sag with depression and blink with alarm.' It was one of the most downright letters he ever wrote, and the reasons for his anger were complex. His resilience was being sapped by increasingly bad health; he disliked the format of the show, preferring something scripted with elegance and polish; he recognised that Lyn, whose judgement he trusted, was convinced that it was the most risky and ineffective programme he had been involved in; and he was annoyed intensely that scripts which he had submitted to Wynford Vaughan Thomas and Patrick Dromgoole, and which he thought were funny and promising, had struck no spark of interest in them. It was time for the parting of the ways, and when renewal of the contract was due, neither side mentioned it. Free now to return to BBC television as well as radio if they wanted him, he looked round for opportunity.

1968 was busy enough without large television commitments, though quite a few projects were doomed to be more talk than action. A sudden call from the BBC had him racing over to London to talk to Robert Morley about education in front of the cameras for Morley's *One Pair of Eyes*, and there were many calls on him for contributions to magazines and books; when the summer season came there were classes to give and lectures to deliver, conferences and summer schools to attend; he rarely stopped. Once the revisions to the autobiography were completed, Sions and Harris were anxious to get Gwyn started on another book. Gwyn and Lyn had been guests at the great birthday party which Richard Burton gave for Elizabeth Taylor at the Dorchester Hotel in February 1967. After hearing how Burton had seized on Gwyn and led him off to enjoy his company and his humour with his private cronies at the party, so that Lyn did not see her husband for hours on end, Sions became obsessed with the idea that Gwyn should write Burton's biography. Nothing could have been further from Gwyn's mind than to attempt such a task. An idea that did come to possess him, however, took his publishers by surprise: he wanted to write a book on banditry, 'roughly speaking from Spartacus to the train robbers', as Juliet O'Hea, his agent, explained. Sir Robert Lusty at Hutchinson told Harris that he thought they should jump at anything Gwyn suggested, but Sions could not be convinced. When the following year a scholarly study of the bject by a university professor was announced, Gwyn dropped the idea, even though the notebooks he was now keeping were bursting with ideas very different from those that anybody else might have conceived.

Meanwhile, Burton had come into the picture again, this time waxing enthusiastic about making a film of *The Keep*, which had continued to be popular over the years. A television version had done well, showing the potential of the piece, and Gwyn signed contracts with Richard McWhorter, who hoped to direct the film, willingly enough but recognising that it would probably not come to fruition – as, indeed, it unfortunately did not.

During the summer he wrote for Lorraine Davies, a BBC producer who felt strongly that Gwyn's particular idiom was far from exhausted, a radio play called *The Giving Time*, to be broadcast at Christmas. Set in his old favourite time and place of Meadow Prospect, with Teilo Dew and Edwin Pugh and the rest of the gang as alive as ever, it reminded listeners of past pleasures and produced a call for more which Lorraine Davies determined to respond to as soon as possible.

The high point of 1968 for Gwyn was the publication of *A Few Selected Exits* in September. Its reception was as warm as he could have wished. John Betjeman wrote to say that it was a wonderful book, that he could hear Gwyn in every page, and many other old friends declared their admiration for it. It was in many ways a very odd book for an autobiography: imprecise, lacking dates, inventing names (and actions, too, many thought), omitting a great deal; but it was amusing, poetic, touching, typically Gwyn Thomas in its linguistic bravura, and it sold well. Together with the book he had called *A Welsh Eye*, it established him as the most charismatic and idiosyncratic watcher of Wales that could be imagined. His final and most colourful claim to such a role came when in 1969 he made a *One Pair of Eyes* film for BBC television with Gilchrist Calder.

Shot in March and April, the programme, entitled 'It's A Sad But Beautiful Joke', was shown on BBC 2 for the first time in September. Against the background of Rhondda hillsides, collieries and chapels, and Harlech's adult education college, wearing his raincoat and slouch hat, Gwyn spoke the words of his commentary with dramatic inflection, passionate love and black humour. Finishing with his favourite story, that of the mourners who forgot that they had left the coffin under the seat of a pub where they sheltered from the rain, he concluded:

> And I think this is one of the great central dilemmas of the Celtic conscience: it never knows where it really left the body, where it really left the death, where it really left the grief. Because these are the compounds, the elements of a massive joke.
>
> There is laughter. Oh, yes, we hear the laughter all right. But we are never quite sure where it's coming from.

The combination of laughter, pain and poetry in his film made it one of those that stay indelibly in the memory. As the praise and thanks flowed in, he braced himself for an uncertain future. His Welsh eye had not failed him yet, but he was worried. The security of the contract was gone, his health was going and, for the first time, he felt that his inspiration was tiring too. He was only fifty-six, but sometimes he felt more like a hundred. What next?

14

Return and End

Though he did not consciously turn his back on Independent Television after the unhappy *Free House* experience, Gwyn's path led him in 1969 to return to the combination of BBC work and general journalism which had begun his separation from the calling of schoolmaster/novelist in the late 1950s. He had twelve years to live (though as far as he knew it could have been twenty or thirty), years in which it might have been hoped that he would recover his ambition in the field of the novel and, with hard-won maturity and leisure, produce the great, definitive work that had been expected of him. It was not to be. His gradually failing health may have contributed to a conviction that his inspiration was waning; he complained in his notebooks of an increasing sense that he had dried up and was doomed to ride henceforward on a roundabout from which there was no exit. It was not that his ability to produce words at will showed any diminution; on the contrary, he could talk and write as entertainingly as ever, with surges of metaphor and pungently expressed comic perceptions that greatly pleased his audiences.

The trouble was at least in part a product of the many reversals and disappointments he had had to face. Although he rarely expostulated with those who turned his work down, or complained about those who let him down, and although he seemed resilient and unaffected by rejection, he was finding it more difficult to cope with the unpleasant shock of failure when it came. There seemed no shortage of matters about which he still had something to say, but his confidence had been eroded by the combination of ill health and lack of appreciation and he found he was slower to get started on a sizeable venture. He worked on a number of quite large-scale nonfiction projects, like the book on banditry and, after that one lost its viability, others on social ideas of various kinds, but found that publishers were not interested in anything other than reworkings of his former vein. The publication in the United States of *A Few Selected Exits*, in a slightly amplified edition complete with a selection of photographs, was greeted with some warmth in September 1969 but it was his swan-song on the other side of the water except for some magazine articles and stories.

Two more books bearing his name were issued in Britain in the 1970s. The first, enthusiastically promoted by Hutchinson in 1972, was *The Lust Lobby*, a further selection of twenty-nine of his *Punch* stories. It was as fully reviewed and as generously appreciated by the reviewers as any of his previous books had been, and did as well in the shops as a book of short stories could be expected to do. A delightfully funny book, it looked back over a long association with *Punch* that had ended with Bernard Hollowood's resignation as editor in 1968; when William Davis took over, he either did not wish to retain the Gwyn Thomas presence in his pages or failed to realise that Gwyn would not write for him unless he was directly invited to do so. Deeply mindful of his dignity, a matter of ever greater significance to him as his body began to let him down, Gwyn had never asked for a commission in his life, and would no more have taken steps to draw the attention of the new editor to his oversight than he would have walked naked down Piccadilly. So it came about that in a further ten years when he was still capable of writing pieces as comical and provocative as anything that did appear in *Punch*, its pages included nothing by him.

Gwyn's last book to be published in his lifetime was *The Sky of Our Lives*, issued by Hutchinson in 1972. Mysteriously promoted as 'Gwyn Thomas's new book, set once again in the wry communities of deepest Wales', it was new only in that the three novellas which it contained had not been printed between the same covers before. They were 'Simeon' and 'Oscar', from *Where Did I Put My Pity?*, and 'The Dark Philosophers', previously issued as Gwyn's first novel. While it was only proper that these early stories should be in print – containing, as some commentators maintain, the very best writing that Gwyn ever did – it was misleading for the publishers to make no reference to their provenance, and it led several reviewers into an unfortunate error; Maurice Wiggin, for instance, in the *Observer*, ɔmmented: 'Mr Thomas is developing.... He is still one of the most ᴁmusing writers in English, but I feel that his innate concern with the flawed dignity of man, the unrealised and thwarted potential, is going to burst through the constraint of sardonic humour.' This perception that Gwyn Thomas was at bottom a serious writer came twenty-five years too late. *The Sky of Our Lives* was successful enough to go into paperback the following year, the only one of Gwyn's books to do so.

In 1969 Gwyn, though just beginning to fear a lessening of his powers as a serious writer, was quite hopeful about the possibilities of the years to come. He had to work, for very little savings had accumulated from some of the relatively good years he had enjoyed in television, and if he didn't ply his tongue and pen there would be no bread. There were plenty of demands for what he could do, his friends in the BBC being particularly pleased to welcome him back as a free agent. The air was still full of exciting possibilities about films and theatre; one Bill Anderson, for instance, now acquired the rights to *Return and End*, and for several months into 1970 it looked very much as if a production would be mounted, until the undertaking came, as so many times before, to a sudden halt. As late as November 1970 it still looked as though the Richard Burton film of *The Keep* was indeed going to be made when from Tenerife came a cable confirming that Gwyn's new treatment was approved: AM SITTING IN THE SUN BLINDED WITH ADMIRATION FOR YOUR BRILLIANCE AS I READ AND AM LEARNING *KEEP* WE START IN FIVE WEEKS OR SO TROUBLE IS THAT ALL THE PARTS ARE SO BRILLIANT I WANT TO PLAY THEM ALL MYSELF—RICHARD. Although *Punch* didn't seem to want him any more, there were many other papers and magazines on both sides of the Atlantic which did. They would manage, as long as his health held out.

About that, however, there were growing worries. When the Norwich Welsh Society asked him to come and be their guest speaker in their autumn programme, Gwyn declined sadly, explaining: 'My body for the last few years has been most seriously on the blink, and a frowning doctor has put me for an indeterminate period on a regime of stillness and silence.' A little later he told Juliet O'Hea: 'I have been surrounded by a picket fence of doctors, all, I would say, intent upon ushering me betimes into the tomb. I spent some delirious weeks doing a programme for BBC 2 called *One Pair of Eyes* and I came down with a thundering case of diabetic collapse. The biggest thing in sugar since Tate said his first Hullo to Lyle.' As it happened, the diabetes was not in his case as problematical as it might have been, and could probably have been controlled by dietary measures. This was just as well, as he was discovered to be allergic to insulin. Dietary care, however, was a finicky and annoying restriction to one not accustomed to give much concern to what he was eating, and sometimes he even took a kind of pleasure in doing the opposite of what his doctor advised. It was still a year or two before the consequences of this self-neglect began to be really serious.

In August 1969 he was well enough to go with Lyn to Rhuddlan Castle in North Wales for a *son et lumière* review of some aspects of Welsh history in which the castle had been involved. Gwyn had written the script for Stanley Baker, the Houston brothers, Gwen Ffrangcon-Davies and others to revel in, the Pendyrus Male Voice Choir supplied the stirring and moving singing, and the programme was a triumph. There is no record of what Gwyn's thoughts may have been as he sat, the guest of Lord and Lady Longford, in the presence of Prince Charles, but it may be guessed that there was still a sardonic edge to them. A couple of months later he was a guest speaker at the Cheltenham Festival of Literature for the second time, and entertained a distinguished audience with a talk on 'The Novelist as Judge and Joker'. In notes which he supplied for the programme he sketched his theme:

> The writer takes the lumps of life dumped in his lap by the accident of place and the time-bombs of heredity. Everything he says about it is a judgment. Every joke he makes about it is an evasion of judgment. The humorist is the juryman who is utterly perplexed by the process in which he is caught up and spends his time during the trial making funny faces at the witnesses, falling asleep, and generally annoying the judge.

There was no limit to the funny faces that Gwyn, as juryman *honoris causa*, continued to pull during the years that followed. He became a prolific journalist, contributing first many book reviews principally to the *Western Mail* and then, to that newspaper's great good fortune, accepting a post as its resident television critic. Throughout much of the decade Gwyn's grumbling, idiosyncratic, immaculately expressed commentary on the television scene gave much pleasure to the readers of the Welsh national daily newspaper.

It was a highly personal column, sometimes quite revealing about the private life of the writer; it was frequently very funny; and it was as pithy in its comments as could be desired. For instance:

> There are moments in watching television when one feels cut off, stranded on a frozen ledge. You try each of the available switches and each time you run into a blast of arctic desolation. Finally you press the switch for the channel that has not yet been given anything to do, grateful that silence and blankness are still an option while remaining vaguely in loyal touch with the medium.
>
> Such an occasion cropped up one evening last week. On BBC1 there was the Miss World contest. Whatever gland makes a man warm eagerly to these exhibitions of beauty in bulk must, in my case, have been fed to the dogs during the lean years. Loveliness is a thing to be savoured in private and in full, not in flashy fragments before an inflamed and gaping throng.

Or again:

> *Stars on Sunday* has, I am sure, a vast following. It is tuneful and makes so little demand on the mind that the following programme, *Please Sir!*, an epileptic saga of life among a group of Cockney scholars, comes over like a postgraduate seminar.

Congenitally Gwyn was a kindly and appreciative reviewer, of books as well as of television; he once rejected an invitation to review books for an American magazine on the grounds that he was not cut out to be a critic, lacking the essential savagery; but when his ire was stirred by some of television's more vapid offerings his words took on a cutting edge. When he found something to which he could respond with pleasure, he did so with generous warmth and praise, and his general observations showed an essential faith in the possibilities of the medium. When someone came along with programmes such as John Ormond's films in the series *A Land Remembers*, or Kenneth Griffith's *Give Me Liberty or Give Me Death*, about America's break from British rule, or Alex Haley's *Roots*, he was eloquent in his admiration. It never occurred to him to collect and publish his television essays, though they might have proved as attractive a proposition as those of Clive James, the equally witty and idiosyncratic screen-watcher of a later day.

For the American magazine *Travel and Camera* Gwyn wrote a fine piece about Wales in 1971. After that there were occasional articles for the *Guardian*, *Times Educational Supplement*, *Wheeler's Review*, *Listener*, *New Statesman*, *Sunday Telegraph*, *TV Times* and anybody else who thought of asking for a contribution. In an article called 'My Day' for a *Vogue* series in 1972, he at last made up to Lyn for having left her out of his autobiography by ending with a sentence which she treasured: 'I raise the last wine-glass of the day to the sedan chair of miracles that has brought me through the years, the master-spirits of word and music who will never deny me enchantment, and a companionship in life-long marriage that will never surrender its magic, nor my astonishment, daily renewed, that it should ever have come my way.' Looking back became his principal theme, and the decade produced a number of articles full of affectionate recall of a way of life that was gone. For Stewart Williams of Barry, who began to publish a series of very successful picture books of areas of South Wales as they had been fifty or a hundred years before, he wrote glittering prefaces to volumes dealing with old Rhondda, old Pontypridd, old Barry and old Cardiff. As late as the spring of 1980 he wrote for the glossy American magazine *GEO* a long and affecting essay about Wales that distilled and summarised almost all he had ever had to say about his country. Till the end of his life his articles showed the same wit and vitality that had always marked his work, allowing no glimpse of the increasingly painful and frustrating physical life he was now enduring.

Although after 1969 he undertook no more work for HTV, he accepted an offer from Thames Television in 1971 to take part in a prestigious series about the British Museum. 'They are doing a series on the Museum's various departments,' he explained to Nana: 'John Betjeman on the Victorian rooms, Tyrone Guthrie on the Greeks, and I, as sworn friend and confidant of Caractacus and Boadicea, on the Britain which the Romans found and occupied in AD 41.' Having spent a day travelling about choosing the exhibits that best set his mind and tongue tapping, he said, he was all in; he took shelter behind a brass rail and rested his head on it for half an hour. He was dusted twice and labelled once. The series, when transmitted, was extensively discussed in the press, and *Treasures of the British Museum*, an impressive book containing the texts of the programmes and a selection of pictures, bade fair to become the coffee-table book of the year.

His return to occasional work for BBC radio after the end of the HTV contract took the form of appearances on all manner of talk programmes from *Woman's Hour* and *Any Questions?* to *Good Morning Wales* and the BBC World Service. His popularity after a contribution to Jack de Manio's Radio 4 programme in 1971 led to many invitations to return over the next two or three years. Here, as in all his broadcasts, his good humour and bustling, image-studded talk suggested a man in good strength and well adjusted to a comfortable middle life, and indeed for the first half of the 1970s he was able to conceal almost completely the symptoms that might have hinted at his uneasy state of health. Appearances on television, as when he met Michael Parkinson on his show in 1971, showed him to be so vital that those who wanted to hate him for the way he was, as they thought, cheapening the image of Wales and the Welsh by his constant joking at their faults, had no compunction in doing so. Unabashed, he continued to state his views on the idiocies that seemed to go with expressions of nationalism, berating 'paintbrush politics' (obscuring road-signs in English with green paint to make the point that they should have been in Welsh), Welsh licensing laws, language fetishism at the National Eisteddfod, the continuing puritanical influence of the chapel, the fecklessness and unscrupulousness of local government, the criminality of extremists who sought to make their point by house-burning, and all other such targets, without a shadow of regret that by such tactics he was distancing himself further and further from the position of elder statesman in the Welsh cultural community that should rightfully have been his. He remained what he had always been, an idealistic internationalist to whom excesses of petty nationalism were an offence against humanity, and he said as much in terms which gave no quarter to those who thought differently.

In response to the persuasive overtures of Lorraine Davies he wrote two more radio plays. *He Knows, He Knows*, performed in 1972, developed an idea which Gwyn had first explored in a *Punch* story, about the mania for quiz games in the media and consequently in the pubs and clubs. His lead character, one of the polymathic know-alls who cannot help imposing his knowledge and skill at answering questions on all around, is eventually turned on by his victims. *The Worriers*, broadcast in 1974, he adapted from a play intended for the stage; a sad-comic tale of a sheep-farmer beset by worries, it ranged over many of the ideas which Gwyn's writings had exploited over the years, giving his characters an opportunity to recreate the sardonic, nostalgic atmosphere which was Gwyn's trademark.

BBC television also sought again to make use of Gwyn's gifts as a dramatist. A teleplay screened in 1973 called *Up and Under*, about the pressures on a brilliant young rugby player not at all unlike Barry John, won the praises of Benny Green, who declared himself amazed that an artist of Thomas's calibre had been so neglected and called for more of his 'wicked and derisive humour'. Two years later another play for television, *The Ghost of Adelphi Terrace*, was roundly admired; a conversation piece between Bernard Shaw and James Barrie, with the ghost of Barrie's adored mother hanging over the proceedings, it was, as Nancy Banks-Smith pointed out, 'a play about a Scotsman and an Irishman written by a Welshman', and as such glittered with Celtic word-wizardry. But the television play on which Gwyn worked hardest and with the greatest personal involvement was doomed never to be performed. Commissioned by John Hefin, it was to explore the life of Aneurin Bevan, not in the fictional way which had been adopted in *Return and End* but in a more documentary style.

In accepting the commission Gwyn pointed out that a straight-forward documentary based on painstaking research was simply not his line of country; his imagination was bound to interpret events and present them in ways quite different from the way someone like Elaine Morgan, for instance, might try faithfully to offer a narrative of the life of Lloyd George. He was urged to proceed nevertheless, and did so, creating a script in which Bevan takes an American historian who wants to write about him and his times on a tour of the places that have been significant to him. Imaginative and poetic, it was a prolonged discussion piece in which Gwyn's projection of Bevan, standing against various backgrounds, reflected on his adventures in the political life in language which any listener would immediately identify as that of Gwyn Thomas. A haunting, penetrating and poetic script, it was not what was wanted at all, and since it was received the BBC in Cardiff have been unable to think of anything to do but sit on it. Fascinated during much of his life by the political game and Bevan's role in it, Gwyn never had much luck in trying to make it the subject of his art.

During the early 1970s there was much talk in Wales about establishing a National Theatre, a campaign in which the Welsh Arts

Council began to take an interest and play a benevolent role. As part of this movement, invitations were extended to Gwyn to resume his hat as a premier Welsh playwright. A letter from an actor called Ronnie Radd urged him to seek a new production for *Loud Organs*, only this time without the music which had been a major cause of its failure in 1962. It was a magnificent *play*, Radd insisted, which the actors had loved but which the public had not appreciated because the music got in the way. Gwyn was sympathetic to this view, but could not find a producer willing to take it up. When he mentioned his play *Sap*, however, to Michael Geliot, the director of the Welsh Drama Company, he found that he had touched a fuse. Refurbished, and provided with a completely different selection of First World War songs and hymns from that with which Gwyn had furnished Gerry Raffles back in 1962, *Sap* was mounted in Cardiff to considerable acclaim in November 1974. Gwyn's old pupil, Keith Baxter, was in the cast and Graham Jones wrote in the *Guardian* that it was 'an absolutely superb production with acting from an all-Welsh cast, the like of which for excellence I have not seen in Cardiff before.' Comparisons with *Oh! What A Lovely War* were inevitably made, but though Gwyn's approach to similar themes and his incomparable flow of language ensured that they were not odious, it may be supposed that perception of the idea's true originality was necessarily lacking. At any rate, it did not transfer to London, although hopes for it briefly ran high.

Persuaded to try again, Gwyn returned to his exploration of the theme of Welshness begun in *The Keep* with a play called *The Breakers*, produced at Cardiff's Sherman Theatre in November 1977. In three acts, set successively in 1776, 1876 and 1976, the history of a Welsh family provides the theme as, dissatisfied with opportunity in Wales, a generation emigrates to America, only for a later generation to wish to come home and rediscover its roots. For a raft of reasons, some of which probably were to do with the play itself, rather too wordy and lacking in action as it was perceived to be, the production was a disaster. The actors did not seem to have had sufficient time to master an intricate script in which each of them had to play three roles, one for each period, and complaints about such elementary matters as fluffing lines and entrances do a production little good. There had been more drama behind the scene than on it, and just a day before the first curtain was due to rise the most celebrated actor in the cast, Ray Smith, caused a sensation by walking out in a passion of annoyance and frustration. When it looked as if there would be no world premiere for his play after all, Gwyn just shrugged and said: 'If the play is wrecked, we'll just have to report it to Trinity House.' Smith, who adored Gwyn and would not willingly have harmed his enterprise, returned to the cast for the first night to go ahead, but he proved to be right in his assertion that the production had been skimped. Despite a magnificently appreciative review from Bernard Levin, who said that if he were the director of the National Theatre he would immediately tip all their present Austrian and Venetian rubbish into the Thames and import this product of the Marches, the play foundered.

Partly as a result of his dramatic work, Gwyn was formally recognised by the Welsh Arts Council in 1976 and granted their Honour Award. Since this included a pleasant ceremony and a cheque for £1000, he was very glad of it. If it ever occurred to him that he was, among prominent Welshmen of his generation, signally without such acknowledgement, he never made any comment about it; a modest man, whose dignity mattered more to him than any trumpery award, he looked with some pleasure at what had been given him but expected nothing more. In an alcove in his house Lyn proudly kept a number of trophies: the weighty statuette of the *Evening Standard* Drama Award for *The Keep*; the plaques given by the *Western Mail* and *South Wales Echo* for his television work; and a shield labelled RHONDDA RECOGNITION AWARD, presented to him by a private group of citizens from his native valley to compensate for the failure of any public body to do as much. If he knew that there were those who on his behalf asked in some bewilderment where were the honorary doctorates, where was the CBE, it did not seem to be a matter of any moment to him.

Although by this stage of the 1970s Gwyn was feeling generally so ill that he hated to go out at all, he allowed himself to be persuaded to write another play. This he did by adapting *The Alderman*, his radio play of 1966, just as its then producer, Herbert Davies, had suggested. Working now with Gareth Jones, whom he allowed to rewrite passages and streamline the action, he produced a script for Theatr yr Ymylon called *Testimonials*, which was competently and successfully produced at the Sherman Theatre in January 1979. A very funny play about moral and political corruption in the valleys of South Wales, it was not appreciated equally by everyone who saw it, despite the fact that, as Jon Holliday pointed out in the *South Wales Echo*, it hardly rated as satire because the author had insufficient malice in him, had too much compassion for all his creations. Gwyn was too ill to go to see the play, and he wrote no more.

The 1970s was a curious decade for Gwyn, partly because of the effort it took him to maintain the profound differences between the image he allowed the public to have of him and the private hell into which he was slowly descending. On radio and on television he continued to seem as funny, vital and cheerful as he had always done. In interview with Joan Bakewell for an HTV programme in 1974, as with Denis Mitchell for a *Private Lives* film for ITV in 1975 and on *Kane at Christmas* for BBC. later that year, he was wonderfully entertaining. In his company Harry Secombe and Cliff Morgan could not contain their laughter at his sallies. Yet at about the same time he was telling Teifion Phillips: 'I hobble along on dwindling reserves of fitness, caught in as stout a web of disquietudes as a diligent neurotic can devise' and when approached to address the Electricity Boards' Conference at Colwyn Bay in 1975 he had to excuse himself: 'Since my illness my outside limit in the way of travel and public utterance has been a quick mutter on the porch.'

In talks with Vincent Kane and others, such as Frank Delaney who came to interview him for BBC radio's *Bookshelf* programme in 1979, he still showed a tremendous appetite for talk, for funny reminiscences, for philosophical reflection expressed in moving, comic and provocative terms. Those who watched carefully might have noticed that his hands trembled a great deal, that he was never seen in motion but always ensconced in a chair, that his complexion was pale; but his gestures were so full, his bushy eyebrows were so expressive, his voice was so plangent and vital, that it was easy to overlook the other signals. Delaney perceived him as a wounded lion and declared that he was adding him to his private pantheon of Welsh gods, such was the power that still emanated from the man.

Successful though he was in concealing a great deal of his pain from the world at large, and even to some extent from his wife, he could not have controlled it as he did without some safety valve, some means of blowing it out of his system. The outlet he found was in the notebooks which he had begun to keep again with an obsessive determination in 1963. While it is not possible to establish exactly why he started to write so compulsively and extensively into his 'Ideal' series 4444/8 and 4444/9 hardback notebooks at this time, one may hazard a guess from their contents that one of the early impulses was a need to supplement a memory that had been almost infallible but that was beginning to become overcrowded.

At first he recorded mainly items from his reading that had amused or impressed him; from a book that had truly riveted his attention he sometimes wrote as much as ten or fifteen pages of quotations. Later he was evidently writing down from memory considerable swathes of poetry, from Tennyson and Wordsworth to A.E. Housman and Edna St Vincent Millay, as if he was afraid that without some such revision the impression might fade from his mind, the mental recording be somehow lost. Sometimes the notebooks change from commonplace book to trial ground: aphorisms of Gwyn's own creation stand next to epigrammatic quotations from many sources, or ideas for stories are noted and partially developed; notes are made of conversations overheard in pubs and stories told by characters he has met.

The habit continued for fourteen years, until the last of forty-five volumes petered out on page 28 in 1977. The neat, immaculate handwriting of the early volumes gradually became a trembling, spidery scrawl as his hand lost its strength, as his legs had done. As the quality of the handwriting deteriorated, so to some extent did the intellectual level of the notes. As the 1960s swung on, although he still read with passionate attention new books of historical and social concerns, he noted increasingly stories that intrigued him in more sensational sources such as the *News of the World* and with greater frequency he jotted down personal memories that had evidently sprung upon him out of the blue. Entries began to appear that were brief, sometimes mysterious, statements, many of them about his appalled perception that death lay ahead and that gradual disintegration of the body was the path towards it. As his physical ability to take pleasure in sex deteriorated, his mental awareness of it suddenly blossomed. Whereas in public life he had generally eschewed an interest in the sexual side of life, or treated it at most with a typical obliquity, and whereas in some published articles at this very time he wryly decried the whole business as part of the absurd joke in which mankind was trapped, in the pages of his notebooks he let out the agony in his skull by writing fantasies of sexual behaviour in circumstances sometimes highly farcical, sometimes bleak and sinister, mostly stimulated by the outpourings of someone to whom he had lent an attentive ear in a pub or by a provocatively expressed story in the gutter press. What emerges from those millions of words more than anything is a picture of a man who has, like Mr Kurtz, seen a vision of the horror, but who has somehow survived by being able to summon up a smile, even to laugh in its face, the picture of a man sorely beset but of great fortitude.

Rarely or never did he permit himself moments of such self-exposure in public, but strove against all the odds to preserve his dignity and appear as whole and hearty as he would have liked to be. In a letter of 1975 he confessed to a friend that he had 'spent some months in the cellar of a grim malaise' from which he was only then making a faltering exit; it was one of the few serious references to his physical condition that escaped him. At a party a year or two later, the degree of immobility in his legs had become such that he had to be supported up the stairs to the bathroom by Gwyn Jones, elected to the honour as the strongest man present; on the painful way back down the stairs, Gwyn had to ask for a moment's respite. Just that once, as Gwyn Jones remembered, there was no joke on his friend's lips, just a low-voiced sentence that stayed long in his mind: 'Oh God, Gwyn; who ever would have thought that it would come to this?'

Still, life in Peterston had its pleasures. The Sportsman's Rest was a sort of second home in which there was no shortage of the kind of people with whom Gwyn liked to be, chatty characters, bawdy storytellers, worldly-wise observers of the scene from farmers to garage mechanics, from teachers to his colleagues in broadcasting. There, as in innumerable other such locations that he had cherished at one time or another, he loved to sit and listen as well as talk, committing to memory a thousand phrases and unlikely tales, relishing the company of non-literary people, many of them with experiences of a world unlike his own of which he never tired of hearing.

In Wyndham Park there lived at various times men with whom he was able to be on terms of some friendship though little real intimacy: Gerry Monte, a frequent broadcaster who admired Gwyn enormously, and who loved the curiously shy charm Gwyn showed towards his children; Tom Davies, an *Observer* correspondent, who in a profile of Gwyn told a story about how he had once tried to enliven a party at his house by importing a couple of strippers, only to see Gwyn watch the performance with weariness before leaving with a muttered comment about the village having enough trouble already with the leaves falling down every autumn; and David Cole, of the Thomson organisation which owned the local newspapers and who recognised how much they owed to Gwyn's contributions over the years. There were other faithful callers, friends made in the worlds of literature and broadcasting, including Glyn Jones, John Ormond, Vincent Kane, Wynford Jones and others, and occasional visitors from England and America to help raise his spirits. Les Robinson and his wife Edna were often there, and from the younger generation there were their son Jeffrey, by then a teacher, who acted almost as an adopted son to the childless couple; Ian Michael, a former pupil of Walter down in Neath, by then a university teacher with a warm affection for Gwyn and a high regard for his achievement, and working on a 'Writers of Wales' monograph about him; and Dai Smith, one of Gwyn's former pupils from Barry, by then making his name as a social historian and keenly interested in making known Gwyn's contribution to the culture of South Wales. Visits from surviving members of Gwyn's family were less frequent. Irene and Eddie came occasionally, but between Gwyn and his brother Walt there had fallen a silence that appeared set to endure, until at last in 1980, hearing that all was not well at Peterston, Nest and Walt made the journey from Neath and did what they could to help. The journey to Wells nowadays seemed a very long one and was seldom made.

When in 1979 Gwyn gave the annual Gwyn Jones lecture he chose as the key image to illuminate his theme 'the subsidence factor', contrasting the stability of the land under the homes of dukes with the eternal threat of slip and movement in the exploited ground on which stood the homes of the workers. Many times in the past he had made audiences laugh happily at stories of victims of subsidence, when tenors disappeared into the cellarage halfway through an aria and so on. This time the point was more serious:

> We applaud the dukes. They pulled off a miracle of lavishly subsidised placidity and achieved a magnificence of style that made the average children's pantomime look drab. But nature demands a balance. If the ducal phenomenon in its glorious phase was freakish, let us concede that

217

alongside it spawned phenomena every bit as outrageous and incredible. I lived in one of them and I look forward one day to a quiet talk with the Duke of Devonshire about Chatsworth, and I will talk about the lower Rhondda, and if we will both admit to having been touched in various ways by a quite bewitching unreality, I think the cause of social wisdom will have been well served.

The argument was powerfully expressed, the vehicle entertaining and typical of Gwyn's mode of expression; but his delivery lacked the fire and edge associated with him. In the minds of more than one observer, including Gwyn Jones in whose honour the lecture was being given, the image remained of Gwyn moving slowly and awkwardly to the rostrum, where he spoke with less than his accustomed panache. The evidence of a sad decline was irrefutable.

In the spring of 1981, John Ormond came to Peterston to record a conversation with Gwyn, intending it to be the first in a series of six talks on and around subjects that interested him. A couple of years earlier Gwyn had filmed contributions to Ormond's television series, *The Colliers' Crusade*, about the Welsh miners' experience in the Spanish Civil War. His eloquence then had been such that Ormond had no doubt that a new series of freewheeling conversations, after the fashion of those that Gwyn had done with Vincent Kane half a dozen years earlier, would be highly entertaining. He found Gwyn as ever ready to talk, and as he let his recorder run the flow and coherence of his words impressed him greatly. Without a note Gwyn spoke for half an hour as if he were reviewing his whole life, as if he were offering the world a valediction, Ormond felt; for despite his good form, there was a something in his voice that, with hindsight, Ormond recognised as a failing of vitality. No further recordings were made, for Gwyn's sufferings intensified until a few weeks later he collapsed.

He was taken into the University Hospital at the Heath in Cardiff. Doctors explained to Lyn that his debility was due to a combination of circumstances related to his diabetic condition; the difficulty he had had in getting around for some years since his legs lost their mobility, the general constitutional weakness and the other symptoms, such as the failing eyesight that had worried Gwyn greatly, were products of a neuropathy which had been exacerbated by a nephropathy; there had been a great strain on Gwyn's heart and a near breakdown of the renal system; treatment would take some time. Gwyn, who all his life had hated hospitals and doctors and illness, who had tried to defy the physical deterioration that affected him by pretending it wasn't there, lay patiently in his bed, weak as a kitten and almost blind, wondering when they would let him go home.

Visitors found him relatively feeble when they compared him with the fizzing bomb of yesterday but thought that a period in bed would sort everything out. He smiled and joked a good deal, and the nurses thought him wonderful. When Dr Tom Hays brought round his group of medical students to look at Gwyn he said, 'Here you see a man who hates doctors' and Gwyn said the things against their kind they hoped to hear. Gwyn Jones called to sort out a last point or two about an article Gwyn had done for *Fountains of Praise*, a book about the Cardiff University College, and the problems were successfully resolved. Glyn Jones was an anxious visitor. 'Are you able to sleep, Gwyn?' he asked, to be answered: 'Why, yes, they're forever giving me a most marvellous array of pills, every colour you can think of – "opium all-sorts" I think they call them.' In his own room, looked after by a most attentive and caring staff, he seemed to be in a stable condition, and Lyn looked forward to bringing him home to Peterston.

While she was with Gwyn on the evening of 12 April 1981, her spirits were raised when Gwyn allowed himself to be persuaded to take some soup and a little bread and butter. It was the first time he had eaten solid food for several days. The sister congratulated her on her efforts: 'Well now,' she said, 'we shall keep our fingers crossed.' But Gwyn, when the nurses were gone and the jokes were done, put out his hand for hers and said: 'Oh dear, Lyn. I'm not much use to you like this, am I, girl?'

When she left him that evening, Lyn turned at the door to say goodnight, see you tomorrow. For the briefest moment a strange feeling made her tremble; it was as if the head she saw on his pillow was that of the young Gwyn she had met and lost her heart to in Cymmer forty-four years before, as if not a moment had passed since that May day in 1937. The perception passed quicker than thought, and she walked away in the mood of hope that had given her courage throughout the evening.

On their midnight rounds the nurses found all well with Gwyn, but when a check was made at four o'clock in the morning of 13

April they found that he had slipped soundlessly away in the small hours. In another three months he would have been sixty-eight. Death had claimed him far too soon.

After the cremation, a farewell ceremony was held by his friends among a stand of trees a stone's throw from the Brynffynon Arms in Llanwonno, the place he had written about in the last words of his autobiography: 'I was home, at my earth's warm centre. The scared monkey was back in the branches of his best-loved tree. I've never had any truly passionate wish to be elsewhere.' Fifty yards away, Guto Nyth Brân slept on in his tumbled grave as Gwyn's ashes were scattered on the grassy hillside.

Gwyn's early death came as a shock to very many who had loved and admired his work, and as 1981 wore on there were numerous tributes to him both in Wales and in England. His obituarist in *The Times*, recalling his career as 'novelist, dramatist, broadcaster and raconteur', said that 'more than any other writer of the twentieth century, Gwyn Thomas captured the significance of the majority of Welsh experience'. In the *Guardian* Norman Shrapnel appreciated 'his hilarious, gab-gifted novels of proletarian life' and called him 'one of the funniest writers the Welsh have ever produced', whose work had been 'part of the wind of change that blew from the regions through the stuffy house of English fiction in the late forties and fifties'. Many felt a sense of loss who did not even know that he had been, before his transformation into a television presenter and critic, the author of some of the most blackly and quirkily comical novels of the immediate postwar period. At intervals during the year or so after his death his delightful broadcasting personality was recalled in programmes on radio and television, and a successful theatrical performance of extracts from his writings known and unknown reminded devotees of the extent of their loss, but as a serious writer he seemed fated to remain in the limbo into which he had effectively drifted almost two decades before.

Some adherents guarded his name and reputation, however, with vigour and conviction that the world would one day rediscover the treasure it had laid aside. The National Library of Wales at Aberystwyth was pleased to acquire the great bulk of his private papers and manuscripts, and the considerable job of sorting and cataloguing the mass of diverse material is still continuing. The University College at Swansea accepted several hundred of his books and housed them with papers and memorabilia in a room called the Gwyn Thomas Room in the South Wales Miners' Library now at Hendrefoilan. Startled to find that none of his books was in print, a number of publishers began cautiously to repair the omission. At the time of writing, however, Gwyn Thomas is still effectively a forgotten force.

It is inconceivable that he will remain relegated to the shadows. Though in his lifetime he made, because of his freely spoken opinions on the Welsh language question and related matters, some keen enemies among the more humourless and fanatical of his countrymen, it seems inevitable that both literary critics and general readers will in time find again the dark poetry and the comic magic of his serious writing. When the television antics and the radio and newspaper journalism are faded memories, when the essays in theatre and even those pioneering radio plays are deemed to have lost all vitality, the focus will return to that small handful of novels and that clutch of short stories in which he made heard a distinct, memorable and outraged voice. It was a voice from the valleys, from a world limited in time and space, but what it said for and about its world was true in its own way about most worlds, and in his relentless and idiosyncratic examination of the ways and manners of the men and women of his imagined Rhondda, Gwyn Thomas portrayed with fiendish exactitude and with a comic sadness a world we may all recognise and which may give us endless pleasure.

Notes on Sources

The principal sources of information for this biography are Gwyn Thomas's books; papers (manuscripts, typescripts, letters, contract notes, notebooks, cuttings, memorabilia) in the possession of Mrs Lyn Thomas; letters, typescripts and notebooks in the possession of Mrs W.D. Thomas; some thirty boxes of papers (manuscripts, typescripts, letters, notebooks, cuttings) held by the National Library of Wales; radio scripts held in the BBC Play Library at Broadcasting House; correspondence materials in the BBC Written Archives Centre at Caversham; television scripts and correspondence held in the HTV Archive at Cardiff; papers (letters, memorabilia) held in the Gwyn Thomas Room at the South Wales Miners' Library; a few letters held by the Harry Ransom Humanities Research Center, University of Texas at Austin; papers (typescripts, letters, cuttings, memorabilia) in the possession of Professor Ian Michael; letters in the possession of Mrs Nest Thomas, Professor Dai Smith and Dr Glyn Jones; and the personal reminiscences of those who knew Gwyn Thomas and to whom I am grateful for talking or writing to me, sometimes at considerable length.

In order to keep this listing as brief as possible, it provides information only about those quotations whose source is not apparent in the text.

1 A HOUSE FULL OF CHILDREN

1 'A View of the Valley', *New Statesman*, 24.2.61, p 301
2 'It's a Sad but Beautiful Joke', BBC2 TV, 6.9.69
3 'Private Lives', talking with Denis Mitchell, Granada TV, 1975
4 'Llef' in 'Out of the Air', *Listener*, 13.3.75, p 338
5 'Arrayed Like One of These', in *Selected Short Stories*, p 18

Notes on Sources

2 COUNTY SCHOOLBOY

1 'One of the Memorable', *Teacher*, 15.5.64, p 20
2 *A Hatful of Humours*, p 9
3 *Ibid*
4 *A Few Selected Exits* (cited from this point as *Exits*), p 85
5 'Not Even Then', in *Gazooka*, p 62
6 'Shed Costumes', in 'Out of the Air', *Listener*, 1.8.74, p 144
7 'The Parkinson Show', BBC1 TV, 1971

3 GWYN THE OBSCURE — A WELSHMAN AT OXFORD

1 Letter on file at St Edmund Hall, Oxford
2 'The Appeal', *Punch*, 5.6.68
3 'Kane at Christmas', BBC Wales TV, 1977
4 'The Colliers' Crusade', Part 1, BBC Wales TV, 1981
5 Letter on file at St Edmund Hall, Oxford
6 *Ibid*
7 *Ibid*
8 Letter to Mrs Peggy Counsell, in possession of Mrs W.D. Thomas

4 FIRST DEATH

1 *Exits*, p 102
2 See Gwyn's account in *Exits*, pp 89–95
3 Letter on file at St Edmund Hall, Oxford
4 *Exits*, p 112
5 *Ibid*, p 114

5 A NOT SO MERRY MERRY-GO-ROUND

1 *Exits*, p 115
2 'Walking Away from the Impotent Halls', *Punch*, 13.9.67
3 *Exits*, p 113
4 In a notebook in possession of Mrs W.D. Thomas
5 'Private Lives', *op cit*
6 *Ibid*
7 *Ibid*

6 A WEIRD TRAFFIC

1 'Rulers of the Town', in *Ingot*, Dec 1959, p 28
2 *Bury Times*, 22.2.40
3 *The Demetian*, 1963

Notes on Sources

7 BURSTING ONTO THE SCENE

1 'A Fresh Breeze across the Sea', *New York Herald Tribune Weekly Book Review*, 11.5.47
2 'A Work of Genius', *Daily Worker*, 28.12.47
3 Notebook in possession of Mrs W.D. Thomas

9 LURE OF THE AIR WAVES

1 Keith Newman in *Sydney Morning Herald*, 17.11.51
2 'D.H.' in *South Wales Evening Post*, 30.6.51
3 Letter in possession of Mrs Nansi Roberts
4 'Forenoon', script in BBC Play Library, Broadcasting House, London

10 RECRUIT TO MR PUNCH

1 'I Want To Be Saved from the Motor Car', *TV Times*, 24.10.63
2 From a letter from Desmond Watkins to MP, 29.10.86
3 'You Can't Help Laughing', in *Books and Bookmen*, Feb 1956
4 'Amis and Thomas', in *Saturday Night* (Canada), 28.4.56

11 INVITATION TO THE THEATRE

1 Quoted in advertisement by Macmillan (NY), cutting in possession of Mrs Lyn Thomas
2 *Exits*, pp 152–5

Selected Bibliography

Gwyn Thomas was a prolific writer of short pieces, so the following list is necessarily selective. It aims to include everything published by Gwyn Thomas in book form, a selection of stories and articles of particular interest but never reprinted in book form, a list of the more interesting of his otherwise unpublished radio and television plays, and a listing of some of his unpublished work. Part 2 lists briefly some of the writings about Gwyn Thomas and his work which may be found of interest, though of such material there is surprisingly little. The fullest existing bibliography of Gwyn Thomas is that appended to *Gwyn Thomas* by Ian Michael in the 'Writers of Wales' series published by the University of Wales Press, and I have used that listing as a starting point for the following.

PART 1

A: BOOKS BY GWYN THOMAS IN ORDER OF PUBLICATION

1946 *The Dark Philosophers* (short novel) in *Triad One*, edited by Jack Aistrop, London: Dennis Dobson Ltd, pp 81–193; published separately in USA as a novel, Boston, Mass: Little, Brown & Co, 1947; reprinted in *The Sky of our Lives*, London: Hutchinson, 1972 and Boston, Mass: Little Brown & Co, 1972

1946 *Where Did I Put My Pity? (Folktales from the Modern Welsh)*, (short stories) London: Progress Publishing Co. (contains 'Oscar', 'Simeon', 'The Couch, My Friend, Is Cold', 'Dust in the Lonely Wind', 'A Spoonful of Grief to Taste' and 'Myself My Desert')

1947 *The Alone to the Alone* (novel) London and Brussels: Nicholson & Watson; published in USA as *Venus and the Voters*, Boston, Mass: Little, Brown & Co, 1948

1949 *All Things Betray Thee* (novel) London: Michael Joseph; published in USA as *Leaves in the Wind*, Boston, Mass: Little, Brown & Co, 1949; reprinted in USA with an Introduction by Maxwell Geismar, New York: Monthly Review Press, 1968; reprinted with an Introduction by Raymond Williams, London: Lawrence & Wishart, 1986

Selected Bibliography

1951 *The World Cannot Hear You (A Comedy of Ancient Desires)* (novel) London: Victor Gollancz; Boston, Mass: Little, Brown & Co, 1952; reprinted Bath: Portway Press for the Library Association, 1968

1952 *Now Lead Us Home* (novel) London: Victor Gollancz; reprinted Bath: Portway Press for the Library Association, 1968

1953 *A Frost On My Folic* (novel) London: Victor Gollancz

1954 *The Stranger at My Side* (novel) London: Victor Gollancz

1956 *A Point of Order* (novel) London: Victor Gollancz

1957 *Gazooka and Other Stories* (short stories) London: Victor Gollancz

1958 *The Love Man* (novel) London: Victor Gollancz; published in USA as *A Wolf at Dusk*, New York: Macmillan, 1959

1960 *Ring Delirium 123* (short stories) London: Victor Gollancz

1962 *The Keep* (play; acting edition) London: Samuel French

1964 *A Welsh Eye* (essays, stories, etc, with drawings by John Dd Evans) London: Hutchinson; Brattleboro, Vermont: Stephen Greene Press, 1965; reprinted London: Hutchinson, 1984

1965 *A Hatful of Humours* (essays reprinted from the *Teacher*) London: Schoolmaster Publishing Co

1968 *A Few Selected Exits* (autobiography) London: Hutchinson; published in USA in slightly expanded version with photographs and with sub-title: *An Autobiography of Sorts*, Boston, Mass. and Toronto: Little, Brown & Co; reprinted Bridgend: Poetry Wales Press, 1986

1971 *The Lust Lobby* (short stories) London: Hutchinson

1972 *The Sky of our Lives* (three novellas reprinted: *The Dark Philosophers*, and 'Oscar' and 'Simeon' from *Where Did I Put My Pity?*) London: Hutchinson; Boston, Mass: Little, Brown & Co; reprinted London: Quartet Books, 1973

1979 *The Subsidence Factor* (The Annual Gwyn Jones Lecture, delivered 27 April), Cardiff: University College Press

1984 *Selected Short Stories*, Bridgend: Poetry Wales Press

1985 *High On Hope*, Selections from G T's writings for the *Western Mail* edited by Jeffrey Robinson and Brian McCann, Cowbridge: Brown & Sons

1986 *Sorrow For Thy Sons* (novel written c. 1936, edited and with an Introduction by Dai Smith) London: Lawrence & Wishart

The following list of translations of books by Gwyn Thomas into foreign languages may be of interest:

1948 *Pastor Emmanuel (The Dark Philosophers)* in Norwegian (Tiden, Oslo)

1951 *Die Liebe des Reverend Emanuel (The Dark Philosophers)* in German (Gutenberg, Zurich)

1954 *The World Cannot Hear You* in Italian (Giulio Einaudi, Milan)

1955 *All Things Betray Thee* in Italian (Feltrinelli, Milan)

1956 *To-Tul Ti-E Potrinnic (All Things Betray Thee)* in Romanian (EPLU, Bucharest)

1957 *Liscie Na Wietrze (All Things Betray Thee)* in Polish (Wydawniczy, Warsaw)

1958 *Bezhvestia Filosofi (The Dark Philosophers)* in Russian (Moscow)

1959 *Osi Vagyak Komediaja (The World Cannot Hear You)* in Hungarian (Europa, Budapest)
  Vesichke Te Izhmenye (All Things Betray Thee) in Russian (Paul List, Leipzig)

1960 *L'Uomo dell'Amore (The Love Man)* in Italian (Feltrinelli, Milan)

Selected Bibliography

1961 *The Alone to the Alone* in Italian (Feltrinelli, Milan)
 Ring Delirium 123 in German (Fretz und Wasmuth, Zurich)
 Das Nest (The Keep) in German (GMBH, Hamburg)
1962 *The Keep* in Swedish and Norwegian (Folmer Hansen, Oslo)
 The Keep in Dutch (IBA, Antwerp)

B: UNCOLLECTED ESSAYS, STORIES AND PLAYS BY GWYN THOMAS IN VARIOUS BOOKS

1946 'The Hands of Chris', short story in *Saturday Saga and Other Stories*, London: Progress Publishing Co
1947 'The Limp in My Longing', short story in *Modern Reading*, Vol 15, edited by Reginald Moore, London: Phoenix House
1955 'Of All the Saints', short story in *The Pick of Punch*, London: Chatto & Windus
1956 'Thy Need', in *Welsh Short Stories*, selected by Gwyn Jones, London: Oxford University Press
1959 'Education', essay in *The New Book of Snobs*, by various hands, London: Museum Press
1960 'Grace and Gravy', autobiographical essay in *The Pick of Punch*, London: Chatto & Windus
1961 *The Keep*, (play) in *Plays of the Year*, Vol 24, edited by J.C. Trewin, London: Paul Elek
 'Brotherly Love' and 'Ripe I Cry', short stories in *The Pick of Punch*, London: Chatto & Windus
1962 'The Seeding Twenties', autobiographical essay in *Pick of Today's Short Stories*, Vol 13, edited by John Pudney, London: Putnam
 'A Quiet Place', essay in *The Complete Imbiber*, Vol 5, edited by Cyril Ray, London: Vista Books
 'I Dreamt that I Dwelt' and 'Beau', short stories in *The Pick of Punch*, London: Chatto & Windus
1963 *Jackie the Jumper* (play) in *Plays of the Year*, Vol 26, edited by J.C. Trewin, London: Paul Elek
1965 *The Loot* (one-act play for sixthformers) in *Eight Plays*, Vol 2, edited by Malcolm Stuart Fellows, London: Cassell
1969 'Some Inns in Wales', essay in *Pub: A Celebration*, edited by Angus McGill, London: Longmans
1971 Autobiographical Essay, in *Artists in Wales*, edited by Meic Stephens, Llandysul: Gwasg Gomer
 'The Romano-British', essay in *Treasures of the British Museum*, introduced by Sir John Wolfenden, London: Collins
1974 'Valley Pilgrims to the Valley Shrine', introductory essay in *The Cardiff Book*, Vol 2, Barry: Stewart Williams
 'Foreword' to *Old Rhondda in Photographs*, with commentary by Cyril Batstone, Barry: Stewart Williams
1977 'Foreword' to *Old Pontypridd and District*, Barry: Stewart Williams
 'Foreword' to *Old Barry in Photographs*, with commentaries by Brian C. Luxton, Barry: Stewart Williams
1981 'Wales' in *Travel in VOGUE*, London: Macdonald

227

1983 'The First Waves', essay in *Fountains of Praise*, edited by Gwyn Jones and Michael Quinn, Cardiff: University College Press

C: Selected essays and stories by Gwyn Thomas never reprinted in book form

1951 'Then Came We Singing', short story in *Coal*, first version of 'Gazooka'

1957 'A Rhondda Bethel', essay in *Times Educational Supplement*, 24 May

1958 'The Little Baron', short story in *Vogue*, April

1959 'I Think, Therefore I Am Thinking', essay in *Anglo-Welsh Review*, Vol 10, no 25, pp 19–21

'Rulers of the Town', essay in *Ingot*, 1 Dec

1960 'Journey Through Wales', essay in *Holiday*, Vol 28, no 3, pp 34–135

'Father's Christmas', essay in *Ingot*, January No, pp 30–32

'Wildcats I Have Known', essay in *Ingot*, 1 March

'Gwyn Thomas's Schooldays', series of 9 autobiographical essays in *Punch*, 22 June–17 August

1961 'We Miss You, Mr Mooney', short story in *The Barrian*

'A View of the Valley', essay in *New Statesman*, 24 Feb

'Border Dispute', essay in *Ingot*, 1 July

'Growing Up in Meadow Prospect', series of 6 autobiographical pieces in *Punch*, 12 April–17 May

1962 'Why I Quit Teaching', article in *South Wales Echo*, c. 12 May

1964 'Martin Luther: The New Piety', essay in *Holiday*, Vol 35, no 1, pp 62–145

'Tranquillity and Warm Beer – The Cotswold Inns', essay in *Holiday*, Vol 35, no 5, pp 80–168

'A Joyful Noise', essay in *Holiday*, Vol 36, no 6, pp 10–18

1965 'The Passionate Authors', essay on Spanish literature in *Holiday*, Vol 37, no 4, pp 10–24

'Castë System at School', article in *Evening Standard*, 22 Feb

'The Longest Evening', story in *Western Mail*, 24 Dec

'Violence and the Big Male Voice', short story in the *Montrealer*, May

1966 'King's Conversation', reports a conversation between GT and Jeremy Thorpe, *King*, 1 Jan

'A Harvest Frenzy', short story in the *Reporter*, 21 April

'A Subordinate Crumb on Television', essay in *Lilliput*, 1 May

'Death Moves in the Valleys Like A Busy Bagman . . .', essay about Aberfan in the *Teacher*, 28 Oct

1969 'Wales – Fact and Fiction', essay in *Wheeler's Review*, Vol XV, no 2

'Lloyd George – Magic Prince of the Welsh', essay in *Radio Times*, 31 July

'One Welshman's Wales', essay in *Travel and Camera*, Vol 32, no 6

1971 'The Very Perishable Vision – or Culture Went Thataway', essay in *Wheeler's Review*, vol XVII, no 1, pp 22–25

1972 'My Day', essay in *Vogue*, 1 Feb

1973 'Paint Brush Politics', essay in *Daily Telegraph Magazine*, 3 Aug

1976 'Mind the Promised Land Doesn't Become Paradise Lost', essay in *Western Mail*, 16 Nov

Selected Bibliography

1980 'Sound and Fury in Wales', essay in *GEO*, May, pp 128–50

To which should be added at least 68 uncollected pieces from *Punch*, at least 45 from the *Teacher* and at least 4 from the *Guardian*, a total of about 117, though there are undoubtedly more which I have not so far discovered.

D: Theatre Plays by Gwyn Thomas

1960 *The Keep*, single performance at Royal Court Theatre, London, Aug 14; new production at Royal Court Theatre, 22 Nov 1961 and thereafter (for published editions, see above)

1962 *Loud Organs*, first performed Blackpool, 22 Oct; subsequently at New Theatre, Cardiff, 29 Oct and thereafter (Unpublished)

1963 *Jackie the Jumper*, performed at Royal Court Theatre, London, 1 Feb and thereafter (published in *Plays and Players*, Feb 1963; for further publication, see above)

1974 *Sap*, performed at Sherman Theatre, Cardiff, 12 Nov and thereafter (Unpublished)

1976 *The Breakers*, performed at Sherman Theatre, Cardiff, 16 Nov and thereafter (Unpublished)

1979 *Testimonials*, performed at Sherman Theatre, Cardiff, 19 Jan and thereafter (Unpublished)

E: A Selective List of Radio and Television Plays and Features by Gwyn Thomas

1950 *Why I Write*, radio interview with Glyn Jones, BBC Welsh, 16 March

1952 *Gazooka (A Rhondda Reminiscence)*, radio play on BBC Welsh Home Service, 11 Jan; new production on BBC Third Programme, 2 Jan 1953, repeated several times

The Orpheans, radio play, BBC Welsh Home Service, 2 Sep

1953 *Forenoon*, radio play, BBC Northern, 25 Jan

The Rich Hills: A Return to the Rhondda, radio feature, BBC Welsh

Festival, radio play, BBC Welsh, 9 April

Our Outings, radio feature, BBC Welsh, 27 Oct

The Deep Sweet Roots, radio feature, BBC Northern, 12 Nov

1954 *Portrait of a Village*, radio talk, BBC Welsh, 24 Oct

1955 *Vive L'Oompa (The Story of a Welsh Brass Band That Went to Paris)*, radio play, BBC Third, 12 Aug

Up the Handling Code, radio play, BBC Welsh, 15 Nov

1956 *To This One Place*, radio play, BBC Welsh, 26 Nov

1957 *Merlin's Brow*, radio play, BBC Welsh, 18 Oct

1958 *How I Came to be a Writer*, radio talk, BBC Welsh, 28 May

The Long Run, radio play, BBC Welsh, 17 July

The Putters-Out, short story read by GT, BBC Welsh, 1 Aug

1959 *How to Become a Welsh Headmaster*, radio play in series on 'Self-Improvement', BBC Welsh, 10 Oct

1960 *On Leaving a School*, radio talk, BBC Welsh, 29 April

Wales and the West, series of six weekly television programmes, with John Betjeman, TWW, from 27 Aug

Selected Bibliography

1962 *A World of Sound*, series of fortnightly radio programmes using archive material so that GT talks to Hilaire Belloc, James Stephens, Gilbert Murray, etc., BBC Home, from 3 Feb

The Slip, television play, BBC1, 14 Oct

1963 *This World of Wales*, television programme for St David's Day, with Richard Burton, TWW 1 March; networked also in USA and Canada

The Hot Spot, television film about Cannes Film Festival, TWW

The Walk Out, radio play, BBC Third, 7 March

The Dig, television play, BBC1, 24 Oct

East Germany Today, television film, TWW

1964 *Self-Interview*, radio interview, Woman's Hour, BBC Home, 13 Jan

Gwyn Thomas in New York, television film, TWW

The Jagged Land, television feature, ABC TV, 1 March

The Entrance, radio play, BBC Light, 29 April

The Keep, television adaptation, 6 May

Venice: The Drowning City, television film, TWW

1965 *Protest*, series of weekly radio programmes on, e.g., Betting, Loneliness, BBC Home, from 2 July

Return to the Rhondda, television film-essay, TWW

As I See It, weekly television talk-show series, TWW

The Way to the King, short story, BBC Welsh, 16 Nov

1966 *The Alderman*, radio play BBC Home, 17 Jan

10.42 and All That, weekly television satirical programme, TWW

The Growing People, television film about Russia, TWW

The Darker Neighbour, television film about Spain, TWW

A Day of Mourning, radio talk, 22 Oct

Wales Today, radio feature, BBC World Service, 27 Dec

1968 *The Gwyn Thomas Lectures*, series of weekly television programmes on aspects of literature, TWW/HTV, 2 Jan–7 April

Free House, weekly television talk-show series, HTV

The Giving Time, radio play, BBC 4, 19 Dec

1969 *One Pair of Eyes: It's a Sad but Beautiful Joke*, television film, BBC2, 6 Sept

1970 *Retreat From Mankind*, radio feature with records, BBC4, 29 July

Good Morning Wales, GT begins contributing regular items to this daily radio programme, continuing for several years, BBC Radio Wales

1971 *Rhondda*, radio feature, BBC World Service, 3 Feb

One Man's Week, television feature, BBC1, 6 March

1972 *He Knows, He Knows*, radio play, BBC4, 3 Aug

1973 *Up and Under*, television play, BBC1, 3 Mar

1974 *The Worriers*, radio play, BBC4, 22 Aug

1975 *Man of Action*, radio feature with records, BBC3 and 4, 1 March

Adelphi Terrace, television play, BBC2, 7 Aug

1977 *The Greatest Welshmen: Lewis Jones*, radio talk, 4 Feb

With Great Pleasure, radio feature with records, BBC4, 19 April

1978 *Spring Meeting*, radio feature with records, BBC4, 23 Feb

The Long Lesson, radio play, BBC Radio Wales, 17 March

Selected Bibliography

A Land Once Distant and Alone: Spanish Echoes, radio feature, BBC Home, 17 Dec
1981 *Torchbearers of Uneasiness*, radio talk, BBC Radio Wales, 13 April

F: SOME SPECIALLY INTERESTING UNPUBLISHED WORKS

Abel; or: O Lost!, a novel (c 1939)

Return and End, a play for theatre inspired by the life of Aneurin Bevan (c 1963)

The Dark Neighbour, a novel in two parts set in Spain at the time of the Moorish domination (c 1950)

Stobo; or: The Thinker and the Thrush, a comic novel of Rhondda life (c 1949)

Schoolman, a reminiscence of a life in teaching together with a number of short stories inspired by teaching and colleagues (c 1972)

A Tongue for a Stammering Time, a play for television about the life of Aneurin Bevan (c 1975)

The Snug, series of half-hour television plays about happenings at the Belmont Bannerman Social and Progressive Club, offered to HTV but not taken up (c 1969)

The Wandering Boy, television play (c 1970)

A Sympathetic Dust, television play

PART 2: WRITINGS ABOUT GWYN THOMAS

1950 *Literature and Reality*, by Howard Fast, New York: International Publishers, pp 67–77

1952 'Barry's Literary Phenomenon' by T.H. Corfe and G. Ingli James, *Barry Herald*, 29 June

'Barry's Literary Phenomenon: Mr Gwyn Thomas Makes His Reply', *Barry Herald*, 4 July

1953 'Laughter from the Rhondda' by Mimi Josephson, *John O'London's Weekly*, Vol LXII, no 1527, 16 Oct, pp 921–2

1956 'You Can't Help Laughing', by Alexander Baron, *Books and Bookmen*, Feb

1957 *The First Forty Years: Some Notes on Anglo-Welsh Literature*, by Gwyn Jones, Cardiff: University of Wales Press

1965 'A Welsh Eye', by Brian Way, *Anglo-Welsh Review*, Vol 15, no 35, pp 138–40

1968 *The Dragon Has Two Tongues*, by Glyn Jones, London: Dent, pp 107–23

1970 'The Magnificent Absurdities of Gwyn Thomas', by Sandra Bisp, *South Wales Echo*, 3 March

'A Study of Gwyn Thomas's Humor', by Pearl Zinober, unpublished MA thesis, Iowa State University

1973 'Gwyn Thomas', by Henry Raynor, *Contemporary Dramatists*, ed. J. Vinson, London: St James Press

1976 'Getting a Laugh out of Devolution', by Jon Holliday, *South Wales Echo*, 3 Nov

'Absurdity in the Novels of Gwyn Thomas', by Roger Stephens Jones, *Anglo-Welsh Review*, Vol 25, no 56

1977 *Gwyn Thomas*, by Ian Michael, Cardiff: University of Wales Press

1978 *The Welsh Industrial Novel*, by Raymond Williams, Cardiff: Cardiff University Press

1979 'Stories of a Life Sentence', by Tom Davies, *Observer*, 9 Sep

The Welsh Industrial Novel, by Raymond Williams, Cardiff: University College Press

The Bandsman's Daughter, by Irene Thomas, London: Macmillan

Selected Bibliography

1980 *Profiles*, by Glyn Jones and John Rowlands, Llandysul: Gwasg Gomer pp 285–91

1981 'A Tribute to Gwyn Thomas', by Glyn Jones, *Anglo-Welsh Review*, no 68

1982 *Random Entrances to Gwyn Thomas*, by Glyn Jones, Cardiff: University College Press
Laughter Before Nightfall, by John Ormond, unpublished script for a tribute to Gwyn Thomas

1984 'Reading Gwyn Thomas', by Dai Smith, *Book News From Wales*, Autumn
'All Things Betrayed Them', in *Wales? Wales!* by Dai Smith, London: Allen & Unwin, pp 140–51

1985 *The Early Gwyn Thomas*, by Dai Smith, reprinted from *Transactions of the Honourable Society of Cymmrodorion*, Denbigh: Gee
'The Human Comedy', by Michael Parnell, *Planet*, no 53, pp 99–102
'Breaking Silence: Gwyn Thomas and the Pre-History of Welsh Working-Class Fiction', by Dai Smith in *Artisans, Pedants and Proletarians: Essays For Gwyn Alf Williams*, ed. by C. Emsley & J. Walvin, New York: Croom Helm

1986 'A Novel History', by Dai Smith in *Wales: The Imagined Nation*, ed. by Tony Curtis, Bridgend: Poetry Wales Press, pp 131–58
Writer's World: Gwyn Thomas, ed. by Dai Smith, Cardiff: Welsh Arts Council
'*Sorrow for Thy Sons* and *All Things Betray Thee*', by Michael Parnell, *Anglo-Welsh Review*, no 84, pp 132–5
'The Young Gwyn Thomas', by Michael Parnell, *Planet*, no 59, pp 64–70

1987 'Kinds of Relating: Gwyn Thomas and the Welsh Industrial Experience', by James A. Davies, *Anglo-Welsh Review*, no 86, pp 72–87

Index